THE ROLE OF EXTERNAL EXAMINING IN HIGHER EDUCATION

INNOVATIONS IN HIGHER EDUCATION TEACHING AND LEARNING

Senior Series Editor: Patrick Blessinger, St John's University and Higher Education Teaching and Learning Association, USA

Associate Series Editor: Enakshi Sengupta, Higher Education Teaching and Learning Association, USA

Published Volumes:

Volume 23	University–Community Partnerships for Promoting Social Responsibility in Higher Education – Edited by Enakshi Sengupta, Patrick Blessinger and Craig Mahoney
Volume 24	Leadership Strategies for Promoting Social Responsibility in Higher Education – Edited by Enakshi Sengupta, Patrick Blessinger and Craig Mahoney
Volume 25	Integrating Community Service into Curriculum: International Perspectives on Humanizing Education – Edited by Enakshi Sengupta, Patrick Blessinger and Mandla Makhanya
Volume 26	International Perspectives on Improving Student Engagement: Advances in Library Practices in Higher Education – Edited by Enakshi Sengupta, Patrick Blessinger and Milton D. Cox
Volume 27	Improving Classroom Engagement and International Development Programs: International Perspectives on Humanizing Higher Education – Edited by Enakshi Sengupta, Patrick Blessinger and Mandla Makhanya
Volume 28	Cultural Competence in Higher Education – Edited by Tiffany Puckett, and Nancy Lind
Volume 29	Designing Effective Library Learning Spaces in Higher Education – Edited by Enakshi Sengupta, Patrick Blessinger and Mandla S. Makhanya
Volume 30	Developing and Supporting Multiculturalism and Leadership Development – Edited by Enakshi Sengupta, Patrick Blessinger and Mandla S. Makhanya
Volume 31	Faculty and Student Research in Practicing Academic Freedom – Edited by Enakshi Sengupta and Patrick Blessinger
Volume 32	International Perspectives on Policies, Practices & Pedagogies for Promoting Social Responsibility in Higher Education – Edited by Enakshi Sengupta, Patrick Blessinger and Craig Mahoney
Volume 33	International Perspectives on the Role of Technology in Humanizing Higher Education – Edited by Enakshi Sengupta, Patrick Blessinger and Mandla S. Makhanya
Volume 34	Humanizing Higher Education through Innovative Approaches for Teaching and Learning – Edited by Enakshi Sengupta, Patrick Blessinger and Mandla S. Makhanya
Volume 35	Humanizing Higher Education through Innovative Approaches for Teaching and Learning
Volume 36	Integrating Research-based Learning across the Curriculum
Volume 37	International Perspectives in Social Justice Programs at the Institutional and Community Level

INNOVATIONS IN HIGHER EDUCATION TEACHING AND LEARNING VOLUME 38

THE ROLE OF EXTERNAL EXAMINING IN HIGHER EDUCATION: CHALLENGES AND BEST PRACTICES

EDITED BY

ENAKSHI SENGUPTA
International Higher Education Teaching and Learning Association, USA

PATRICK BLESSINGER
International Higher Education Teaching and Learning Association, USA

ANDREW SSEMWANGA
Family Enterprise Support Initiative (FESI), Uganda

and

BARBARA COZZA
St John's University, USA

Created in partnership with the
International Higher Education Teaching and Learning Association

https://www.hetl.org/

United Kingdom – North America – Japan
India – Malaysia – China

Emerald Publishing Limited
Howard House, Wagon Lane, Bingley BD16 1WA, UK

First edition 2021

British Library Cataloguing in Publication Data
A catalogue record for this book is available from the British Library

ISBN: 978-1-83982-175-2 (Print)
ISBN: 978-1-83982-174-5 (Online)
ISBN: 978-1-83909-880-2 (Epub)

ISSN: 2055-3641 (Series)

ISOQAR certified Management System, awarded to Emerald for adherence to Environmental standard ISO 14001:2004.

Certificate Number 1985
ISO 14001

CONTENTS

LIST OF CONTRIBUTORS

Patrick Blessinger	International Higher Education Teaching and Learning Association, New York, USA
Mikhaila Burgess	Noroff School of Technology and Digital Media, Norway
Sarah Cooper	York St John University, York, UK
Beth G. Costner	Winthrop University in Rock Hill, USA
Barbara Cozza	St John's University, New York, USA
Juliet Hinrichsen	Independent Educational Consultant, Derbyshire, UK
Lisa E. Johnson	Winthrop University in Rock Hill, USA
Helen Kay	Sheffield Hallam University, Sheffield, UK
Fareeda Khodabocus	University of Mauritius, Moka, Mauritius
Henri Li Kam Wah	University of Mauritius, Moka, Mauritius
Kay Maddox-Daines	University of Suffolk, Ipswich, UK
Victoria L. O'Donnell	Laureate Online Education, Netherlands & University of Liverpool, UK
Sara Pearman	UCR Rotherham, Rotherham, UK
Helen Phillips	Cardiff University, Cardiff, Wales
Amudha Poobalan	University of Aberdeen, Aberdeen, UK
Megan Schramm-Possinger	Winthrop University in Rock Hill, USA
Enakshi Sengupta	International Higher Education Teaching and Learning Association, New York, USA
Padam Simkhada	University of Huddersfield, Huddersfield, UK
Andrew Ssemwanga	Family Enterprise Support Initiative, Kampala, Uganda
Edwin van Teijlingen	Bournemouth University, Dorset, UK

Dionisia Tzavara Laureate Online Education, Netherlands & University of Liverpool, UK

Deepanjana Varshney City University College of Ajman, United Arab Emirates

SERIES EDITORS' INTRODUCTION

The purpose of this series is to publish current research and scholarship on innovative teaching and learning practices in higher education. The series is developed around the premise that teaching and learning is more effective when instructors and students are actively and meaningfully engaged in the teaching-learning process.

The main objectives of this series are to:

1) present how innovative teaching and learning practices are being used in higher education institutions around the world across a wide variety of disciplines and countries,
2) present the latest models, theories, concepts, paradigms, and frameworks that educators should consider when adopting, implementing, assessing, and evaluating innovative teaching and learning practices, and
3) consider the implications of theory and practice on policy, strategy, and leadership.

This series will appeal to anyone in higher education who is involved in the teaching and learning process from any discipline, institutional type, or nationality. The volumes in this series will focus on a variety of authentic case studies and other empirical research that illustrates how educators from around the world are using innovative approaches to create more effective and meaningful learning environments.

Innovation teaching and learning is any approach, strategy, method, practice or means that has been shown to improve, enhance, or transform the teaching-learning environment. Innovation involves doing things differently or in a novel way in order to improve outcomes. In short, Innovation is positive change. With respect to teaching and learning, innovation is the implementation of new or improved educational practices that result in improved educational and learning outcomes. This innovation can be any positive change related to teaching, curriculum, assessment, technology, or other tools, programs, policies, or processes that leads to improved educational and learning outcomes. Innovation can occur in institutional development, program development, professional development, or learning development.

The volumes in this series will not only highlight the benefits and theoretical frameworks of such innovations through authentic case studies and other empirical research but also look at the challenges and contexts associated with implementing and assessing innovative teaching and learning practices. The volumes represent all disciplines from a wide range of national, cultural, and organizational contexts. The volumes in this series will explore a wide variety of teaching and learning topics such as active learning, integrative learning, transformative learning, inquiry-based learning, problem-based learning, meaningful learning, blended learning, creative learning, experiential learning, lifelong and lifewide learning, global learning, learning assessment and analytics, student research, faculty and student learning communities, as well as other topics.

This series brings together distinguished scholars and educational practitioners from around the world to disseminate the latest knowledge on innovative teaching and learning scholarship and practices. The authors offer a range of disciplinary perspectives from different cultural contexts. This series provides a unique and valuable resource for instructors, administrators, and anyone interested in improving and transforming teaching and learning.

Patrick Blessinger
Founder, Executive Director, and Chief Research Scientist, International HETL Association

Enakshi Sengupta
Associate Editor, International HETL Association

PART I

ROLES AND RESPONSIBILITIES OF EXTERNAL EXAMINERS

CHAPTER 1

INTRODUCTION TO THE ROLE OF EXTERNAL EXAMINING IN HIGHER EDUCATION – CHALLENGES AND BEST PRACTICES

Enakshi Sengupta, Patrick Blessinger,
Andrew Ssemwanga and Barbara Cozza

ABSTRACT

Using an external examiner in an institution is not a new phenomenon; the evidence of having an outsider to scrutinize the quality control process has been prevalent since the 1800s. However, the concept has undergone considerable changes and has been subjected to mounting criticism and validity of the process. There are several challenges that are faced by institutions in recruiting and defining the role of external examiners and the assumption that they are assessment literate. Universities are engaged in safeguarding the procedure, and at the same time, enhancing the quality standards. Researchers have been collaborating to create best practices and working on key developments that would ensure that degree standards are maintained in higher education. There is no "one size fits all" guidelines, but hiring an external examiner with the view to safeguarding academic quality is the prevalent norm across the globe. The book on the role of external examiners put forth such challenges and best practices by academia in various parts of the world. Authors have written about how to mitigate disadvantages and how to create opportunities without compromising the quality assurance process. International standards have been discussed with the view to make external examining a rigorous process that is fair, reliable and consistent.

The Role of External Examining in Higher Education: Challenges and Best Practices
Innovations in Higher Education Teaching and Learning, Volume 38, 3–11

ISSN: 2055-3641/doi:10.1108/S2055-364120210000038001

Keywords: External examiners; quality assurance; higher education; standards; benchmarking; assessment; standards; universities; accountability

EXTERNAL EXAMINING – ROLE AND RESPONSIBILITIES

Recent years have seen a massification of higher education around the world and an increasing demand for accountability and auditing of the existing system to enhance the quality control of external examining along with other educational paradigms. This has also led to a complexity in the existing practices in universities (Gaunt, 1999). Constant change has resulted in multi-faceted role of the external examiners and an increased scrutiny about their scope of work and the procedures implemented by them toward increasing the quality of the underlying practices. Researchers have been engaged in exploring the various facets of this concept and practice although, such engagement has been scanty and doesn't instill confidence in the findings revealed to date (Cuthbert, 2003; Orr, 2007).

Issues such as the effectiveness of external examiners, the impact created by them, consistency, reliability, comparability, and the overall contribution of such a practice toward enhancement of higher education still remains debatable (Brooks, 2012; Murphy, 2006). The various interpretations of external examination standards provided by academics are mainly due to lack of agreement among examiners (Medland, 2015). The evaluations tend to overlook the substance that is being evaluated and the processes involved (Harvey, 2002). The new UK Quality Code for Higher Education (QAA, 2012) "appears to signal a tentative downgrading of the external examiner as the prime guardian of standards and a subtle transformation in official views of the role" (Bloxham & Price, 2015, p. 196).

Medland (2015) proposed two general areas of expertise that an external examiner should engage in: their subject expertise and their assessment expertise. However, expertise in the subject is often the most compelling criteria in involving an external examiner in the institution. Some of the criteria laid down by guidelines and principles for appointing external examiners are competence, experience, qualifications, and sufficient standing, credibility and their breadth of experience within the discipline to be able to command respect of colleagues (Finch Review, 2011, p. 14) Orr (2007) argues that assessment to be "co-constructed in communities of practice and standards [that] are socially constructed, relative, provisional and contested" (Orr, 2007, p. 647). Such arguments highlight the need to be "situationally contingent" and embedded in local cultures (Shay, 2005, p. 669) and being unfamiliar with such concepts will limit the capabilities of the examiners. Bloxham and Boyd (2012) further stated that

> there is an obligation to ensure that examiners are sufficiently experienced, alert to the vagaries of professional judgment and conscious of developments in good assessment practice – in other words, that they are assessment literate. (p. 631)

However, the system which still lacks development and is mainly based on assumptions raises doubt "that the average external examiner has the 'assessment literacy' to be aware of the complex influences on their standards and judgement processes" (Bloxham & Price, 2015, p. 12).

Generally, external examiners are appointed by institutions to offer an independent assessment of the academic standard and practices that are currently prevalent in the institution. External examiners are meant to exercise check and balance of the quality standards in practice. The role and scope of work are limited to reviewing of exam scripts, as a second or third examiner to thesis or assignments and at times being involved in an informal engagement to discuss and assess the examination board. External examiners rarely meet with the students, unless when they are defending their thesis. Their interaction is limited to the staff members in collegiate discussion and working toward enhancing the standard of the institution of higher education. External examiners have adopted the role of being a critical friend who is capable of identifying the weakness and strength of the prevalent system and promote good practices.

Various quality control bodies are now assessing the role of the external examiners and a review in the UK assessed the effectiveness of appointing external examiners and discussing to what extent they can be used effectively in safeguarding the academic quality standard and suggest possible changes to make the system more robust in nature (Higher Education Funding Council for England (HEFCE), 2015). One of the main recommendations of the review which was undertaken by the Higher Education Academy (HEA) concerned the need "to professionalize external examining … so that those conducting the role are skilled and knowledgeable about assessment and the assurance of academic and quality standards" (HEFCE, 2015, pp. 92–93). The review further emphasized the ways that the system could calibrate the existing standards, the subject or even the discipline so that they are at par with the academic benchmark. Such accomplishment cannot be worked alone and needs constant support from the other institutional staff and further stated that "development of staff for the role, clear reward and recognition for the role, appropriate resourcing including time, and effective use of examiner knowledge and experience" (HEFCE, 2015, p. 95).

The induction of newly appointed external examiners is an important component to map the expectations and goals of an institution. A handbook or a code of practice helps in inducting the newly appointed individual in familiarizing with the institutional information, regulation of the assessment and characteristics involved in the curriculum design.

Advance HE (2019) have advocated certain paradigms that can be covered in the induction program (p. 5) as stated below:

- the validation history of the program being held
- emphasis on the design and delivery characteristics of the program as outlined in the program specification
- conducting an assessment of the regulation including detailed explanation of institutional policy with particular focus on condonation and/or compensation, resits, retakes and other mechanisms used to enhance student progression

- provision for arrangements and reasonable adjustments to assessment procedures for students with disabilities
- clearly stating the marking and moderation protocols (question and assignment setting; model answers; double marking; blind marking; moderation)
- dissemination of information on sampling and selection of student work to provide the evidence base for ensuring smooth functioning of the system
- enlisting the entire examination procedures and requirements for attending examination boards, including dates for board meetings
- granting access to recent external examiner reports and minutes of examination boards
- creating an annual report of the external examiner and how it is used effectively by the institution
- ensuring contact protocols and details for key staff members.

External examiners look for professional recognition that comes with their appointment and at the same time, they get the opportunity of exposure to alternative ideas and practices which in turn enhances their credibility and status as an academic. Quality Code's Advice and Guidance on External Expertise states that higher education providers "ensure that external experts are given sufficient and timely evidence and training to enable them to carry out their responsibilities" (p. 5). Induction sessions, regular meetings, and annual events helps external examiners to gain experience and at times mentor new external examiners. Assessment literacy has been associated with teacher's training (DeLuca & Klinger, 2010). However, some academics are of the opinion that assessment literacy is still in its infancy and lacks adequate research findings to support the practice (Price, Carroll, O'Donovan, & Rust, 2011). Smith, Worsfold, Davies, Fisher, and McPhail (2013) is of the opinion that assessment literacy in students requires awareness from the examiners of the purposes and processes involved in assessment and is involved in learning trajectory, as well as the ability of an individual to evaluate personal responses to assessment tasks. The concept has been further defined as:

> [an] understanding of the rules surrounding assessment in [the] course context … use of assessment tasks to monitor or further learning, and ability to work with the guidelines on standards in their context to produce work of a predictable standard. (Smith et al., 2013, p. 46)

CONCLUSION

In most institutions, it is assumed that the senior academic staff will work as external examiners and appointment in such a post indicates seniority in candidate's curriculum vitae. The challenge lies in giving formal recognition to the teaching staff to become an external examiner and in most cases, often, it is not a criterion that is equated with the promotion or some kind of incentive for the academics. Institutions often fail to recognize the responsibilities and role of a senior academic working as an external examiner as a demonstration of their capability and commitment toward higher education. The post of an external examiner demands long and well-established relationships from the awarding institution and recognition to their contribution for quality enhancement of the institution.

CHAPTER OVERVIEWS

"Acting as External Examiners in the UK: Going Beyond Quality Assurance," by Amudha Poobalan, Padam Simkhada and Edwin van Teijlingen, describes the traditional role of the external examiners in UK universities or more formally Higher Education Institutions as that of quality assurance. Typically, an experienced academic who is not affiliated with the Higher Education Institution (i.e., someone from another university) is invited to act as an external examiner for a particular course or a module. The external examiner's primary role is to provide impartial and independent advice to ensure academic standards are upheld for a degree program; and that the degree is comparable with similar programs across the country and that the achievements of students are also comparable with students on courses at other universities. This primary role makes external examiners highly valued people in UK universities, and as a result, their views are nearly always taken seriously. Over and above this recognized primary role of quality assurance, external examiners can also be engaged by the host university in other ways. These additional roles or tasks of the external examiner can help enhance teaching and learning in higher education. This chapter will reflect on the range of roles, including the ones that go beyond quality assurance.

"Promoting Access to External Examining Roles Through Professional Development," by Helen Kay and Juliet Hinrichsen, is about external examining activity as a recognized indicator of subject expertise and peer esteem. It also evidences understanding of quality assurance, course, and assessment design. As such it contributes to the enhancement of an academic CV and may impact on promotion and career prospects. Fair access to external examining opportunities is thus an equity issue for universities. In the context of race equality, where both staff and students of color in academia show consistently differential outcomes to their White counterparts, professional development can mitigate disadvantage, especially where it is focused on access to opportunity. Professional development for external examiners has been an underdeveloped area but the recent establishment in the UK of the Degree Standards Project has begun to address this. The authors propose that there is nevertheless a gap in provision to support academics who aspire to become external examiners but who have had no previous experience. This chapter describes an institutional initiative to promote access to initial external examining roles through professional development and reports on participant outcomes. Evaluation data suggest that an approach such as this can support obtaining a first appointment and may help to mitigate some of the barriers of access to external examiner roles for staff of color. The authors argue that the sector urgently needs to diversify the ethnicity of the external examiner pool in order to provide an essential critical lens which could impact on the equity of degree outcomes for Black, Asian and Minority Ethnic (BAME) students.

"Authentic Assessments and the External Examiner," authored by Mikhaila Burgess and Helen Phillips, explores the key role of the external examiner which is to review student work submitted for assessment plus the feedback and grading undertaken on that work by academic staff. The aim of this is to ensure equitability between the assessments of individual students' achievement and consistency and comparability across courses throughout the program and with commensurate study levels and programs at other institutions, whilst safeguarding academic standards. The variety of assessment-types that an external examiner may review can be diverse. When the primary focus of the work being assessed is tangible, such as with written examinations or assignments, external examiners are able to view student achievements and assessor actions through a lens comparable to that of the original assessors. However, this process cannot adequately capture assessment-types where the only evidence is proxies to the original achievement. In this chapter, the authors explore the concept of authentic assessments, the benefits of incorporating them within study programs, identify challenges pertaining to their presence to holistic quality assurance processes in general, and the role of the external examiner in particular. The authors will demonstrate how adopting non-intrusive technologies for recording and verifying authentic assessment practices can strengthen the QA process for the benefit of all stakeholders. For illustration, a case study is employed to demonstrate how these challenges have been tackled regarding performance-based authentic assessments at an institution in Norway. The chapter concludes with a summary plus a call to arms for further research into how quality and consistency can be assured when authentic assessments are employed.

"Is There Such a Thing as 'Comparableness'? The Challenges Facing the EEs of Higher-Education Courses Delivered Within Further-Education Institutions," by Sarah Cooper and Sara Pearman, explores the numerous considerations that an external examiner (EE) of an undergraduate degree within a further-education (FE) college must be mindful. There may be the perception that one's academic experience of lecturing within a university equips us with the knowledge to collaborate with colleagues within an FE institution. However, this is a valid point only to a certain point. There is a spectrum of contrasts between the higher education (HE) and FE environments, that are reflected within the comparisons that this chapter highlights between the teaching-and-learning experiences. If we think back to the original purpose of an EE (where Oxford scholars were invited by Durham University to provide external guidance in the nineteenth century), we can appreciate the key task of an EE and its aim: to assess the comparability of student achievement. The landscape of HE has changed considerably since then, and now undulates with numerous opportunities for learners to gain a HE qualification. It is this difficulty in assessing comparability that an EE of a HE courses within an FE environment must be willing to acknowledge. The fact that the student-and-learning experience varies wildly in HE and FE muddies the waters for the EE: how can comparableness be assessed?

"A Study of the Effectiveness of the External Examining System of Postgraduate (MBA) Dissertations and the Mismatch Between Expectations and Practice: Evidence from India," authored by Deepanjana Varshney, explores external examining as one of the pivotal means for ensuring the monitoring of the guidelines and standards within private autonomous universities and institutes. External examiners are considered independent individuals who can provide unbiased, objective evaluation, and informed comment on the student's quality of the project as compared to the standards. Hence, the role of the external examiner is vital and has a strong influence on institutional quality assurance.

The qualitative research has primarily aimed to study the external examining practices involving a private university in India. Interviews were conducted mainly with the external appointed examiners; however, the internal faculty guides or supervisors were also made to participate in separate interviews. The results were coded following the Content Analysis framework. The research unraveled the pandora's box of the system bottlenecks and challenges concerning the expected and actual practices. Limitations, recommendations, and future research implications were discussed.

"External Examining the Professional Doctorate as Distinct from the Traditional PhD: Differentiating and Developing Policy and Practice," by Dionisia Tzavara and Victoria L. O'Donnell, speaks about professional doctorates (PDs) who have been added to the curriculum of many universities worldwide, as an alternative to the traditional Philosophy Doctor (PhD). PDs are more focused on practice-based knowledge that advances professional practice and contributes to society, industry, and the economy. The dominance of the PhD as the typical higher degree by research, has led universities to develop frameworks for their PDs which are very similar to the PhD framework. This includes the assessment of the PD, which in many cases follows the same process and is based on the same criteria as for the PhD. This similarity in the assessment of the two types of doctorates creates challenges for External Examiners, who are invited to evaluate the contribution of the PD within frameworks which are tailored around the PhD. In this chapter, the authors focus their investigation on the Doctorate in Business Administration (DBA) and conduct a review and analysis of institutional documents from universities in England in an attempt to understand the similarities and differences between the examination process of the PD and the PhD and the extent to which the examination process of the PD supports the evaluation of the practice-based contribution that is at its heart. Through this review and analysis, the authors identify the challenges that exist for External Examiners who are called to assess PDs, and make recommendations which will support External Examiners to evaluate the contribution of the PD.

"External Examining Policies at the University of Mauritius," written by Fareeda Khodabocus and Henri Li Kam Wah, talks about the primary roles of external examiners at the University of Mauritius (UoM) which is designed to assist the university in ensuring that degrees awarded meet international standards. It ensures that assessment is valid and that procedures and arrangements for assessment, examinations, and determination of awards are sound and conducted rigorously, fairly, reliably, and consistently. External examiners come from a wide range of highly reputed institutions across the globe and the UoM has a set of external examining policies that act as a guide to external examiners. At the end of their visit, the external examiners submit their signed reports to the Vice-Chancellor. The reports, which include their concerns, are circulated to all administrators and academic staff for their review and analysis. Analysis of the external examiners' reports for 2016–2019 reveals that 28% of the UoM external examiners come from the United Kingdom, 39% were from South Africa and the remaining 33% from Australia, India and other European countries.

Overall, 98% of external examiners have rated the UoM programs as average and above compared to institutions where they had experience of external examining. The contributions of external examiners are highly valued in the continued growth of the new vision of the institution aspiring to be a research-engaged and entrepreneurial institution.

"Benchmarking: A Comparative Case Study Analysis of Quality Assurance Across the Private and University Sector in the UK," by Kay Maddox-Daines, is a study which compares quality assurance across two case studies in the UK; a commercial organization operating in the private sector and a university. Case Study A is a private education organization specializing in the delivery of business and management programs. Case Study B is a university that delivers courses across four academic schools and through a number of partnerships. The business school offers a range of undergraduate and postgraduate degrees in business management, economics, accounting, events, tourism, marketing, entrepreneurialism, and human resources. Semi-structured interviews were conducted with 11 organizational members from across the 2 organizations including 8 academics/tutors, 6 of whom are also employed as external examiners and/or external quality assurers. The study compares the remit of both External Quality Assurers (EQA) working on behalf of awarding bodies and external examiners working on behalf of universities. The EQA role is conceptualized as an "arbiter of standards" whereas the external examiner is more likely to be considered as "critical friend." This variance in conception has important implications for the way the process of quality assurance is conducted and utilized in support of program and institutional development. The research finds that one of the most significant differences between quality assurance processes in Case Studies A and B is the way in which student feedback is collected and utilized to support and enhance the process of review. The chapter provides recommendations designed to capitalize on the value of the quality assurance process through greater alignment of teaching and assessment strategy and policies and procedures in practice.

"Building Without a Foundation: Efforts in Higher Education to Meet External Examiners Requirements in the Absence of Statewide Data," written by Megan Schramm-Possinger, Lisa E. Johnson, and Beth G. Costner, is about the United States (US) accreditation agencies that assess higher education in a manner analogous to external examiners in the United Kingdom. An example accreditor, the Council for the Accreditation of Educator Preparation (CAEP), requires university-level Educator Preparation Program providers (EPPs) to evaluate the degree to which (a) their graduates feel prepared to assume their professional roles as a result of their EPP training and (b) their impacts on PK-12 students' learning. These are meaningful forms of programmatic assessment, however, governmental agencies in the United States do not uniformly collect these data. This has required many EPP providers to do so, with unintended negative consequences. The authors use this context as a case study to examine what must be done when reporting guidelines do not align with the data available. Although a single example, readers are asked to consider analogous situations within their own contexts. Presented in this chapter is the accreditation landscape, a description of the challenges listed above, common solutions, and recommendations for greater coordination among stakeholders in order to expand the systematic conferral of data in safe, ethical, and meaningful ways.

REFERENCES

Advance HE. (2019). Degree Standards project. Retrieved from https://www.heacademy.ac.uk/degree-standards

Bloxham, S., & Boyd, P. (2012). Accountability in grading student work: Securing academic standards in a twenty-first century quality assurance context. *British Educational Research Journal, 38*(4), 615–634.

Bloxham, S., & Price, M. (2015). External examining: Fit for purpose? *Studies in Higher Education, 40(*2), 195–211.

Brooks, V. (2012). Marking as judgement. *Research Papers in Education*, *27*(1), 63–80.

Cuthbert, M. (2003). The external examiner: How did we get here? [Online]. Retrieved from http://78.158.56.101/archive/ law/resources/assessment-and-feedback/cuthbert/index.html

DeLuca, C., & Klinger, D. A. (2010). Assessment literacy development: Identifying gaps in teacher candidates' learning. *Assessment in Education: Principles, Policy and Practice*, *17*(4), 419–438.

Finch Review. (2011). Review of external examining arrangements in universities and colleges in the UK: Final report and recommendations. Report commissioned by Universities UK and GuildHE. [Online]. Retrieved from www.universitiesuk.ac.uk/highereducation/Documents/2011/ReviewOfExternalExaminingArrangements.pdf

Gaunt, D. (1999). The practitioner as external examiner. *Quality in Higher Education*, *5*(1), 81–90.

Harvey, L. (2002). Evaluation for what?' *Teaching in Higher Education*, *7*(3), 246–263.

Higher Education Funding Council for England (HEFCE). (2015). A review of external examining arrangements across the UK. Report to the UK higher education funding bodies by the Higher Education Academy, June 2015.

Medland, E. (2015, December). Examining the assessment literacy of external examiners. *London Review of Education*, *13*(3), 21–33.

Murphy, R. (2006). Evaluating new priorities for assessment in higher education. In C. Bryan & K. Clegg (Eds.), *Innovative assessment in higher education* (pp. 37–47). London: Routledge.

Orr, S. (2007). Assessment moderation: Constructing the marks and constructing the students. *Assessment and Evaluation in Higher Education*, *32*(6), 645–656.

Price, M., Carroll, J., O'Donovan, B., & Rust, C. (2011). If I was going there I wouldn't start from here: A critical commentary on current assessment practice. *Assessment and Evaluation in Higher Education*, *36*(4), 479–492.

QAA. (2012). UK Quality Code for Higher Education. [Online]. Retrieved from www.qaa.ac.uk/AssuringStandardsAndQuality/quality-code/Pages/default.aspx

Shay, S. (2005). The assessment of complex tasks: A double reading. *Studies in Higher Education*, *30*(6), 663–679.

Smith, C. D., Worsfold, K., Davies, L., Fisher, R., & McPhail, R. (2013). Assessment literacy and student learning: The case for explicitly developing students "assessment literacy". *Assessment and Evaluation in Higher Education*, *38*(1), 44–60.

CHAPTER 2

ACTING AS EXTERNAL EXAMINERS IN THE UK: GOING BEYOND QUALITY ASSURANCE

Amudha Poobalan, Padam Simkhada and Edwin van Teijlingen

ABSTRACT

Traditionally the role of the external examiners in UK universities or more formally Higher Education Institutions (HEIs) is that of quality assurance (QA). Typically, an experienced academic who is not affiliated with the HEI (i.e., someone from another university) is invited to act as an external examiner for a particular course or a module. The external examiner's primary role is to provide impartial and independent advice to ensure academic standards are upheld for a degree program; and that the degree is comparable with similar programs across the country and that the achievements of students are also comparable with students on courses at other universities. This primary role makes external examiners highly valued people in UK universities, and as a result, their views are nearly always taken seriously. Over and above this recognized primary role of QA, external examiners can also be engaged by the host university in other ways. These additional roles or tasks of the external examiner can help enhance teaching and learning in higher education. This chapter will reflect on the range of roles, including the ones that go beyond QA.

Keywords: External examiner; quality assurance; higher education institution; mentor; strategic sounding board; referee; critical friend; arbiter of standards; adjudicators; assessment improvement

---

The Role of External Examining in Higher Education: Challenges and Best Practices
Innovations in Higher Education Teaching and Learning, Volume 38, 13–23

ISSN: 2055-3641/doi:10.1108/S2055-364120210000038002

BACKGROUND TO EXTERNAL EXAMINING IN THE UK

Higher Education Institutions (HEIs) in the UK often have a large number of external examiners on their books. We realize that having external examiners for undergraduate and postgraduate courses is not universal. For example, having an external examiner in the United States is uncommon; Columbia University's twenty-first century Public Health Master's program does not mention external examiner at all (Begg et al., 2014).

In 2018, the UK Quality Code for Higher Education published by the Quality Assurance Agency (QAA), a national body for higher education, states that the role of the external examiner is to "provide each degree-awarding body with impartial and independent advice, as well as informative comment on the degree-awarding body's standards and on student achievement in relation to those standards" (The Quality Assurance Agency for Higher Education, 2018). External examiners are hence perceived as crucial for maintaining the academic standards within higher education settings. Careful and well-balanced advice provided by experienced external examiners reflects their experience and awareness of many higher education providers in the UK and sometimes overseas experience. They are then able to compare the standards of assessment process and students' assessed work between the institutions and provide independent feedback in an annual written report. These external examiners' reports are often seen by senior personnel in the university. For example, the University of Aberdeen states this clearly on its "External Examiners Annual Report" form that:

> Your comments are central to the university's quality assurance mechanisms. Your report will be considered by the relevant School and College and by the Quality Assurance Committee and may be made available to other appropriate university committees. (University of Aberdeen, 2017)

This is an indication that the examiner's assessment is taken seriously and comments or observations are being used by HEIs to take actions to improve quality. In the instance of systematic serious breach of quality standards, the external examiners can write to the head of the school or faculty in confidence and, in extreme cases, have the remit to ask the QAA to investigate any serious concerns or failings. All universities in the UK have clearly defined the roles for external examiners. We list in Table 1 the roles and responsibilities of external examiners at a typical UK university:

Table 1. Roles and Responsibilities of External Examiners at a Typical UK University.

- To ensure that the standard of any award is comparable to the standard of similar awards conferred by universities in the UK.
- To evaluate all forms of assessment which contribute to students' degree results.
- To evaluate, and help ensure fairness and consistency in, the assessment process.
- To moderate summatively assessed work at module and program level.
- To comment on draft examination papers and assessment tasks as appropriate.
- To report on the structure, content, academic standards, and teaching of programs.
- To comment, if invited to do so, on any alleged cases of assessment irregularities.
- To produce an annual report for consideration by the appropriate board and the relevant department of academic quality.

Usually, each degree program has at least one external examiner, while the larger programs may have several external examiners. External examiners can be selected for specific modules or sub-disciplines in a program or to individual years in an undergraduate degree (Durham University, n.d.). External examiners are typically appointed for three or four years, to ensure some consistency over a longer period (QAA, 2018). External examiners often receive a small annual honorarium. The quantum of which could dependent on the number of students on the course (University of Reading, n.d.) or a standard rate set by the university per program (University of Bristol, n.d.). External examiners are expected to attend the university at least once a year usually to attend the exam board meeting at the end of the academic year. Some HEIs expect external examiners to attend twice a year, either once a term or for the final exam board meeting and the resit exam board meeting (Advance HE, 2019).

While the primary role of external examiners is quality assurance (QA), the role of external examiners may go beyond this with a call to improve the standards of teaching and assessments and improve student experiences. In this chapter, the following external examiners' roles will be addressed: (a) transforming student experience; (b) being a strategic sounding board; (c) becoming mentors or role models to less experienced staff; (d) acting as a referee; and (e) being a supportive but critical friend. Last but not least, we will highlight the advantage for the external examiner's home institution. The latter benefits through examples of good practice and ideas for innovation brought home by the external examiners.

Transforming Student Experience

Universities, first and foremost, will normally use external examiners only for QA, whom they see primarily as the person doing the overall quality control of the course. For example, the policy and guidelines for external examiners published by the University of Oxford in 2018 regard external examiners as "arbiters of standards":

> Individuals may be nominated to serve as external examiner in one of two categories: either (1) as an external arbiter of standards; or (2) to provide academic expertise not otherwise obtainable within the university. (University of Oxford, 2018)

Medland (2015) noted two areas of expertise to underpin the external examiners' role: "subject and assessment expertise (or assessment literacy)". With subject expertise and level of experience of assessing university assignments and examinations, external examiners assure quality by making sure the subject-specific content of the individual courses/modules fits with the overall program. They also make sure that assessments are appropriately designed and organized, marking adheres to the standard criteria set using a marking rubric. They ratify this by looking at standards across the sector and ensure adherence to faculty and/or university policies (University of Oxford, 2018). External examiners accomplish these tasks through the pedagogical knowledge, confidence and the teaching experience, both in understanding the QA approaches relevant for the country and understanding the academic standards for a given course or a module. This QA monitoring involves checking and approving the questions for a sample of continuous assessments and all examination papers. This same monitoring usually involves commenting and editing questions prior to exams as well as assessing model answers drafted by academics on the course. External examiners also check a sample of work by the students to ensure consistency in marking and making sure a fair assessment process was followed. Typically, external examiners sample a few of the top, middle, and bottom marks to assess the accuracy and fairness of the marking.

Some universities deploy the external examiners as an independent referee either to give a third (or second) opinion on students' work or for course-related issues such as discrepancies between the internal markers of a thesis or dissertation. HEIs can also invite the external examiners as a moderator where the internal exam board could not arrive on an agreement. All of these approaches used and activities carried out by the external examiners can either be hands-on or be very much hands-off (Newcastle University, 2009). For example, external examiners might never meet any students on the course in person nor many of the lecturers on the course. On some occasions, however, HEIs may introduce the external examiners to all or selected number of students, perhaps at a semi-informal meeting, such as poster presentations or oral presentations. Our experience is that meeting of students, tutors, and lecturers on the course helps the external examiner to make a more holistic assessment of the course. External examiners will sometimes ask to directly examine the student performance in the form of a viva, to endorse the level of degree classification to be awarded to the student (e.g., pass/fail or distinction/commendation categories) (University of Oxford, 2018).

The role of an external examiner, in its absolute, can be done without meeting any students or other lecturers on the course/module. The reliable judgments on the academic side can be desk-based, that is, made with no interaction with the students at all. However, in these varied processes of external examining, in addition to bringing in the independent evaluation of the courses or modules and their standards of achievement, the external examiner can improve the learning process and experience of the students. For example, the interaction with the independent evaluator in the form of an external examiner does provide the students with richer experience extending the learning process beyond the end of the exams. From the authors' experiences, interactions with students ranged from examining every student for a 10-to -15 -minute viva in order to determine the level of award to examining every borderline category (fail/pass; normal pass/commendation; commendation to distinction) to have the assurance that the right classification was awarded. It is a matter of striking a balance between the strict process of QA by making the external examiner meet all the students in the exam setting and not meet any students at all.

At one HEI where one of the authors acted as external examiner in Medicine, the external examiner first assessed the written portfolios for the year and after that quality assessment observed a number of students during an Objective Structured Clinical Examination (OSCE). In this HEI, the medical students would have, for example, 3-minute clinical examination OSCE with a patient partner playing a patient with specific symptoms, followed by a communication skills assessment, differential diagnosis assessment or injecting a mannequin. Observing the students gave the external examiner an insight into the examination processes and allowed for informal discussions with the students afterwards about their experience of undergoing an OSCE.

In a second example, the normal practice was that the external examiner conducted a viva for all the students who were in the borderline classification. These viva exams took up a lot of time, which left the external examiner with little time to meet the other students to gain a more general impression of the course. So instead of the external examiner conducting a viva with all the students with borderline classification, the following year this particular HEI only examined those students for whom the internal exam board could not come to a decision. This freed up the time and gave the external examiner an opportunity to attend a poster presentation by all the students. This interaction helped motivate the students to meet the external examiner and also met the objective to enhance the learning through conference style presentations. Interestingly, the way external examiners are being used in different HEIs is hardly ever studied. For example, there appeared to be no published evidence on the student satisfaction or the general student experience in relation to external examiners' roles and/or involvement.

Strategic Sounding Board

Some of the HEIs are a little more strategic in their approach in using the external examiners for advice on curriculum development and the future directions of a program, or the way forward regarding ways of marking or specific course content (University of Aberdeen, 2017). Nearly all external examiners come with experience of coordinating their own programs, have experiences of reviewing programs to improve the quality of the courses and ways of attracting more and better students. Often, they also have past experience from acting as external examiners in other HEIs or from teaching elsewhere, including teaching abroad. This makes them experts in understanding the national and international level thresholds of the quality of teaching and learning. With this wider experience, external examiners can bring in the "outsider" and "unbiased" perspective to the strategic development of courses. They can become a critical friend by casting a fresh eye over the course content, not constrained by the internal politics of the institution. Course coordinators may ask the advice from their external examiners on developing a new module on an existing program or coordinators may seek advice on changing assessment methods for a particular module or the balance of various assessment methods across all modules of a program. External examiners can provide honest and sincere feedback, be encouraging and supportive but speak truthfully and constructively. They can also bring their experience from the university where they are employed and from other HEIs where they have acted as external examiners.

Simple suggestions, based on what works elsewhere, can help program coordinators a lot, for example, offering statements like; "Are you aware that the University of XXX does this slightly differently, namely they …….."; or

> When I was an external examiner at the University of YYY, the programme team decided that it would be better to change the assignment to oral exams from written exams on a similar module to what you are discussing today. Initially, this did not work, but it went much better and was much better appreciated by the students after they also did ....

Some of the critical comments that external examiners provide might be uncomfortable for teaching staff, program coordinators, or heads of department to hear, however such reliable judgments based on experience, advice on good practices and impartial advice can help the institutions to enhance the quality of the programs/modules.

Mentors or Role Models to Less Experienced Staff

Sometimes, the role of the external examiner goes beyond QA in acting as a mentor for slightly less experienced teachers/coordinators. Experienced external examiners use their own experience of being lecturers, coordinators, and external examiners to offer reassurance and support to less experienced staff. Unlike more traditional academic mentorship arrangements, the external examiner as a mentor is not part of the same HEI making it easier for the junior mentee to express issues and concerns related to their work. Mentorship combines psychological and practical support, which unlike supervision or line management, is voluntary (Arnesson & Albinsson, 2017). It can be difficult for a junior member of staff and new coordinators to bring about a change in the way the courses are run, assessments are conducted and feedback are provided. The external examiners, with their experience, can provide sound advice in helping the new members assess the robustness of the proposed changes and to help negotiate the changes with the institution. In some circumstances, the external examiners can vocalize the support for the changes proposed by the junior member of staff. An agreement from the external examiner will be respected by the HEI and will carry a great deal of weight to bring about changes, which otherwise the department or faculty or HEI might be resistant to (Benes et al., 2014).

Observing an experienced external examiner in action at the external exam boards is, in itself, a great learning experience for junior members of staff. When junior members are first appointed as external examiners, they can believe that their appointment as external examiner is to be critical, that they have an obligation to highlight every shortcoming of the course and to provide a list for improvement. As mentors, external examiners can gently teach the junior members of staff to get the right balance into accomplishing the QA role of identifying any weaknesses and bringing it to the attention of the department at earliest opportunity, while stepping back from interfering with institutional policies. For example, while some universities follow the policy of terminating the student's study period immediately if they plagiarized their work, some have a policy of warning the students in the first instance or investigate the issue through a devolved committee with a penalty and only terminate the registration of students when it is repeated. In our experience, junior external examiners, either out of compassion to the students or feel a sense of injustice, can try to resist the university policies. Experienced external examiners are more likely to be skilled to have that balance and can provide mentorship to juniors in handling this sensitively and constructively (Manchester Metropolitan University, 2017).

Mentoring junior members of staff in the context of external examining can become a long-lasting and sustainable mentorship. Our experiences have shown that experienced external examiners continue to support the junior staff beyond the fixed term of exam board interactions, both in terms of developing their skills in educational context and also in furthering research collaborations if they have similar interests. The social interactions that happen over coffee and working lunches/dinners in the exam board context with coordinators and lecturers can lead to discussions and academic exchanges with colleagues, which later on can trigger collaborative research projects. For example, we have previously taken forward ideas that gradually developed into a funded international educational workshop, visiting new places and institutions. Such innovative collaborative projects, initiated during the informal conversations in the external exam board context, further the learning experience for all involved in teaching. It could help understanding the student views in international context, which can then be brought back to the UK to suggest possible improvements. This is a really rewarding experience that can continue beyond the mentoring that happens during the external examining.

Acting as Referee

Some HEIs use external examiners as adjudicators in difficult situations. These can be tricky situations between colleagues teaching on a program or situations dealing with difficult students. Since the external examiner is not a stakeholder in the situation and therefore not advantaged or disadvantaged by the decisions made, he or she can act more independently than other decision-makers. For example, a conflict between colleagues about the relative weight of a module in a program or an assignment in a module can affect the status of the module or the workload of certain members of staff. In our experience, such education management decisions are assigned to a dean or a director of education, and occasionally the outcomes might affect the dean's workload or the director of education's module. In these circumstances, the HEIs might consider it safer to seek advice or arbitration from the external examiner, for the same reason that companies hire external consultants to help take the difficult decisions. For example, one of the situations encountered by the external examiners was where there was an on-going conflict between pragmatists and purists in a particular discipline. The purists found that their module (i.e., their specific discipline) was not valued enough within the overall program, whilst the pragmatists argued that this one module should not dominate the overall postgraduate program. This had been a long-running issue for years, and when the internal efforts were not effective to address the issue, it was brought to the attention of the newly appointed external examiner by a senior staff in the school. This examiner, as an independent referee, was able to look at it objectively without being influenced by the internal conflicts. The external examiner's adjudication brought an end to this long-running conflict by effective mediation, while ensuring the university rules are adhered to, which the HEI internally had not managed to solve.

One of the common situations where the external examiner will be asked to be a referee is when there are wide discrepancies between two internal markers. Normally within the institutions, the solution would be that both the markers will discuss the students' work to reconcile the marks. However, in a situation when this is not achieved, the next line of action will be to bring in another internal independent marker with the subject and/or methodological expertise to give it a mark. If the issue is still not resolved, either due to personality clash or deeper conviction of either of the markers that they have judged it rightly, then the external examiner will be called in to referee and assess this piece of work. In one of these situations, the refereeing was more difficult for the external examiner as there was no documentation of the marking process for the external examiner to comprehend the whole situation. Then it falls to the external examiner to read through the whole thesis with no insight into the process or issues identified by the individual markers. This issue would have been solved much more easily and smoothly if time and space were provided to the markers to have a good discussion and to document the reasons. In this situation, the external examiner provided a suggestion to the markers to use an individual mark sheet with scores and comments given by each marker; and then a clear documentation of overall mark sheet, logged in a consistent format, explaining how differing marks were reconciled by staff generating a definitive score. This improved the process and transparency of the marking. With the clear documentation, it also became easier for the external examiner, coming in as a referee, to evidence the quality and consistency of the marking while improving the clarity and saving time.

Growing emphasis of students as "education customers" among UK universities, makes the students more demanding (Tomlinson, 2016), which perhaps makes dealing with poor and/or difficult students more problematic. One of the tricky situations experienced by the external examiners related to a student with issues. This particular student was seen by the external examiner as one of the pass/fail students in an oral exam. The student performed poorly (not just in the oral exam) and as a result, failed the final year. However, the student appealed arguing that the university had not followed the correct procedures. In most UK universities, students cannot appeal against the academic judgment linked to their marks, but can appeal only against the incorrect use of procedures that led to the poor performance by the student. To prove that the correct procedures had been followed, the HEI asked the external examiner to give evidence to help defend the university. At about the same time, the student also contacted the external examiner directly. This is something that is highly unusual in the UK, especially as the student demanded access to notes taken at the oral exam under the freedom of information act. On this occasion, the external examiner emailed the student in reply stating that (a) the concerned HEI had followed its own procedures; (b) that the external examiner's report does not include students' names; and (c) that the HEI has agreed to make the external examiners' report publicly available. The external examiner's diplomatic approach to both helped solve the issue for the university concerned.

Being a Supportive but Critical Friend

Where external examiners go into HEIs as an outsider and as a referee, it is quite easy to display a hawk-like (threatening) behavior toward the members of staff. This could come from a keen sense to be objective, uphold high standards of excellence and an elevated sense of privilege. In addition, given the time pressures for marking and strict turnaround times for the institutions, sometimes the external examiners do not receive the samples of work or the final exam spreadsheet in time to review properly. External examiners sometimes are required to return the feedback within the frame of a few days. If external examiners are required to conduct oral examinations for borderline fail/pass candidates, a short period of time to read several theses can put a strain on the examiners. In those situations, it is easy to display impolite behavior with the academic and administrative staff. This could create an uncomfortable and tense atmosphere at exam boards where the constructive and supportive element can become lost. In these situations, it is recommended that the external examiners gently encourage the admin team to provide adequate time for commenting on students' work in the future. This gentle behavior can inculcate a supportive atmosphere while being a critical friend.

While some universities provide exam board dates well in advance (provide all the dates for the whole year), some universities are not well organized. If several external examiners are involved per program, getting dates for exam boards that will suit all examiners can be complicated. Negotiating the dates for exam board attendance is quite important as the presence of external examiner at the exam board can be quite constructive, to facilitate an improved service to students. Sometimes while when sending the external examiner report to the institutions, it is important that an appropriate language that is supportive is used, while being transparent to highlight any weaknesses identified, retaining the critical element. It is also very important to highlight the positive elements of the program, and appreciate the admin and the support staff. Sometimes, if in doubt, it is helpful to send a draft report to staff to ensure that the external examiner has not penned anything factually incorrect, before submitting the formal report. Recognizing that it is not just a one-way transfer of ideas from a visiting expert to the host institution but a two-way process encourages staff to share issues and opportunities with their external examiner and to exchange ideas. This notion of being a critical friend is not without its own problems as Bloxham and Price (2015) note, since there are concerns about clarity in the external examiners' role in assuring standards when they are more a critical friend than an arbiter of standards.

There are other times when external examiners have to be critical, while being supportive. For example, situations around support systems for staff, such as when the virtual learning environments (VLEs) are clunky, unwieldy, or incompatible with the external examiners institutions. They also might still be based on hard copies or only partly electronic, all of which can pose problems for the external examiner. In these situations, external examiners will be confronted with delays in accessing the relevant information before the exam board or faced with piles of papers on arrival to check things over in a restricted time period. In these scenarios, the external examiner has to be supportive of the teaching and admin staff, accepting the issues that electronic platforms can cause, however, highlighting the issues. For some external examiners, this can be a burden. For example, one of the authors is an external examiner at a UK university where they use a fairly similar VLE as the one at the home HEI. As in all good bureaucracies, fairly similar means in practice that there are subtly incomprehensible differences.

Being used to one operating system at home, and as an external examiner, navigating the visiting HEI's system only occasionally can be frustrating, difficult, and time consuming.

Lessons for Home

Our experience is that over the years, we as external examiners have brought back evidence of good practice from the places we visited as external examiner to our home HEI. Thus, being an external examiner may help the academic, who might be coordinating their own program or leading other teaching staff in their institutions to adopt some of the lessons learnt in their own practice. We have brought back to our respective institutions, many innovations related to improving assessment, or ideas for new modules. We have also returned home with insights that are wider than just the course or module we acted as an external examiner for, such as novel ideas about the marketing of our own courses and/or ways of academic working. For example, one of us came across a good working example of academic writing weeks which was discussed at an external examiners' meeting at one of the reputable universities in the UK. Listening to both the staff's enthusiasm and the evidence they provided, one of us used this to draft a one-page proposal for their own university. After presenting this to our dean, it resulted in the introduction of a similar scheme at the home HEI. A second example of learning as an external examiner, relates to funded postgraduate places. Gaining insight into the kind of funding that another HEI has gained for its MSc students, motivated one of us to discuss studentships with their HEI's director of education and to apply for similar funding the following year.

FINAL THOUGHTS

Being an external examiner can be a demanding and definitely underpaid role. However, in the UK, external examiners volunteer to do it to enhance their career (i.e., something to add to one's CV), for motivation to learn from the other institutions and out of a sense of duty to academia (France & Fletcher, 2004). From our experience, it is unlikely that external examiners do it for the financial gain. As we have summarized, external examiners go beyond the primary role of quality control to become referees, mentors, and strategic sounding boards. In the process, they develop friendships and help support each other. However, not all HEIs make best use of the external examiners. A recent study of staff and students on the Doctor of Physical Therapy (DPT) program at Riphah International University in Islamabad, Pakistan identified "use of external examiners, reliability and validity of assessment tools, scrutiny of assessments by external examiners" as the program's key weaknesses (Shakil-Ur-Rehman et al., 2018). Having external examiners elsewhere can also be beneficial for the external examiner's own university, not just in status of the academic who is involved, but also in gaining insight into elements of good practice at similar HEIs. In spite of the valuable role, the external examiners play in upholding the standards of academia with HEIs and safeguarding student interests, there are no standard protocols across the UK to identify and recruit external examiners. Some of the time, these are informal invitations or personal contacts (France & Fletcher, 2004). There is a lack of strategies to provide professional development and support for the academic staff to take on the role of examining externally. In conclusion, external examiners do go beyond the role of assisting with maintaining the function of the academic system and QA; and there is a need to provide opportunities for professional development for aspiring and serving external examiners to support them in enhancing their roles.

REFERENCES

Advance HE. (2019, February). Fundamentals of external examining. Retrieved from https://www.heacademy.ac.uk/system/files/downloads/Fundamentals%20of%20External%20Examining%20AHE%20-%20%20Feb%202019%20v2.pdf

Arnesson, K., & Albinsson, G. (2017). Mentorship: A pedagogical method for integration of theory and practice in higher education. *Nordic Journal of Studies in Educational Policy*, *3*(3), 202–217.

Begg, M. D., Galea, S., Bayer, R., Walker, J. R., & Fried, L. P. (2014). MPH education for the 21st century: Design of Columbia University's New Public Health Curriculum. *American Journal of Public Health, 104*, 30–36. https://doi.org/10.2105/AJPH.2013.301518

Benes, J., Roskovec, V., & Sebkova, H. (2014). The Czech Case: Students, governance and the interface with secondary education. In H. Eggins (Ed.), *Drivers and barriers to achieving quality in Higher Education* (pp. 127–142). Rotterdam/Boston/Taipei: Sense Publishers.

Bloxham, S., & Price, M. (2015). External examining: Fit for purpose? *Studies in Higher Education*, *40*(2), 195–211. https://doi.org/10.1080/03075079.2013.823931

Durham University. (n.d.). Number of external examiners for a programme. Retrieved from https://www.dur.ac.uk/learningandteaching.handbook/section_10/3/

France, D., & Fletcher, S. (2004). The motivations and professional development needs of aspiring and serving external examiners in the GEES disciplines. *Planet*, *13*(1), 30–34. https://doi.org/10.11120/plan.2004.00130030b

Manchester Metropolitan University. (2017, March). Guidance notes for Programme Leaders on Mentoring arrangements to be provided for new/inexperienced Subject External Examiners. Retrieved from https://www.mmu.ac.uk/academic/casqe/examiners/docs/mentoring.pdf

Medland, E. (2015). Examining the assessment literacy of external examiners. *London Review of Education*, *13*(3), 21–33.

Newcastle University. (2009). Meetings between external examiners and students. Retrieved from https://www.ncl.ac.uk/ltds/assets/documents/qsh-extexam-meetingstudents.pdf

Shakil-Ur-Rehman, S., Ahmad, S., & Yasmin, R. (2018). Study of curriculum of Doctor of Physical therapy programme based on World Federation of Medical Education standards. *Pakistan Journal of Medical Science*, *34*(6), 1582–1585. http://doi:10.12669/pjms.346.15926

The Quality Assurance Agency for Higher Education. (2018). UK quality code for higher education: Assuring and enhancing academic quality. Chapter B7: External examining. Retrieved from https://www.qaa.ac.uk/docs/qaa/quality-code/chapter-b7_-external-examining.pdf

Tomlinson, M. (2016). Students' perception of themselves as 'Consumers' of higher education. *British Journal of Sociology of Education*, *38*(4), 450–467. https://doi.org/10.1080/01425692.2015.1113856

University of Aberdeen. (2017). Academic quality handbook: Roles and responsibilities of external examiners. Retrieved from https://www.abdn.ac.uk/staffnet/teaching/external-examiners-6107.php

University of Bristol. (n.d.). Fees and expenses for external examiners for taught programmes. Retrieved from http://www.bristol.ac.uk/academic-quality/assessment/exexs/fees.html

University of Oxford. (2018). Policy and guidance for examiners and others involved in university examinations. Retrieved from https://academic.admin.ox.ac.uk/files/pandgforexaminerspdf

University of Reading. (n.d.). External examiner payment bands. Retrieved from https://www.reading.ac.uk/web/files/exams/EE_Payment_bands.pdf

CHAPTER 3

PROMOTING ACCESS TO EXTERNAL EXAMINING ROLES THROUGH PROFESSIONAL DEVELOPMENT

Helen Kay and Juliet Hinrichsen

ABSTRACT

External examining activity is a recognized indicator of subject expertise and peer esteem. It also evidences understanding of quality assurance, course, and assessment design. As such, it contributes to the enhancement of an academic CV and may impact on promotion and career prospects. Fair access to external examining opportunities is thus an equity issue for universities. In the context of race equality, where both staff and students of color in academia show consistently differential outcomes to their White counterparts, professional development can mitigate disadvantage, especially where it is focused on access to opportunity. Professional development for external examiners has been an underdeveloped area but the recent establishment in the UK of the Degree Standards Project has begun to address this. The authors propose that there is nevertheless a gap in provision to support academics who aspire to become external examiners but who have had no previous experience. This chapter describes an institutional initiative to promote access to initial external examining roles through professional development and reports on participant outcomes.

Evaluation data suggest that an approach such as this can help with obtaining a first appointment and may help to mitigate some of the barriers of access to

The Role of External Examining in Higher Education: Challenges and Best Practices
Innovations in Higher Education Teaching and Learning, Volume 38, 25–41

ISSN: 2055-3641/doi:10.1108/S2055-364120210000038003

external examiner roles for staff of color. The authors argue that the sector urgently needs to diversify the ethnicity of the external examiner pool in order to provide an essential critical lens which could impact on the equity of degree outcomes for Black, Asian and Minority Ethnic students.

Keywords: Appointment; Black, Asian and Minority Ethnic; confidence; degree standards project; evaluation; external examiner; finch report; professional development; UK Quality Code for Higher Education; under-representation

CONTEXT

In response to an institutional objective to increase the number of academic staff with external examiner roles, members of the central academic development team at Sheffield Hallam University designed and delivered a professional development workshop with the aim of increasing the number of academic staff successfully securing external examiner appointments. This initiative fell within the scope of the academic developers' remit and as such was a practical initiative and not a research project. However, the approach was informed by the literature on external examining and by the developers' participation in the UK Degree Standards Project (Advance HE, 2018a), further explained below. The program was evaluated, for both internal and external reporting purposes. The high percentage of staff of color attending the workshops was of note, and evaluation data were correlated with ethnicity in order to follow their outcomes. The term Black, Asian and Minority Ethnic (BAME) staff is widely used in the HE sector and beyond but is not unproblematic. It is used in this chapter with that reservation and with the preferred alternative wording "*Minoritised.*"

CAREER VALUE OF EXTERNAL EXAMINING

Benefits to Individuals

Hannan and Silver (2006) found that the motivations for becoming an external examiner focus on both what can be gained as well as what can be contributed through the process. An important motivator for participants was collegiality; the instinct to reciprocity and a sense of obligation, a belief that without the commitment and good will of academics from across the sector the external examining system would not be able to function. They also identified the value of engaging with academics in the same discipline to enhance one's personal reputation and to promote the reputation of the home institution. An interest in how other institutions' courses are organized, managed, and delivered, and how any good practice observed could be shared amongst colleagues in home institutions, was also reported. In other words, external examining was seen as an aspect of professional development, providing a means of keeping up with current practices and issues. Rust et al. (2015) also found that these were the most frequently reported reasons for being an external examiner, referred to by over half of the 600 respondents in their study.

The acquisition of an external examining role is still generally regarded as indicative of subject expertise and academic authority: the UK Quality Code advises that external examiners "will have sufficient standing, credibility and breadth of experience within the discipline to be able to command the respect of academic peers" (The Quality Assurance Agency for Higher Education (QAA), 2018a, p. 1). The role of the external examiner as part of the sector's formal quality assurance system confers a particular status to this activity which is believed by academics to enhance their CV (Hannan & Silver, 2006, Rust et al., 2015). The adoption of teaching and academic citizenship strands within institutional promotion frameworks (Locke, Whitchurch, Smith, & Mazenod, 2016) may frame external examining activity as contributing evidence toward promotion. For example, Sheffield Hallam University recognizes external examining within the Grade 8 and Grade 9 indicators on its Academic Careers Framework (Sheffield Hallam University, 2019). Quite apart from its value to the sector and to disciplines, then, the role of external examiner also has intrinsic career value to the post holder. This raises the question of equity in access to external examining opportunities.

Under-representation of BAME Staff

There is clear evidence of the under-representation of BAME staff in the HE academic population and, in particular, in senior leadership, the professoriate and other high status roles (Leathwood, Maylor, & Moreau, 2009; Sanders & Rose-Adams, 2014). The difficulties that ethnic minority people experienced in getting promoted was the single most important complaint that emerged in the discussions and achieved the most consensus. (Carter et al., 1999: p. 53 in Leathwood et al., 2009).

Staff of color within the academy experience marginalization, lack of opportunity in higher value activities such as research and formal development (Bhopal, 2014; Bhopal & Brown, 2016). External examining activity could have an impact on such marginalization through its value as indicative evidence in academic careers frameworks and through the influence and credibility conferred by the implied expertise of its status. However, selection practices are localized and tend to rely on informal approaches through disciplinary networks and word-of-mouth communication (France & Fletcher, 2004). BAME academics are less likely than their White counterparts to have access to these powerful "insider" networks in which job offers are made and opportunities for career advancement are discussed (Bhopal, 2014). Pilkington (2013) has also identified that staff of color are less likely to be seen as leaders or experts, and informal recruitment mechanisms are clearly more exposed to such biases. This compounds the barriers to appointment for aspiring externals of color and presents challenges to the academy in diversifying external examiner profiles. The data on external examiner diversity are very scarce, however Harris and Bone (2002) found that 96% of 128 respondents from 60 Law Schools were White. Providing continuing professional development opportunities which attract BAME academics can support the diversification of university senior leadership teams and the career progression of individual BAME academics (Arday, 2018; Bhopal & Brown, 2016). Professional development opportunities which support promotion are therefore significant for this group of staff, who may struggle to access external examining positions.

PROFESSIONAL DEVELOPMENT AND EXTERNAL EXAMINING

The need to increase the professionalism of the external examining role has been highlighted in the Higher Education Academy's (HEA) sector review of external examining in the UK (Rust et al., 2015), with initial and continuing development being identified as a key aspect of professionalization. However, the inductions provided to new external examiners by host institutions are limited to a focus on the practicalities of undertaking the role within a specific organization and the requirements of its local processes and procedures. The need for professional development has become more urgent as a number of studies have highlighted weaknesses in the UK external examining system, such as inconsistences in practice norms and in conceptions and assurance of academic standards (Bloxham & Price, 2015; Hudson, Bloxham, den Outer, & Price, 2015; O'Connell et al., 2016; Rust et al., 2015; Universities UK, 2011).

At the same time, there is more scrutiny on the role of institutions in relation to the support and recognition of staff who take on external examining roles. The HEA review identified that, whilst there is an expectation that academic staff will engage in external examining, there is no formal recognition of this activity by the home institutions. Frequently they do not know or record which of their staff are external examiners (Rust et al., 2015). The review also suggests that institutions tend to focus on visiting external examiners and overlook their own staff who are externals. Crucially, institutions do not exploit their experience as a valuable resource. They note the need highlighted in the Finch Report (Universities UK., 2011) for "institutions recognising the involvement of their own staff in external examining and agreeing time for the work" (Universities UK., 2011, p. 6). They recommend that the sector

> undertakes to support and recognise external examiners in their home institutions including development of staff for the role, clear reward and recognition for the role, appropriate resourcing including time, and effective use of examiner knowledge and experience. (Rust et al., 2015, p. 13)

The Degree Standards Project

The UK Quality Code advises that externals should be established experts, but it does also allow for a developmental approach: "experienced in acting as an external examiner *or are supported by the provider… for example through training and mentoring*" (QAA, 2018b, p. 7, our italics). Whilst the Code does direct providers to "ensure that external experts are given sufficient and timely evidence and training to enable them to carry out their responsibilities" (QAA, 2018b, p. 5) this only addresses an institution's responsibilities to the externals that it appoints.

In response to the need to increase the professionalism of the external examining role, a sector-owned professional development course for external examiners has been developed in the UK as part of the Degree Standards Project (Advance HE, 2018b). The course is open to aspiring, new, and experienced examiners and aims to enable participants to develop their understanding of the role in relation to the UK Quality Code for Higher Education (QAA, 2018a) with a focus on academic standards and professional judgment in the context of external examining. Alongside this is a trainer training strand which prepares institutional nominees to deliver the professional development course internally. This enables the sector to build capacity toward a systematic and consistent development offer for external examining.

The Degree Standards Project is a demanding course which draws on a significant knowledge base and thus may not suit those at an exploratory stage. It is particularly appropriate for those with external examining experience, or who have already acquired a role. Since many calls for external examiners require or prefer prior experience of external examining, the challenge lies in acquiring an initial appointment. It is also important that successful new externals are effective in post; and as peers will look to the appointee for expertise and professional judgment it is important that they can feel confident in role. We suggest that there is a significant opportunity for institutions to provide professional development for their own staff in relation to accessing external examining appointments.

The provision of support by home institutions to become externals could have institutional benefits such as increasing the internal pool of examiners; improving the quality of staff performance in role and hence the institution's reputation; and facilitating access/removing barriers, hence also supporting the promotion and career progression of under-represented groups of staff.

We describe, below, a professional development approach developed at Sheffield Hallam University which appears to be effective in mitigating the problem of access to external examining appointments. Whilst it has benefits to all participants, it has proven notably attractive to BAME staff and has contributed to significant rates of appointment where there was no previous experience of external examining.

THE WORKSHOP

Background

A half-day workshop was developed and led by a central academic developer with inputs from Academic Quality and Standards and experienced external examiners from the academic departments. The purpose of the workshop was to (a) increase the likelihood of appointment by supporting aspiring staff in preparing for application and (b) improve the effectiveness of newly appointed externals in role by facilitating engagement with key technical and conceptual elements of external examiner practice.

During the period December 2018 to December 2019, 7 workshops were delivered to a total of 74 participants.

Design

The workshop was designed around four key elements which were intended to scaffold both acquisition of, and competence in, a first appointment. It sought to develop a broad understanding of the requirements associated with the role, to provide participants with peer support, develop their confidence in applying for roles, and to create a sense of preparedness for taking on the role of an external examiner. The four areas covered in the workshop were:

1. Sector context and the external examining role
2. Applying to be an external examiner
3. Interrogating data
4. Experiences from the field.

These are outlined in more detail below.

Sector Context and the External Examining Role

Framing the role within the context of the UK Quality Code (QAA, 2018a) and sector reports is the first step in "externalising" the external role. Many externals' dominant perception of the role lies within the critical friend (i.e., supportive peer) and quality assurance (regulatory scrutiny) domains (Hannan & Silver, 2006; Rust et al., 2015). The facilitators' own participation in Degree Standards Project workshops provided an opportunity to give more focus to the importance of external benchmarks. Input was also provided from the central Academic Quality team on formal requirements and the institutional expectations of external examiners (e.g., what makes a good external examiner report?)

Applying to be an External Examiner

Given that prospective external examiners are expected to be experienced, it can be very difficult for aspiring candidates to procure an initial appointment. The two elements tackled in the workshop to address this are *profile* and *sources of information*. In the case of the latter, few participants were aware of the JISCmail service [JISCmail (n.d.); https://www.jiscmail.ac.uk/external-examiners] and they may have underestimated the importance of specialist discussion lists. There is an in-workshop demonstration and search, based on participants' own disciplinary areas. Seeing actual calls advertised concretizes this as a key usable resource rather than just "a link."

With regards to profile, Medland (2015) identifies the issue of assessment literacy as a key area of expertise of equal importance to that of disciplinary knowledge and experience. There is also a range of other domain knowledge which informs the role and can prove of contextual value to courses seeking externals with expertise in, for example, learning technology/social media, internationalization, or employability. Participants are therefore sent a pre-workshop call for an external for Study Hard University and are asked to complete an application. They then participate in a peer exercise where they give and receive feedback on their application. This activity is followed by a short presentation which aims to focus on the skills and experience participants generally neglect; for example, assessment initiatives and course design experience; teaching recognition such as grants, internal awards or HEA fellowship. In general, participants believe that their publications, research, and subject expertise are key to appointment and have not fully considered their teaching expertise as an important contribution to their profile.

Interrogating Data

Awards Board documentation is provided containing several issues which an external might be expected to surface from the data. For example, more students being awarded first class honors than upper second class; a very high proportion of students requiring reassessment; modules with widely different spreads of marks taken by the same student cohort. As much of the data are numerical, or statistical, this can be an area of concern for new externals. Confidence in interpreting data from a course which is not their own is essential. As this is a group exercise, there is an opportunity for peer learning, and a check is made for understanding of acronyms and technical terms used in the Boards, for example, 'compensation'.

Experiences from the Field

Several experienced external examiners from within the institution contribute by reflecting on their role through the following structure: Why do it? (my motivations; how have I benefited); starting out (my experience of being a new EE – how I got my role; support I did/did not have and how I learned the job); top tips ("dos and don'ts"; what I wish I had known when I started…). This encourages participants to adopt a metacognitive appreciation and critical reflection of their preparedness and how they might approach the role. Open discussion of mistakes and misconceptions by experienced and successful examiners also helps participants to build confidence and future resilience should inevitable slip-ups or uncertainties occur.

EVALUATION OF THE WORKSHOP PROGRAM

An evaluation of the program of workshops was conducted. The purpose of the evaluation was twofold: firstly, to establish whether the program was effective in building institutional capacity in external examining (Did the program result in first-time appointments to EE positions?). Secondly, to provide developer feedback on the content and pedagogical design of the workshop (Did the workshop content and design meet the needs of participants?). Correlations with ethnicity were also analyzed to identify the specific outcomes of BAME participants. Ethics approval was obtained and the evaluation was undertaken by an educational developer, who had also been involved in the facilitation of the workshops.

Evaluation Methods

An electronic survey and a semi-structured interview were used to evaluate participants' perceptions of the workshops and their experiences of gaining appointments as external examiners. An invitation to participate in the survey was sent to all workshop participants in January 2020 and the survey was open for three weeks. The semi-structured interviews were conducted with an opportunity sample of workshop participants in January 2020.

The survey comprised both quantitative and qualitative questions. Participants also completed a series of diversity monitoring questions. An individualized link to the electronic questionnaire was emailed to all workshop participants, with two follow-up emails sent at weekly intervals. The response rate to the survey was 55%, comprising 41 of the 74 workshop participants. The workshop participants responding to the survey are referred to as "respondents." The data obtained from the survey was analyzed using Microsoft Excel.

Sixteen workshop participants were also contacted by email and invited to participate in an interview. Eleven people agreed to be interviewed, six men, and five women (note: some but not all of the interviewees completed the survey). Interviewees completed consent and diversity monitoring forms prior to the interviews. The interviews lasted approximately 20 minutes and provided insights into interviewees' opinions and experience of attending the workshop. Interviewees were asked "What did you find the most useful element of the workshop? Why?" A thematic approach was taken to analyzing these responses, with the responses being grouped according to the four key elements of the workshop. Interviewees were also asked "What motivated you to come to the workshop?" and "What do you think are the benefits of attending the workshop?" For these questions, an inductive thematic approach was taken to analyzing the interviewees' responses.

EVALUATION QUESTION 1: DID THE WORKSHOP RESULT IN FIRST-TIME APPOINTMENTS TO EE POSITIONS?

External Expert Appointments

Analysis of the 41 responses to the questionnaire indicated that three respondents had already been appointed to a role before attending the workshop. Of the 38 remaining respondents, 47% had applied for external examining roles following the workshop and 56% of these had been appointed to external examining posts. A further two respondents indicated that they had been appointed to an external examining role but apparently had not "applied." So, 12 of the 38 respondents (32%) had gained appointments as external examiners after attending the workshop. Thirteen of the respondents had been appointed as external panel members at validation events (34%). In total, 18 (47%) of the 38 respondents had gained "external expert" (external examiner or external panel member) posts after completing the workshop. Only one respondent indicated that they had decided external examining was not for them.

Previously Unsuccessful Applicants

Twenty percent (8) of the respondents indicated that they had previously applied for roles and had been unsuccessful. Four of the six respondents cited that they had not been successful due to a lack of experience.

> "Applied few times and was not nominated so basically gave up due to lack of experience I thought." (Respondent 25)

> "I did not have previous experience of external examining." (Respondent 34)

> "Many of the advertised post specified previous EE experience which I did not have." (Respondent 36)

Following the workshop, only one of these previously unsuccessful respondents had not been appointed. However, this respondent's comments suggest they were confident and prepared.

> "It was a great workshop, very engaging and enlightening and I now feel suitably prepared to apply and enquire about EE roles if and when they arise." (Respondent 22)

These previously unsuccessful respondents were asked whether they had done anything differently after attending the workshop when applying for subsequent roles. Comments included:

> "I took more of an active approach to finding external examiner opportunities." (Respondent 10)

> "Personally I think the change in my CV, lots of things I have done that never thought of mentioning on CV, but after the workshop I changed my CV and was appointed for my first application." (Respondent 25)

One respondent did say that they did nothing differently.

Confidence about What to Include in an Application

Respondents were asked to reflect retrospectively on how confident they felt about what to include in an application for an external examining role before and after they had attended the workshop. Fig. 1 indicates that their responses suggest a marked increase in the confidence of respondents after the workshop. Those indicating they felt extremely confident or very confident increased from 20% (8/41) to 51% (21/41).

Preparedness for Taking on an External Examining Role

Respondents were also asked to consider retrospectively how prepared they felt about taking on the role of an external examiner again focusing on before and after they had attended the workshop. Fig. 2 indicates that their responses suggest

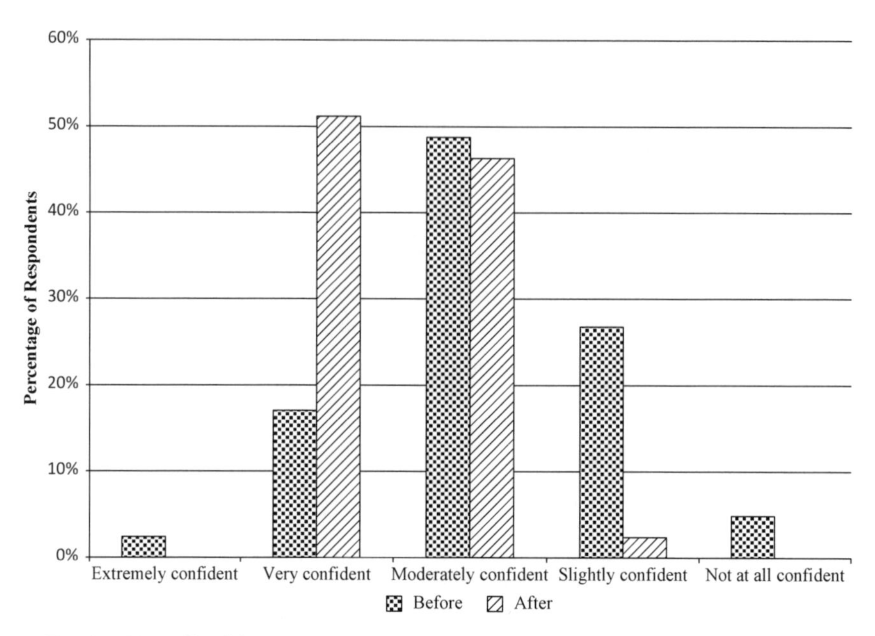

Fig. 1. How Confident Do You Feel About What to Include in an Application?

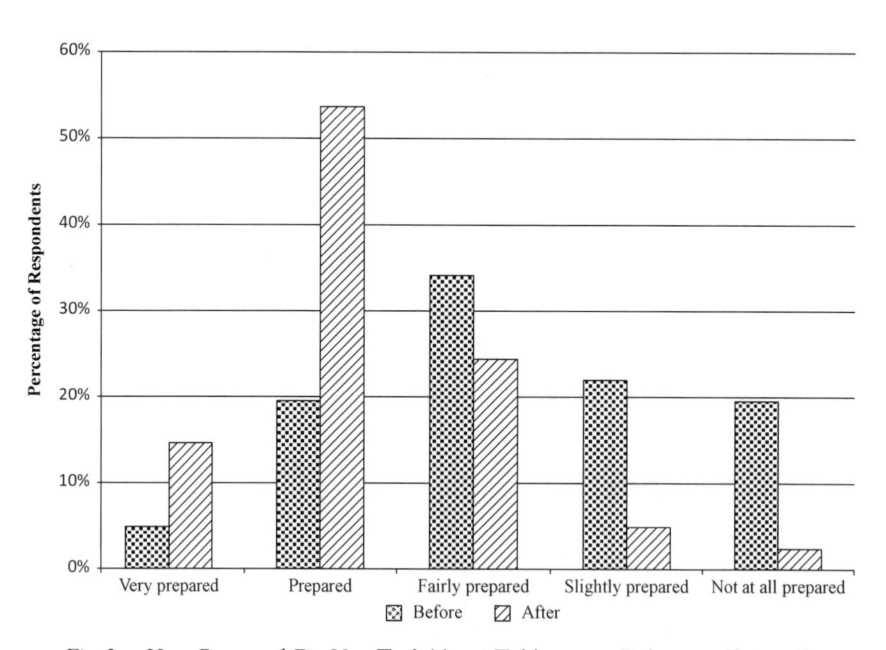

Fig. 2. How Prepared Do You Feel About Taking on a Role as an External Examiner?

that there was a sizable increase in their feelings of preparedness after the workshop. Those indicating they felt very prepared or prepared increased from 24% (10/41) to 68% (28/41).

Summary

The data suggest that the workshop was an effective tool in building institutional capacity in external examining. Almost half of the respondents had been appointed as external experts either in an external examining role or as an external member of a course validation panel. Furthermore, its effectiveness in supporting participants with the application process is shown when the success rate of those who had been previously unsuccessful is considered, as all but one had secured a position. The evidence presented indicates that there was an increase in the confidence of survey respondents about what to include in their applications and their perceptions of their preparedness for taking on the role of an external examiner.

EVALUATION QUESTION 2: DID THE WORKSHOP CONTENT AND DESIGN MEET THE NEEDS OF PARTICIPANTS?

Sector Context and the External Examiner Role

The sessions focusing on the sector context and the external examiner role were valued and considered important aspects of the workshop. Some had not considered fully the quality and academic standards aspects of the role.

> "What was interesting, I thought, was the aspect that you are effectively part of the quality assurance process of that University and therefore the governance of that University and I think that really brought it home, the importance of the role and it should be taken seriously. I think that was really useful because I think that it made some very useful and important points that helped me understand the role a little better." (Interviewee 10)

> "......understanding the types of roles that the external examiner fulfils – provided a really useful understanding." (Interviewee 11)

Applying to be an External Examiner

The pre-workshop call for Study Hard University and completion of a mock application form, followed by an exercise providing peer feedback was seen as a very valuable aspect of the course.

> "Tailoring the application: I didn't want to do the exercise before the workshop I was quite irritated! Whilst I had seen positions coming up I didn't know how to write that letter or put the CV together. Physically doing something, bringing it along, getting the positive and negatives, people saying you've got quite a lot haven't you! You never look at yourself in that way. I went away and did it, thinking I can do this. And something came up the next day. The workshop definitely pushed me to get it done. When you're putting stuff out there you want it to be right." (Interviewee 9)

> "A really good opportunity to cast an eye over your credentials in terms of your CV, your experience, that was really good because then it allowed us to plug the gaps." (Interviewee 2)

"The activity I thought was brilliant because it allowed me to think yes this is what I can include, this is what I haven't included, and that whole peer sort of support…Because in doing that, and then sharing the ideas, it really emphasised what could go in there. What was important and how to present it. And that was so different to what I'd done previously…. So yeah, that really helped sort of shape things." (Interviewee 1)

Knowing where to find information about external examining posts was also identified as an important take away from the workshop. Some interviewee said they were unaware of the JISCmail list prior to the workshop.

Critically Analyzing Data

The exercise requiring participants to explore and comment on a spreadsheet of marks presented at a board was identified as having helped build confidence.

"I just felt a bit more confident to be able to look at other people's marks." (Interviewee 5)

"Looking at results and module scores and things like that in a format that's not like the ones I'm used to on my course. I think that helped with me looking at some unfamiliar documentation at a different institution." (Interviewee 8)

"It was really useful to get different people's perspectives on what they would see from that data and that was a great way to get started with it. Actually what would you do and how you need to notice things." (Interviewee 4)

Experiences from the Field

A session provided by an experienced external examiner was identified by most interviewees as being user friendly and very helpful.

"There was a gentleman that spoke about his experiences of being an external examiner. I found that really useful." (Interviewee 8)

What Other Needs Where Met by Participating in the Workshop?

The motivations and benefits of attending a workshop were also explored in the interviews. A key motivation was getting a better understanding of what the external examiner role entailed, together with a desire to gain an objective and authoritative view of the topic.

"I think going to a workshop like that just helps put a lot of context to things that you don't always get when you're hearing things on the grapevine….you don't understand the full context of what's expected…….understanding more about it from an objective point of view is helpful." (Interviewee 5)

Some attended as part of their self-development or because they did not feel they had the confidence to just apply. Others thought attendance would be useful to have on their CVs.

"it makes me feel a lot more confident" (Interviewee 5)

"It made the EE role doable…taking some of the fear about what's going to be involved." (Interviewee 9)

"Definitely made it clear for me….By attending the workshop, it's given me more scope for what the external examiner can do for the [my] course." (Interviewee 11)

The importance of meeting other people from across the university to draw on their experiences was also a motivator. Building confidence and gaining clarification through conversations with peers were identified as an important aspect of workshop attendance, as was the potential for forming a support network.

> "reassurance you can have conversations with colleagues....it gave me peace of mind that I could do the role...that is was something within my capabilities....it helped me create a working relationship with the institution I'm working with because it gave me some good steerage." (Interviewee 10)

> "....spending time with other people who were in a similar position, it's useful to talk to other people." (Interviewee 6)

> "I realised when I came to the workshop that there were quite a lot of people in my situation, who were still looking, so I felt it's not just me!" (Interviewee 7)

> "And just the general way that the training was set up, it was very informal, is really good, there was a lot of discussions and opportunities to get other people's views and opinions." (Interviewee 2)

Summary

Feedback from those interviewed suggested that all of the four key elements of the workshop were valued and provided people with opportunities to explore aspects of the role they had not considered, share ideas, and build confidence. As a central offer facilitated by a range of experienced practitioners, interviewees felt that the workshop had provided them with an objective and authoritative overview of the external examining role and its requirements. The peer conversations made possible through the workshop were seen as boosting their confidence in relation to applying for and being successful in the role.

WHAT WERE THE OUTCOMES FOR BAME STAFF?

External Expert Appointments

The survey data were analyzed to explore differences between the experiences of the White and BAME respondents. Sixty-three percent of the respondents were White, 32% were BAME, and 5% did not indicate their ethnicity. The percentage of White respondents applying for external examiner posts after the workshop was very similar (46%) compared with (42%) of the BAME respondents. Of these, 60% of the White respondents had been successful in their applications compared with 40% of the BAME respondents.

Thirty-eight percent of the White respondents had been appointed as external examiners compared with 17% of the BAME respondents and 38% of the White respondents had been appointed as external panel members at validation events compared with 33% of BAME respondents. Overall, 50% of the White respondents had gained "external expert" appointments compared with 42% of the BAME respondents.

Confidence about What to Include in an Application

Comparisons were made between the answers of White respondents and the BAME respondents when asked to reflect retrospectively on how confident they felt about what to include in an application for an external examining role before and after they had attended the workshop. This showed that there was a comparable change in the confidence of respondents after the workshop, Fig. 3. The White respondents indicating they felt extremely confident or very confident increased from 19% (5/27) to 52% (14/27) and the BAME respondents from 17% (2/12) to 50% (6/12).

Preparedness for Taking on an External Examining Role

Comparisons were also made between the answers of White respondents and the BAME respondents when asked to consider retrospectively how prepared they felt about taking on the role of an external examiner, again focusing on before and after they had attended the workshop. This showed a comparable change in perceptions of preparedness (Fig. 4). The White respondents indicating that they felt very prepared or prepared increased from 19% (5/27) to 67% (18/27) and the BAME respondents from 33% (4/12) to 75% (9/12). These represent a 48-percentage point change and a 42-percentage point change, respectively.

Summary

Although not part of the evaluation, it is important to note that the workshop attracted particularly high numbers of BAME staff (24.4% compared to the institution population of 9.7%). It may be significant that (a) the offer is explicit in its relevance to the role of external examining; (b) it is clearly aimed at those without

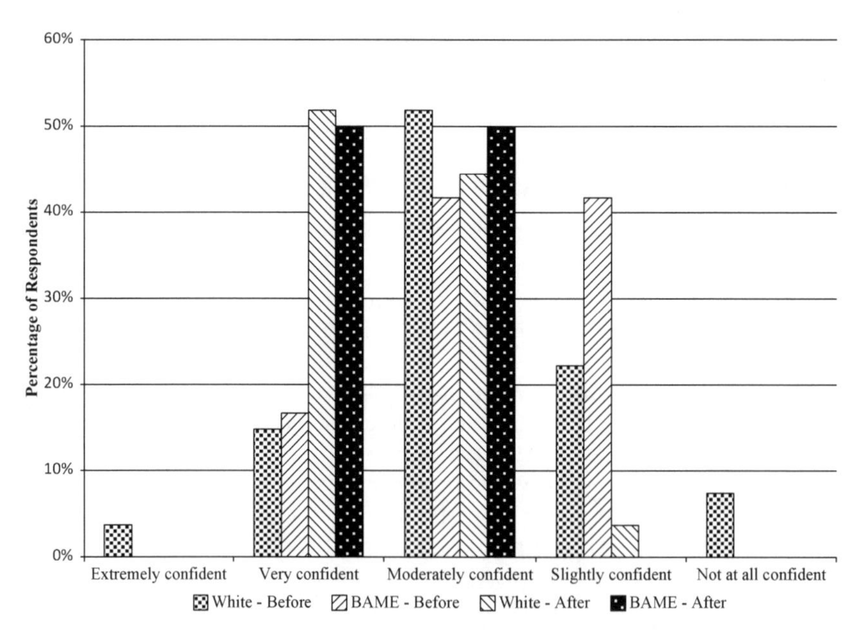

Fig. 3. How Confident Do You Feel About What to Include in an Application?

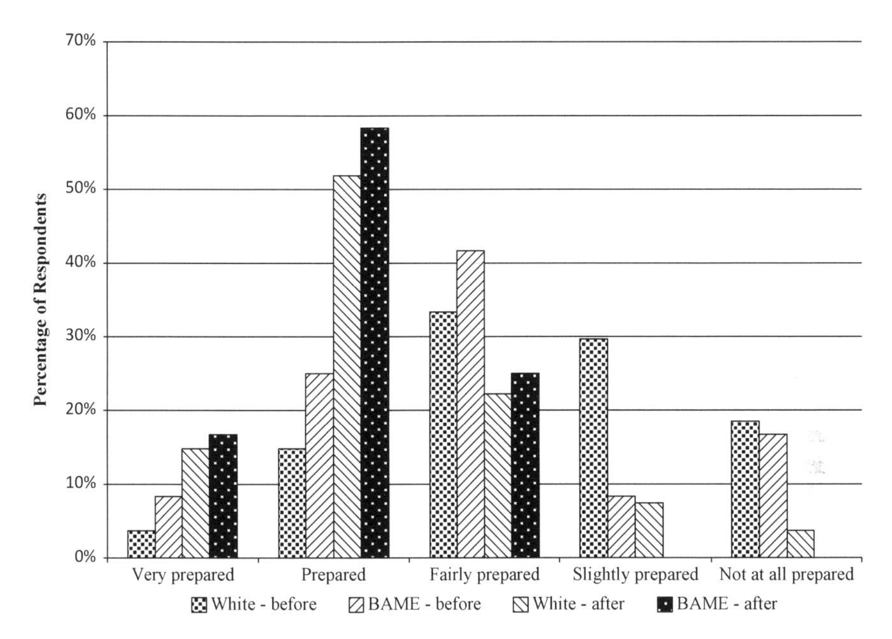

Fig. 4. How Prepared Do You Feel About Taking on a Role as an External Examiner?

such roles currently; and (c) it is a central offer with open access and cross-institutional publicity via an all-staff email as well as website listing. In combination, these factors may have helped to neutralize some of the barriers to access such as gatekeeping behaviors. These figures also suggest a demand from this group for professional development which supports career progression.

There remains a differential in appointment to examiner roles between White and BAME staff but this is reduced when other external roles are included. There is also some dependency on external factors beyond the scope of the workshop (i.e., the recruiting institutions). There does appear to be a strong effect for both groups in relation to increased confidence and preparedness. Arguably this is an outcome which goes beyond external examining specifically and may contribute to resilience or readiness to take up other opportunities. Clearly, the samples are not large and we were unable to access the outcomes of those who did not participate in the evaluation but there appear to have been positive outcomes for BAME staff. There is potential for further mentoring and follow-up to provide additional support, including fostering peer support communities with experienced externals.

THE NEED TO DIVERSIFY THE EXTERNAL EXAMINER POOL

The UK Quality Code expects that externals will be "drawn from a relevant variety of institutional or professional contexts and traditions" for the purpose of "wide-ranging external scrutiny" (QAA, 2018b, p. 8) but makes no mention of diversity, which can bring a form of scrutiny which could otherwise be lacking. For example in the UK, the disparity in good degree outcomes for students of color is both consistent and persistent (Universities UK & the National Union of Students, 2019). The term "Degree Awarding Gap" acknowledges systemic and structural factors which HE institutions need to address. Increasing the racial diversity of the external examining pool contributes to this agenda in two ways: by supporting access to esteem and promotional indicators for individual academics of color; and through the critical surfacing of unconscious bias within academic practice. The premise of 'externality' in quality assurance is based on the notion of distance from local, familiar and parochial practices and norms. In addition to its benchmarking function, there is the opportunity to view procedures, pedagogic and assessment practices through an "impartial" lens. It allows for the supportive interrogation of both individual and collective methods, assumptions and beliefs. The "Why Is My Curriculum White?" campaign (Hussain, 2015) draws attention to the project of decolonizing the curriculum. This should be a legitimate area of scrutiny for an external examiner, as is the potential for unconscious bias in marking, feedback, placement experience, etc. A racially diverse external examiner community is better positioned to ensure such scrutiny:

> "Decolonising the curriculum relies upon who we recruit and promote within the academy, training teachers and researchers of different backgrounds who will contribute to reshaping the academic canon as well as pedagogical practices and creating new institutional norms." (Begum & Saini, 2019, p. 198)

Additionally, the Finch Report (Universities UK, 2011) makes two recommendations relating to students (a) having access to reports (Recommendation 12, p. 10) and (b) knowing who their external examiners are (Recommendation 13, p. 10). The presence of external examiners of color might be seen as role models to BAME students whilst also exposing White students to diverse academic authority figures.

From our data, it appears that institutional support such as this workshop may have a positive effect in improving BAME access to external examining roles. Alongside other measures, such as improvements in recruitment and advertising, institutions can contribute to the diversity of appointments by providing high-quality development for academics new to external examining.

REFERENCES

Advance HE. (2018a). Degree Standards project. Retrieved from https://www.heacademy.ac.uk/degree-standards

Advance HE. (2018b). Professional development course for external examiners. Retrieved from https://www.heacademy.ac.uk/training-events/professional-development/external-examining-course

Arday, J. (2018). Understanding race and educational leadership in higher education: Exploring the Black and ethnic minority (BME) experience. *Management in Education, 32*(4), 192–200. https://doi.org/10.1177/0892020618791002

Begum, N., & Saini, R. (2019). Decolonising the curriculum. *Political Studies Review, 17*(2), 196–201. https://doi.org/10.1177/1478929918808459

Bhopal, K. (2014). *The experience of BME academics in higher education: Aspirations in the face of inequality. Stimulus paper.* London: Leadership Foundation for Higher Education. Retrieved from https://www.lfhe.ac.uk/en/components/publication.cfm/BhopalST26

Bhopal, K., & Brown, H. (2016). *Black and minority ethnic leaders: Support networks and strategies for success in higher education*. London: Leadership Foundation for Higher Education.

Bloxham, S., & Price, M. (2015). External examining: Fit for purpose? *Studies in Higher Education, 40*(2), 195–211. https://doi.org/10.1080/03075079.2013.823931

France, D., & Fletcher, S. (2004). The motivations and professional development needs of aspiring and serving external examiners in the GEES disciplines. *Planet, 13*(1), 30–34. https://doi.org/10.11120/plan.2004.00130030b

Hannan, A., & Silver, H. (2006). On being an external examiner. *Studies in Higher Education, 31*(1), 57–69. https://doi.org/10.1080/03075070500392300

Harris, P., & Bone, A. (2002). The experience of external examiners for undergraduate law degrees: A research survey. *The Law Teacher, 36*(2), 168–183. https://doi.org/10.1080/03069400.2002.9993103

Hudson, J., & Bloxham, S., den Outer, B., & Price, M. (2015). Conceptual acrobatics: Talking about assessment standards in the transparency era. *Studies in Higher Education, 42*(7), 1–15. https://doi.org/10.1080/03075079.2015.1092130

Hussain, M. (2015, March 11). *Why is my curriculum white?* NUS – National Union of Students. Retrieved from https://www.nus.org.uk/en/news/why-is-my-curriculum-white/

JISCmail. (n.d.). Retrieved from https://www.jiscmail.ac.uk/external-examiners. Accessed on September 29, 2020,

Leathwood, C., Maylor, U., & Moreau, M. (2009). *The experience of black and minority ethnic staff working in higher education*. London: Institute for Policy Studies in Education, [ebook]. Retrieved from http://www.ecu.ac.uk/wp-content/uploads/external/experience-of-bme-staff-in-he.pdf

Locke, W., Whitchurch, C., Smith, H. J., & Mazenod, A. (2016). *Shifting landscapes: Meeting the staff development needs of the changing academic workforce*. York: The Higher Education Academy.

Medland, E. (2015). Examining the assessment literacy of external examiners. *London Review of Education, 13*(3), 21–33. https://doi.org/10.18546/LRE.13.3.04

O'Connell, B., De Lange, P., Freeman, M., Hancock, P., Abraham, A., Howieson, B., & Watty, K. (2016). Does calibration reduce variability in the assessment of accounting learning outcomes? *Assessment & Evaluation in Higher Education, 41*(3), 331–349. https://doi.org/10.1080/02602938.2015.1008398

Pilkington, A. (2013). The interacting dynamics of institutional racism in higher education. *Race Ethnicity and Education, 16*(2), 225–245. https://doi.org/10.1080/13613324.2011.646255

The Quality Assurance Agency for Higher Education (QAA). (2018a, May). *The UK Quality Code for Higher Education*. Retrieved from https://www.qaa.ac.uk/quality-code#

The Quality Assurance Agency for Higher Education (QAA). (2018b, November). *UK Quality Code for Higher Education, Advice and Guidance, External Expertise*. Retrieved from https://www.qaa.ac.uk/en/quality-code/advice-and-guidance/external-expertise

Rust, C., Bloxham, S., Hudson, J., den Outer, B., Price, M., & Stoakes, G. (2015). *A review of external examining arrangements across the UK*. Report to the UK higher education funding bodies by the Higher Education Academy. Retrieved from https://www.researchgate.net/publication/279512279_A_review_of_external_examining_arrangements_across_the_UK_Report_to_the_UK_higher_education_funding_bodies_by_the_Higher_Education_Academy

Sanders, J., & Rose-Adams, J. (2014). Black and Minority ethnic student attainment: A survey of research and exploration of the importance of teacher and student expectations. *Widening Participation and Lifelong Learning, 16*(2), 5–27. https://doi.org/10.5456/WPLL.16.2.5

Sheffield Hallam University. (2019, June). *Academic Career Framework*. Retrieved from https://blogs.shu.ac.uk/acf

Universities UK & the National Union of Students. (2019). *Black, Asian and minority ethnic student attainment ay UK universities: # closing the gap*. London: Universities UK & the National Union of Students. Retrieved from https://www.universitiesuk.ac.uk/policy-and-analysis/reports/Pages/bame-student-attainment-uk-universities-closing-the-gap.aspx

Universities UK. (2011). *Review of external examining arrangements in universities and colleges in the UK: Final report and recommendations (Finch Report)*. London: Universities UK. Retrieved from https://www.universitiesuk.ac.uk/policy-and-analysis/reports/Pages/external-examining-arrangements-review.aspx

CHAPTER 4

AUTHENTIC ASSESSMENTS AND THE EXTERNAL EXAMINER

Mikhaila Burgess and Helen Phillips

ABSTRACT

A key role of the external examiner is to review student work submitted for assessment plus the feedback and grading undertaken on that work by academic staff. The aim of this is to ensure equitability between the assessments of individual students' achievement and consistency and comparability across courses throughout the program and with commensurate study levels and programs at other institutions, whilst safeguarding academic standards.

The variety of assessment-types that an external examiner may review can be diverse. When the primary focus of the work being assessed is tangible, such as with written examinations or assignments, external examiners are able to view student achievements and assessor actions through a lens comparable to that of the original assessors. However, this process cannot adequately capture assessment-types where the only evidence is proxies to the original achievement. In this chapter, the authors explore the concept of authentic assessments, the benefits of incorporating them within study programs, identify challenges pertaining to their presence to holistic quality assurance (QA) processes in general, and the role of the external examiner in particular. The authors will demonstrate how adopting non-intrusive technologies for recording and verifying authentic assessment practices can strengthen the QA process for the benefit of all stakeholders. For illustration, a case study is employed to demonstrate how these challenges have been tackled regarding

The Role of External Examining in Higher Education: Challenges and Best Practices
Innovations in Higher Education Teaching and Learning, Volume 38, 43–59

ISSN: 2055-3641/doi:10.1108/S2055-364120210000038004

performance-based authentic assessments at an institution in Norway. The chapter concludes with a summary plus a call to arms for further research into how quality and consistency can be assured when authentic assessments are employed.

Keywords: Authentic assessment; performance assessment; external examiner; quality assurance; lecture capture technology; higher education; Norway; UK; external quality monitoring

An external examiner needs to complete a number of tasks during their role. One of these is to review student work submitted for assessment plus the feedback and grading undertaken on that work by academic staff. The aim of this is to ensure equitability between assessments of individual students' achievement as well as consistency and comparability across courses throughout the program and with commensurate study levels and programs at other institutions, whilst safeguarding academic standards. The variety of assessment-types that an external examiner may review can be diverse, covering traditional written exams, practical work, and performance-oriented activities. Reviewing assessment and grading practices across a program through the critical consideration of samples of students' submitted work provided in evidence, along with the subsequent evaluations by academic staff, is a standard practice across UK Higher Education. When the primary focus of the submitted work being assessed is tangle, such as term papers, essays, and traditional written exams, this system enables external examiners to view student achievements through a lens comparable to that of the original assessors. However, this process cannot adequately capture all current assessment practices, such as performance-oriented authentic assessments where the sole evidence of student activities are typically proxies to the original achievement, such as student or staff notes pertaining to the learning activity undertaken.

QUALITY ASSURANCE CHALLENGES

Experiential learning activities and authentic assessments are incorporated into Higher Education (HE) programs in order to enhance the employability of graduates (Sotiriadou, Logan, Daly, & Guest, 2019), whereby learning and assessment activities mimic skills and practice required in the relevant professional workplace, with an emphasis on the process followed to achieve the final results. As such, these activities and assessments often incorporate some degree of performance, where a student demonstrates their application of knowledge and skills to a domain-relevant challenge within some environment.

The external review usually focuses on the static products of such practice-oriented assessment (written transcripts, minutes, logbooks, etc.) rather than the actual process and performance (the running of assessment by academic staff, involvement of industry professionals, and their completion by students) which means external examiners are unable to scrutinize and evaluate the complete body of evidence pertaining to students' learning and achievements. This restricts their ability to express comprehensive opinions about the quality of the assessment process and the standards of learning across that program.

Excluding authentic and, specifically, performance-oriented assessments from the external examination review process can result in:

- Gaps in assessment literacy of both the original assessors and the external examiners relating to the use of authentic assessments in a study program remaining unidentified by the institution, external bodies, and the examiners themselves.
- An incomplete external quality monitoring (EQM) process, potentially resulting in inconsistencies and variable practices across assessment implementation and grading remaining unidentified and therefore unchallenged, and thus undermining the veracity of the EQM process.

Such a gap in the quality assurance (QA) system limits its efficacy, to the detriment of all stakeholders. The first step in combating this issue is to explore and confirm the details of this gap and explicitly acknowledge its existence. The second is to identify methods for eliminating this gap as far as possible by developing a domain-specific toolkit for institutions to employ in order to improve transparency of assessment practices and procedures that support the QA process in general, and the external examiners in particular.

CHAPTER OVERVIEW

In this chapter, we explore the concept of authentic assessments, the benefits of incorporating authentic assessments, both formative and summative, within HE study programs, identify challenges pertaining to the presence of these assessments to holistic QA processes in general, and the role of the external examiner in particular.

We will argue that adopting a variety of non-intrusive technologies for appropriately recording and verifying authentic assessment practices in action can:

- increase the transparency of assessment and grading practices;
- add to the body of evidence of student learning available to examiners;
- increase the rigor, validity, and utility of external examiner reviews and reports;
- strengthen the QA process for the benefit of all stakeholders.

In the next section, we explore the concept of authentic assessments, the difference between these and traditional assessments, and outlining the specific challenges pertaining to performance-based authentic assessments. We then continue by identifying the gaps currently associated with the review of such assessment practices in the external examination process. The following section focuses on one subject domain, that of computing, in order to propose a toolkit for adaption and adoption across institutions to start reducing that gap. We follow that with a case study to illustrate how this toolkit has been employed in practice, specifically to computing undergraduate education in Norway. Due to the narrow focus of this illustrative case study, the chapter concludes by emphasizing the limitations of this work with a recommendation for others to develop these ideas further in other subject domains.

AUTHENTIC ASSESSMENT

One traditionally associates university assessments with time-constrained written exams and essays (McKie, 2019). Whilst these can be effective at testing a student's ability to recall memorized facts under pressure, the need for this skill is questionable during this fourth industrial revolution, the age of easily accessible and ever-growing online reference resources. This "learn and regurgitate" approach to assessment is not conducive to effective learning (McKie, 2019). In some professions, such as medicine, quick recall of facts is essential, but increasingly it is the ability to process and demonstrate knowledge and apply it to the challenge at hand that is required and valued more highly. This is illustrated within the European Higher Education Area through the skill-related level descriptors outlined in the European Qualifications Framework for Lifelong Learning, whereby the learning outcomes for HE explicitly state the requirement for students to be able to demonstrate skills relevant to the profession. For example, the learning outcomes for bachelor study at level 6 explicitly require "advanced skills, demonstrating mastery and innovation, required to solve complex and unpredictable problems in a specialised field of work or study" (European Commission, 2018, p. 13).

As such there has been a growing interest in, and adoption of, learning activities and assessments that aim to equip students not only with theoretical knowledge and its application within an academic environment, but also with the ability to apply such knowledge to practical real-world situations (Darling-Hammond & Snyder, 2000).

Experiential Learning & Authentic Assessment

The concept of authentic assessment, which complements the traditional assessment-types, is based upon the close alignment of assessments with the requirements of specific, relevant professional practice, mimicking appropriate activities and tasks as present within the workplace. It is typically focused on developing and testing higher-order thinking skills, such as problem-solving and critical thinking, rather than memorization, through exercises that are more realistic within the context of the "real world" (Weliwita & Witharana, 2019). When designed well, these activities are therefore of greater benefit to all stakeholders:

- Students – in developing and practicing relevant skills in a supportive education environment that will be invaluable to them after graduation,

- Educators – in supporting students in becoming professionals in their field, and
- Future employers – through the growth of a workforce-ready pool of graduates, already practiced in a range of practical skills required in the profession in addition to having sound theoretical knowledge.

In conjunction, the assessment practice also needs to be aligned with instruction and learning activities. Increased constructive alignment of instruction, learning, and assessment (ILA), as explained by John Biggs (Biggs & Tang, 2011), is essential for facilitating students developing knowledge, skills, competence and attitudes that directly enhance their employability prospects (Berger & Wild, 2017; Kinash, McGillivray, & Crane, 2018; Sotiriadou et al., 2019). In order to run effective authentic assessments, appropriate instruction and learning activities therefore also need to be employed, supporting students in their development of profession-related knowledge and skills through discovery and experience. The employment of experiential learning activities (Kolb, 2015) is therefore essential for ensuring full constructive alignment of ILA.

One of the crucial underlying premises of authentic assessment is that it values the thinking that's been undertaken behind the work, the process of arriving at the final result, as much as the finished result itself (Savin-Baden, 2003). By focusing on the process rather than product, both student engagement and educator feedback are actively encouraged. It replaces the students' focus on "getting the right result by any method(s) available" with the need to develop the ability to use acquired knowledge and develop their problem-solving skills, both of which are vital to any profession where independent professional thinking and working is valued over following direct instructions and/or repetition of standard tasks.

Authenticity of Learning Activities

Experiential learning activities and authentic assessments incorporated into study programs are varied but can include, for example:

- Interactive oral examinations;
- Peer interactions, including debates and discussions;
- Deliveries and/or presentations to external or industry clients;
- Individual and/or Team problem solving;
- Practical, hands-on experiments;
- Work-integrated learning;
- Mock practical scenarios, potentially involving role play;
- Demonstrations of relevant subject mastery in simulated or real professional environments.

The common feature of these apparently diverse activities is the simulation of skills required within the professional workplace and the live performance nature of the work being undertaken, and an emphasis on the process followed to achieve the final result(s).

Authenticity is not, however, absolute. It cannot be judged on a scale from not authentic to highly authentic. Neither is authenticity consistent across subject areas. What could be considered an authentic assessment in one domain of practice may not be considered as such in another. The designers of such learning activities need to consider the competencies required within the relevant professional field of practice. For example, performance assessments such as presentations and vivas may be considered authentic when these, or closely comparable activities, are also used within the professional domain to communicate and discuss ideas, plans, achievements, etc. to groups of others through structured presentations, which are common in the domains of IT and Management. However, the same assessment type would not be authentic in a domain where this type of activity is not common practice, such as nursing, where the practical Objective Structured Clinical Examination (OSCE) method of assessment would instead be deemed authentic.

The types of assessment used as "authentic" therefore need be determined based upon consideration of the specific subject domain and future careers of program graduates, and relevant employability skills, in order to determine what will directly relate to and support the potential future career of the students.

Performance-Based Authentic Assessments

"Authentic assessment" and "performance assessment" are often considered synonymous, but it is important to point out that although related they are not necessarily the same. In performance assessments students undertake some live activity to demonstrate to their assessor(s) their ability to complete a defined piece of work, whereby the assessor can evaluate their behavior and approach. Performance-based authentic assessments are therefore those designed to assess live demonstrations of relevant skills within a real-world context (Meyer, 1992).

Inclusion of performance-based authentic assessment activities poses a particular challenge for external examiners and the QA process. Traditional static assessment submissions cannot realistically capture a performance-oriented assessment. The only evidence usually available of the undertaken assessment are proxies to the original achievement, such as student or staff notes about a presentation or live demonstration, or minutes from meetings. Such proxies can be highly variable in quality and detail due to these being produced in support of the original assessments, potentially as afterthoughts and not necessarily at the time of the performance. These proxies thus provide some insight into the assessment but are distinct from the activity that was originally performed and assessed.

Performance assessments are used across a wide variety of fields, wherein they're used to evaluate student achievements in many areas including, but not limited to:

- Presentation skills and communication (oral & visual) skills in order to communicate ideas and achievements to specific target audiences (e.g., stakeholders, employers, peers);
- Ability to appropriately and directly engage with field-relevant individuals such as investors, patients, clients, or other stakeholders;
- Demonstrating explicit ability to critically evaluate their work and learning;
- Ability to engage in professional and/or academic discussion with others;
- Ability to defend and explain achievements, demonstrating awareness of process and professional practice;
- Practical, live, and commentated demonstration and/or presentation of achievement, such as developed hardware or a produced documentary (i.e., the tangible deliverables as developed by the student for their assessment);
- Demonstration of an ability to apply knowledge, methods, and professional-level practices to solve potentially new and unseen problems.

The exclusion of such assessments from consideration and evaluation by external examiners therefore leaves a significant gap in the education QA process where these are determined authentic to the domain and as such are incorporated within a study program's portfolio of assessment methods.

EXTERNAL EXAMINERS AND AUTHENTIC ASSESSMENTS

External examiners are used throughout the HE system. It is well known that they are an essential part of the QA process across UK and Ireland, but they are also present in many other systems across Europe, including Norway. Some systems are well established, and some are relatively young. For example, the UK external education system was born in the mid-nineteenth century out of an agreement for the University of Oxford to supply external reviewers to the then newly formed Durham University (Higher Education Academy (HEA), 2013). In Norway, the system is considerably younger, with explicit consideration of QA in education only being explicitly present since the 2003 establishment of the Norwegian Agency for Quality Assurance in Education (NOKUT) (Danø & Stensaker, 2007; Lycke, 2004; Welle-Strand & Thune, 2002). Irrespective of the system, implementation and the length of time this has been adopted, the fundamentals of the role of the external examiner remains relatively consistent.

Role of the External Examiner

The HEA's[1] *Handbook for External Examiners* describes the external examiner as "experienced higher education teachers who offer an independent assessment of academic standards and the quality of assessment to the appointing institution" (HEA, 2013, p. 5). However, rather than being solely an independent inspector of consistency and standards the current external examiner role also includes being a "critical friend," supporting the program and institution, with the additional expectation that they will "identify strengths, weaknesses and good practice of the provision and play a role in quality enhancement" (HEA, 2013, p. 5).

Through this dual role, external examiners ensure that:

- students are treated and assessed consistently and fairly across the program to which they are attached and in line with practices, levels and standards with other comparable programs and institutions;
- academic staff are supported and developed through the provision of feedback and guidance, thus supporting the development of the program, eliminating identified issues in the future, and improving the quality of education provision and therefore also, indirectly, the student experience.

This role is only possible with the support of the institution to which the examiner is appointed, including provision of access to all relevant information and documentation, and clear evidence of assessed student achievements.

Direct & Indirect Quality Assurance for Authentic Assessments

In order to review the quality of student assessment across a study program, or specific sections of a program, external examiners are provided access to a variety of documents pertaining to assessments in every course. This can include one, more or all of the following:

- Assessment tasks as provided to the students;
- Assessment criteria or rubrics, as used by assessors when evaluating submissions (may also be provided to students to facilitate their understanding of, and engagement with, assessment criteria);
- Evidence of assessment moderation (where the external examiners have not been directly involved at this stage of assessment creation);
- Samples of student submissions, usually distributed across the grading range and boundaries;
- Assessor evaluations and grades for the sample submissions;
- Evidence of moderation of evaluations and grading, ideally also containing indication of scholarly discussion between the moderator and assessor;
- Grade listing for each class showing all grades attained and supporting statistical data (such as grade distribution, mean, and standard deviation);
- Explicit documented course staff reflections on the student cohort and assessment practice(s).

The traditional review of assessment tasks and related practices are relatively straightforward when these are designed and set within the program with criterion referenced assessment supporting a clear task description, whereby tangible, static deliverables produced by learners are assessed against the pre-determined set of competencies. This is not the case with authentic assessments, in particular those incorporating an element of performance, due to the often lack of tangible evidence of the work being assessed available to the external examiner.

An additional challenge arises when multiple assessors evaluate the performance, such as two assessors participating in a final year project viva. Where this happens, the only evidence of the student's achievement and evaluation process available to the external examiner may be one or more final grading sheets from the assessors pertaining to an assessment invisible to anyone not present at the original performance. This excludes not only external examiners from undertaking their QA responsibilities but also precludes any additional faculty internal assessment moderation due to the lack of a static student deliverable. In addition, this also adversely impacts on the transparency of the assessment process undertaken by the original assessors.

The Quality Assurance Gap

Although the inclusion of performance-oriented authentic assessments poses a significant challenge for the external examiner in undertaking their QA role, this should not result in the QA gap being ignored nor education practices adapted to eliminate such assessments from study programs. What is needed is an approach for reducing and, where possible, eliminating this gap. Technology may provide a solution.

Technology in Education

The availability and use of supporting technology within education has developed significantly from the basic content management systems of a decade ago, whereby teaching materials, such as lecture slides were provided to students though some online portal. Although some materials are still provided to students in this way, increasingly technology is being used to enhance and facilitate new methods of ILA and the provision of feedback to learners, such as through flipped classrooms (Hwang, Yin, & Chu, 2019), digital simulation of experiments and the development of programs for online or blended delivery. Both teaching staff and their students are therefore familiar with using various technologies throughout education settings. Such familiarity means technologies used in learning environments are often no longer seen as intrusive and a hinderance to learning and development but are expected to be supportive in a variety of ways, including the fostering of experiential learning (Dabbagh & Fake, 2017).

As Davies, Mullan, and Feldman (2017, p. 16) explain, "Technology-enhanced learning can improve the efficiency of [education] provision." The adoption of such technologies provides the opportunity for programs to develop new, more appropriate assessment methods to better align with the intended learning outcomes. They also support the incorporation of a wider variety of realistic, authentic assessments as relevant to the professional domain. In conjunction, such technologies can also be used to make student achievements more transparent to both internal assessment moderators and external examiners.

Technology Supported EQM

Due to the time involved in identifying, testing, and then adopting technologies to support learning and assessment, and facilitate education QA, this task should not be delegated solely to individual academic staff. A set of tools needs to be identified across each subject domain to support academic staff in identifying and then implementing those which are most appropriate for adoption within their specialist field. This toolkit should be developed through solid research and experimentation, in collaboration with academic staff (as appropriate, whilst minimizing unnecessary additional workload), then made available to academic staff in the most appropriate manner to seamlessly support their professional practice, with minimal disruption and zero enforced change to ILA practices.

Many digital tools already exist within HE environments that could be repurposed for inclusion in such toolkits, due to their prior identification, selection, and installation to support the specific needs of pedagogic practice within each specialized subject domain. The first proposed tool in this toolkit, applicable across a wide variety of subject domains, is lecture capture or recording technologies. Due to their prevalence across the HE sector, irrespective of subject area, these could be incorporated into authentic learning and assessment practices to provide a clearer record of the activity, student performance, and academic assessors in action.

Reutilization of Lecture Capture Technologies

Increasingly across the sector, lecture capture technologies are being used with the aim of supporting student learning and widening availability of education to students who may not be able to attend every scheduled teaching session, due to work or family commitments. Although drawbacks of such practices are present and the impact on academic practice of educators are unclear (Joseph-Richard, Jessop, Okafor, Almpanis, & Price, 2018), the presence of recording equipment in campus rooms is becoming an increasingly familiar sight and, as such, are becoming less intrusive into daily learning activities.

Due to the technological developments and the gradual shift to acceptance and familiarity of lecture capture tools, the potential exists for these to be reutilized and incorporated, non-intrusively, into performance-oriented learning and assessment activities. For example, they enable students to practice their presentation skills, watching the recordings of themselves and others and evaluating the performances for self and peer development, and provide students with the opportunity to more fully engage with feedback received on their performance (Bickerton, 2018). When such facilities can also be used for recording performance assessments, these can then be used by internal assessors to facilitate both the provision of additional feedback and the internal moderation of grading, and then by external examiners to review the student performance and achievements. It is therefore important that discussions external examiners have with the course teaching team at the start of their engagement includes lecture capture technology or equivalent used as part of the assessment process and externals access to this material.

AUTHENTIC ASSESSMENTS IN COMPUTING

In order to test and demonstrate our premise that lecture capture technology is one viable tool to incorporate into the toolkit, in this section, we focus upon one subject domain, that of Computing and IT, and outline a number of specific authentic performance-oriented learning and assessment activities where such technologies could be utilized. This is followed in the next section by a case study illustrating the use of such technology within one specific institution.

Domain Diversity

The discipline of computing is diverse in its variety of specializations. These specializations can be:

- Technically focused – e.g., software development and cyber security;
- Theoretical – e.g., algorithmics and applied mathematics;
- Applied, focusing on an external domain – e.g., design and development of insilico environments for pharmaceutical experimentation or climate modeling;
- Focused on interactivity and/or entertainment – e.g., design and development of computer games, animation, and alternative realities.

As such it is also diverse in the types of learning outcomes present across education programs and the ILA methods employed.

For example, within Cyber Security education you can find extended (potentially full day) activities whereby students demonstrate their ability to defend significant IT infrastructure from attack, mimicking the type of situation they could face as a Cyber Security professional. In the related field of Digital Forensics, however this type of assessment would not be considered authentic, being outside of the normal operating practice of such an occupation. Instead, one is more likely to find simulated crime scenes with digital devices to be seized, processed and analyzed according to professional standards whilst operating within relevant legal and regulatory frameworks. An authentic activity and assessment in both domains could then also comprise a mock courtroom and trial, whereby the student demonstrates their ability and skills as an Expert Witness, presenting the results of their work to a court according to professional practice and standards. None of these assessment methods would however be deemed authentic within Software Engineering, Games Development or Artificial Intelligence specializations, which each have their own individual professional needs and requirements.

At present, the results of the aforementioned assessment activities are usually accessible to external examiners only through a selection of static deliverables, created by staff and/or students pertaining to the activity either prior or post performance, such as preparatory notes and resulting assessor comments.

Utilizing Available Technology

A number of non-intrusive technologies are already being used throughout the computing domain for capturing data in order to reduce the incongruity between the demands of the original assessment and the available static deliverables, without putting the onus on students or assessors to undertake additional work in producing such static evidence in support of their achievements to explicitly clarify their learning and development. These include the use of:

- Change management and progress tracking systems such as GitHub (https://github.com/), a tool commonly used within software development projects that can also be used by assessors to review project activity and engagement by all students, particularly invaluable when working on team assessments, and confirm the students' ability to follow a specific software development methodology (such as Waterfall, Agile, or SSADM);
- Computer activity recordings capturing the live solving of domain-relevant problems, such as Ethical Hacking challenges (e.g. https://www.hackthebox.eu/), explicitly demonstrating the students' application of domain-relevant skills and abilities, and their competence in following agreed practices, standards, and regulations for undertaking work within realistic simulated environments;
- Recording equipment to capture live student performance during the completion of such discussion-focused assessment activities as group debates, classroom Q&A's, peer feedback and student presentations.

In the next section, we focus on one example to demonstrate how lecture capture technologies have been used in one institution to provide access to final year student vivas and the accompanying academic debate for both internal moderators of assessments and the external examiners. This case study is presented to illustrate this in practice, with the aim of stimulating debate and further work in this area.

CASE STUDY: NOROFF UNIVERSITY COLLEGE

Noroff University College (NUC) is a private university college in Southern Norway offering NOKUT approved bachelor programs in the areas of Computing and Interactive Media. Part of Noroff School of Technology and Digital Media (https://www.noroff.no/), NUC was established in 2012 as an expansion of Noroff Education, which itself was established in 1987 for providing high school and vocational education programs both online and at four physical campuses across Norway. Noroff no longer provides high school education but instead has focused on expanding its Vocational School and University College, under the guidance and approval of NOKUT.

NUC's education delivery model is based on the synchronous delivery of courses to students regardless of their geographic location, delivering courses simultaneously to both campus and online students. Live streaming and recording technologies, in addition to online chat systems, underpin this model and as such are pervasive throughout all programs and campus facilities. They also support a distributed academic community whereby lectures can be streamed directly to relevant campuses and online students when delivered by staff from any geographic location, both nationally and internationally. As a result of this education model and setup, students become familiar with cameras and live streaming systems in their work environment from the first day of their studies – both within the campus environment and online through the use of webcams.

Authentic Assessments and the External Examiner at NUC

A wide repertoire of assessment forms are used throughout NUC's bachelor degree programs, including both traditional assessments, such as term papers, portfolios of work, and online tests, and authentic assessments, as relevant to each program. The most common authentic assessments that also include a performance element are where students present the results of their work to others (considering various relevant specified target audiences), and student project vivas.

Project vivas in particular are considered authentic within the domains of Computing and Interactive Media in respect of the assessment requiring students to demonstrate their ability to:

- Clearly and concisely communicate the results and achievements of their individual or group work to relevant stakeholders;
- Discuss the process and methodology adopted and followed with relevant peers in their professional community of practice;
- Justify their approach, decisions, and results to others, including peers, line manager(s) and other project stakeholders;
- Debate domain-related topics with others within the professional community of practice.

As with all performance-focused activities, initially only the proxies to vivas were available post assessment: student created presentation plans and/or slides, and session notes produced by those assessors present at the live activity following assessment completion. Although additional supporting materials are often also produced by student(s) during their project work, such as a thesis or portfolio of work, these are commonly submitted for separate assessments with appropriate yet different assessment criteria. As such those related deliverables do not form part of the performance assessment as they do not provide evidence of the student's skills and ability within the performance activity.

The challenge of including vivas in the external examination process was identified during the inaugural graduation year of NUC, when the first cohort of students reached the end of their studies and was assessed using vivas in their final year projects prior to study completion and graduation. Due to NUC having existed for less than three years by this time, this was also the first year where external examiners were recruited to review educational quality for all bachelor degrees.

Having identified this gap within the NUC education QA process during the first year of assessment boards, potential solutions were explored in order to increase external examiner involvement in this process. Due both to the ready availability of unobtrusive lecture streaming and capture technologies across NUC and student familiarity with these systems, it was decided to supplement the static, written records of student achievement in project vivas with recordings of every live performance, made using the already present, and familiar, lecture capture system.

When undertaking project vivas, NUC students present the results of their final year project to 2–3 academic staff. This is then followed by academic questioning, discussion, and debate. These vivas are typically undertaken in rooms equipped with a CISCO streaming and recording suite, irrespective of whether the student and staff are in the same room, or geographically distributed. Where more appropriate, the vivas of online students can take place at other locations using other tools such as Skype (https://www.skype.com/), Zoom (https://zoom.us/), or Discord (https://discordapp.com/) with webcams. In both scenarios, students use technologies present throughout their studies (no alterations to the environment are made), and where the unobtrusive recording of such sessions is supported. Having identified the inability of the external examiner to engage with such assessments the recording facilities offered by those systems were then used for all vivas to determine the impact of the availability of viva recordings on the QA process.

After the first year of implementation, the feedback from external examiners was very positive. The resultant library of viva recordings for the academic year enabled the external examiner to review samples of those performance assessments as required during their review of assessment practices and activities without relying on static proxies, thus enabling them to complete their vital role within the education QA process. They enabled the examiner to complete their vital role within the education QA process more effectively, with the additional benefit of also capturing assessor discussions providing additional insight into the internal assessment and moderation processes.

As expressed by one examiner in their annual report:

> "As an external examiner I found the opportunity to view the recorded final year project presentations invaluable." NUC External Examiner, 2017–2018 External Examiner Annual Report.

Due to the ease of making such recordings and including them within the external examination process, this activity is now standard practice for all final year project vivas across all NUC computing bachelor study programs.

Storage, Dissemination, and Disposal of Performance Recordings

Availability, ease of use, and non-intrusiveness of such technologies are of course pertinent to the consideration of their use in such environments. However, other factors also need examination when using such tools for recording live student performance assessments. Adherence to all legal and regulatory requirements in the storage, dissemination and final disposal of such recordings is essential. This includes regulations within the education domain and the specific institution, plus relevant national and international legislation, such as the General Data Protection Regulation in the EU (European Commission, 2018). It is therefore essential that when employing such an approach in any institution, in any country, that such assessment tangibles are handled appropriately, as with all other work created and submitted by students throughout their studies.

SAFEGUARDING STANDARDS IN HE

Through the experience at NUC, we have demonstrated that it's possible to support the educational QA process, and specifically the role of external examiners, through the utilization of available technology. Practically, great care must be taken to ensure neither assessments nor the behaviors of participants are altered in any way by the inclusion of any such technologies. Supporting the QA process must not be done at the expense of good pedagogic practice. For example, placing a camera in front of a student, pressing record then requiring them to perform naturally is not conducive to authenticity when considering fields where being recorded on camera is not a standard activity within that profession. Discrete, non-intrusive cameras can however be used effectively where they are already present within the education environment to such an extent that neither staff nor students view them as anything other than a regular feature. Compromising ILA practices and impacting upon student performance must always be avoided.

The use of recording equipment is, however, only one tool. We have demonstrated its applicability to authentic assessment capture within the computing domain at NUC, but further work still remains to be done. A toolkit of methodologies and candidate technologies needs to be explored and developed for the variety of authentic assessments present across the HE sector and across each discipline. There will be some commonality across domains and assessments, meaning research results, developments and best practice from other fields should not be dismissed outright but disseminated to ensure domains are not working in disparate silos but communicating and sharing both experiences and best practice (Baker, 2020), whilst also ensuring adherence to all applicable legal and regulatory frameworks.

In this regard, we therefore propose a Call to Action. Across each relevant field of practice further work needs to be done:

- Review and cataloguing of authentic assessment strategies used throughout the field;
- Exploration into the gaps present between these assessment practices and the QA process;
- Explicit discussions on the issues, and potentially relevant solutions, with relevant stakeholders (including teaching staff and students);

- Development and testing of candidate toolkits of non-obtrusive technologies, with guidance for use, for incorporating into those authentic assessments relevant to the field.

As progress is made the gap in our education QA processes can, over time, be reduced and finally closed, increasing transparency throughout the assessment process whilst also supporting the need of authentic assessments throughout our sector.

CONCLUSION

Through our experience of recording performance assessments at NUC and working closely with our external examiners, we have shown it's possible to reduce the gap in the QA process resulting from the use of proxies to authentic assessment submissions by providing external examiners access to recordings of the original student performance, thus enabling them to review the original demonstration of learning undertaken by each student. However, this is just the beginning. The QA gap needs identifying and exploring within other institutions and across other fields to improve transparency of the assessment process and students' individual learning achievements. Digital toolkits can be developed in support of this challenge, but these need to be appropriate to the authentic assessments used within each field, and non-obtrusive to ensure that neither the design and implementation of these assessments, nor the students' ability to demonstrate their knowledge and abilities is compromised in any way.

NOTE

1. Since renamed to Advance HE (https://www.advance-he.ac.uk/).

REFERENCES

Baker, S. (2020, February). *Higher education researchers 'stuck on their own islands.'* Times Higher Education (THE). Retrieved from https://www.timeshighereducation.com/news/higher-education-researchers-stuck-their-own-islands

Berger, D., & Wild, C. (2017). Enhancing student performance and employability through the use of authentic assessment techniques in extra and co-curricular activities (ECCAs). *Law Teacher*, *51*(4), 428–439. https://doi.org/10.1080/03069400.2016.1201745

Bickerton, D. (2018, November 30). The opportunities of Panopto within the School of Music. Cardiff University. Retrieved from https://www.cardiff.ac.uk/learning-hub/view/using-panopto-in-the-school-of-music

Biggs, J., & Tang, C. (2011). *Teaching for quality learning at university* (4th ed.). Berkshire, UK: Open University Press.

Dabbagh, N., & Fake, H. (2017). College students' perceptions of personal learning environments through the lens of digital tools, processes and spaces. *Journal of New Approaches in Educational Research*, *6*(1), 28–36. https://doi.org/10.7821/naer.2017.1.215

Danø, T., & Stensaker, B. (2007). Still balancing improvement and accountability? Developments in external quality assurance in the Nordic countries 1996–2006. *Quality in Higher Education, 13*(1), 81–93. https://doi.org/10.1080/13538320701272839

Darling-Hammond, L., & Snyder, J. (2000). Authentic assessment of teaching in context. *Teaching and Teacher Education, 16*(5), 523–545. https://doi.org/10.1016/S0742-051X(00)00015-9

Davies, S., Mullan, J., & Feldman, P. (2017). *Rebooting learning for the digital age: What next for technology-enhanced higher education?* HEPI Report, 93, 46. Retrieved from http://www.hepi.ac.uk/wp-content/uploads/2017/02/Hepi_Rebooting-learning-for-the-digital-age-Report-93-02_02_17Web.pdf

European Commission. (2018). Data Protection in the EU. Retrieved from https://ec.europa.eu/info/law/law-topic/data-protection_en. Accessed on February 15, 2020.

Higher Education Academy (HEA). (2013). *Handbook for external examiners*. York: The Higher Education Academy, UK.

Hwang, G.-J., Yin, C., & Chu, H.-C. (2019). The era of flipped learning: Promoting active learning and higher order thinking with innovative flipped learning strategies and supporting systems. *Interactive Learning Environments, 27*(8), 991–994. https://doi.org/10.1080/10494820.2019.1667150

Joseph-Richard, P., Jessop, T., Okafor, G., Almpanis, T., & Price, D. (2018). Big brother or harbinger of best practice: Can lecture capture actually improve teaching? *British Educational Research Journal, 44*(3), 377–392. https://doi.org/10.1002/berj.3336

Kinash, S., McGillivray, L., & Crane, L. (2018). Do university students, alumni, educators and employers link assessment and graduate employability? *Higher Education Research and Development, 37*(2), 301–315. https://doi.org/10.1080/07294360.2017.1370439

Kolb, D. A. (2015). *Experiential Learning: Experience as the source of learning and development* (2nd ed.). New Jersey, USA: Pearson Education.

Lycke, K. H. (2004). Perspectives on quality assurance in higher education in Norway. *Quality in Higher Education, 10*(3), 219–229. https://doi.org/10.1080/1353832042000299504

McKie, A. (2019). *Does university assessment still pass muster?* Times Higher Education (THE). Retrieved from https://www.timeshighereducation.com/features/does-university-assessment-still-pass-muster

Meyer, C. (1992). What's the difference between authentic and performance assessment? *Educational Leadership, 49*(8), 39–40. Retrieved from http://www.ascd.org/ASCD/pdf/journals/ed_lead/el_199205_meyer.pdf

Savin-Baden, M. (2003). *Facilitating problem-based learning*. Berkshire, UK: Open University Press.

Sotiriadou, P., Logan, D., Daly, A., & Guest, R. (2019). The role of authentic assessment to preserve academic integrity and promote skill development and employability. *Studies in Higher Education*, 1–17. https://doi.org/10.1080/03075079.2019.1582015

Weliwita, J., & Witharana, S. (2019). A case study on the authentic learning and assessments in the university education. In *2019 Advances in Science and Engineering Technology International Conferences, ASET 2019*. Institute of Electrical and Electronics Engineers Inc. https://doi.org/10.1109/ICASET.2019.8714257

Welle-Strand, A., & Thune, T. (2002). The ambiguous quality agenda in Norwegian higher education policies. *European Education, 34*(2), 74–92. https://doi.org/10.2753/EUE1056-4934340274

CHAPTER 5

IS THERE SUCH A THING AS "COMPARABLENESS"? THE CHALLENGES FACING THE EEs OF HIGHER-EDUCATION COURSES DELIVERED WITHIN FURTHER-EDUCATION INSTITUTIONS

Sarah Cooper and Sara Pearman

ABSTRACT

This chapter explores the numerous considerations that an external examiner (EE) of an undergraduate degree within a further-education (FE) college must be mindful. There may be the perception that our academic experience of lecturing within a university equips us with the knowledge to collaborate with colleagues within an FE institution. However, this is valid only to a certain point.

There is a spectrum of contrasts between the higher education (HE) and FE environments that are reflected within the comparisons that this chapter highlights between the teaching-and-learning experiences. If we think back to the original purpose of an EE (where Oxford scholars were invited by Durham University to provide external guidance in the nineteenth century), we can appreciate the key task of an EE and its aim: to assess the comparability of student achievement. The landscape of HE has changed considerably since

The Role of External Examining in Higher Education: Challenges and Best Practices
Innovations in Higher Education Teaching and Learning, Volume 38, 61–74

ISSN: 2055-3641/doi:10.1108/S2055-364120210000038005

then, and now undulates with numerous opportunities for learners to gain a HE qualification.

It is this difficulty in assessing comparability that an EE of a HE course within an FE environment must be willing to acknowledge. The fact that the student-and-learning experience varies wildly in HE and FE muddies the waters for the EE: how can comparableness be assessed?

Keywords: External examiner; further education; higher education; benchmarks; Quality Assurance Agency; Ofsted; widening participation; partner university; higher-education institutions; further-education institutions

INTRODUCTION

Picture an undergraduate student on a sociology degree at an "elite university" (Lucas, 2006, p. 35). Our implicit bias may shape that picture into one that is comprised of an individual who has excelled at A levels and is the product of a middle-class background. Now envision that student's teaching-and-learning experience: engaged, eager to learn, supported by research-active teaching staff. League tables provide a quantitative overview of this particular andragogical experience, with the student:staff ratio of 11.2, strong career progression and an average entry tariff of 224 points (*The Guardian*, 2020). Those institutions ranked within the lower 10 of the table demand a higher student:staff ratio with less robust career progression and a lower average entry tariff (at the time of writing, none of the institutions in this lower-10 bracket required entry points above 127).

Clearly, there are variations within the student-and-academic experience related to higher education (HE). And in among this, the external examiner (EE) is expected to bring consistency in a role created to provide external guidance – but a role of which the definition has not diversified since the 1800s (Jackson & Lund, 2000) – to the numerous HE provisions within varying environments as ranked within this arguably overly statistical league-table system (Bloxham & Price, 2015).

Already, you may feel discombobulated. "Varying environments" within a "league-table system" from 2020 and a consistent approach that was first established in the nineteenth century, wherein Oxford scholars were invited to the University of Durham in an external consultancy role (Jackson & Lund, 2000). As an academic, you will undoubtedly have collaborated (and it *is* a collaboration) with an EE in some capacity, even before you have the privilege of assuming the role of EE yourself. The collaborative nature of this role is the nugget of the relationship: being afforded the opportunity to reflect on practice and be inspired outside of your own HE "bubble" (this, of course, is applicable to both the EE and the institution team).

The "variation of environments," however, becomes all the more acute when it comes to being an EE of a degree that is delivered in a further-education (FE) college. If we refer back to the 1800s, and the Durham-and-Oxford collaboration

(Jackson & Lund, 2000), then we might assume that the experience of both learners and lecturers in that environment was comparable. In the 2000s, however, there is the argument that this is not the case. And it is this point that we propose to explore within this chapter.

This chapter has been co-written by two people: Sarah Cooper and Sara Pearman. Cooper was the EE for an undergraduate course that Pearman delivered in an FE college. Cooper has also fulfilled the role of EE on two additional courses at HE institutions, and has conducted primary research in terms of consulting colleagues who have worked as an EE on a HE degree delivered in an FE environment and/or have taught within this scenario. This is, therefore, an informed overview as to the challenges facing those delivering HE degrees within an FE environment, and those challenges facing the EE who assumes that role – and may previously have only had experience of delivering and/or external examining HE courses within a HE environment.

The first section of this chapter will be from the perspective of Pearman, as a lecturer on a HE course within an FE institution. It is from the lecturer's perspective that we can ascertain the challenges that face the teaching staff, and that therein inform the contribution of the EE. The second section of this chapter will be from the perspective of Cooper, as an EE attempting to contribute to the team's provision, but who was unaware of the difficult terrain that faces these teams in comparison to colleagues delivering HE courses within HE institutions.

THE CHALLENGES FACING FE LECTURERS WHEN REQUIRED TO DELIVER A HE PROVISION

The purpose of this section is to explore the challenges facing the EE when fulfilling the role on a degree course delivered within the environment of an FE institution. To be able to enhance our understanding of the contrasts between the HE and FE environments, it is important to deepen our awareness of the practices, resourcing and responsibilities that face those lecturers working to navigate this environment. As such, an EE – to be fully effective in the role – must undertake the added responsibility of gaining an insight into the differences and similarities facing colleagues within this environment, and to not simply apply their own experiences to that of the colleagues on the provision they are EE for. With this in mind, we aim to strip back the "mystique" (as one participant in our primary research referred to it) of the FE environment by providing an overview of the key challenges facing lecturers within FE.

The landscape for FE lecturers delivering HE in an FE setting is challenging and can be fraught with highs and lows. For a vast majority of lecturers, attempting to find balance and understanding is essential, yet daunting. Most lecturers who deliver HE in an FE setting teach across both sectors, have a full teaching commitment and receive little or no remission for this cross-sector delivery. Lecturers delivering HE in an FE setting are likely to have more teaching hours than "colleagues in HEIs" (Department for Business Innovation and Skills, 2012, p. 11). This can create a stressful workload for those lecturers, especially for those who are new to delivering at HE level. For an EE working in this environment with no prior experience of FE staff delivering HE, it is likely that this will be the first conundrum they will witness the staff encounter. The EE will quickly ascertain the many variables that the staff are balancing, especially given their high teaching commitment.

An understanding is required by the EE that these staff are considering the requirements of both Ofsted in FE and the Quality Assurance Agency (QAA) in the HE setting. These lecturers have limited time for duties outside of their teaching commitment, which can mean that understanding the role of an EE can often become a working process. McGhee (2003, p. 123) provides insight here:

> The external examining system is designed to uphold standards across the sector, both in a sense of monitoring the consistency with which a university implements its own standards but more generally in the sense of maintaining (largely undefined) sector wide standards.

There can be a misconception of what exactly the role of an EE is and perhaps the most supportive definition is that of a "critical friend," an experienced HE practitioner, who brings with them a wealth of knowledge and a critical eye to the course they are externally examining. Therefore, for both the EE and the teaching team, this process can be a steep and valuable learning curve, in a pressured environment. It can often be the case that FE senior managers have a limited understanding of the requirements of the HE sector. As a result, the support of an EE is a crucial element to a successful delivery of a HE program in FE. The EE and/or the moderator (from the partner university) can often be the person that the teaching team will reach out for support, understanding and clarification. In order for a program to be delivered successfully it is often the combination of a supportive EE and moderator who are the key – a key contrast, and one that an EE previously only experienced in working with courses within the HE sector must be mindful of.

WORKLOAD

Staff delivering in FE work in a high-pressured, target-driven environment, where most are delivering the maximum amount of hours possible and across levels one to level six. It can be difficult to respond to the needs of the college, Ofsted, QAA, the partner university, moderators, EE and the students themselves. All staff will be involved in planning, delivery and assessment, second marking and internal verification processes. Staff can be tasked with the delivery of a session to level one students before moving on to level six teaching and this mental adjustment can be difficult to adapt to. For this reason, the role of the EE is exceptionally important: the impartiality of this role can offer a true reflection of how well the students work is being delivered and assessed. The EE often helps the college to benchmark their provision in comparison to other universities and/or other colleges delivering HE in an FE setting.

SCHOLARLY ACTIVITY AND SUPPORT IN GAINING HIGHER LEVEL QUALIFICATIONS

There is an expectation that a lecturer at HE level will undertake research, scholarly activity and professional updating. However, Tummons, Orr, and Atkins (2013, p. 84) suggests that "FE colleges do not primarily position themselves as engaging in research." In a university, staff are likely to be given remission (albeit to wildly varying degrees) to support these activities. Most universities will have a culture of research and understand the value of research. In most FE settings these values are very different, lecturers are likely to have the same teaching commitment, regardless of whether they teach FE or HE. The contact hours for a lecturer delivering HE in FE environment is likely to be around 25 hours per week and includes cross-sector delivery. With the other duties that a lecturer will be responsible for, it is likely that they will not have much time for scholarly activities. It can be challenging and frustrating for staff to breathe new life into the HE curriculum and their own skillbase.

WORKING ACROSS SECTORS

A key consideration for the FE teaching team is the negotiation of the collaborative landscape, in terms of teaching on and/or the coordination of degrees with different partnering institutions. This requires staff to understand and implement the rules and regulations of more than one university. An EE who is experienced in working with only one set of institutional regulations can appreciate the complexity of navigating this bureaucratic climate. It can be a challenge to separate Ofsted requirements (Ofsed, 2019a, 2019b, 2019c) from the QAA (QAA, 2013a, 2013b) and FE awarding bodies from universities. The support of the EE is vital to guide the team through this landscape of ever-changing rules and regulations.

When FE teams teaching HE first start to assess work at levels four, five and six, it can be difficult to initially "find" the level of student work. This is a skill which is developed over time. The role of the EE is vital, to support with the appropriate awarding of grades, levelness and ensure quality of feedback for students regarding their work. The EE brings with them a wealth of knowledge to support the team and build their confidence in making these decisions. It can be very reassuring for a team to know if they are assessing in line with universities and consider how comparable the students experience is, in terms of assessment. The moderator from the partner university is also instrumental in the team's confidence to award the full range of marks available for assessment. FE teams can be hesitant to award higher grades, and may need support to understand where grade boundaries lay. It may take several visits from the EE and moderator before the team is completely confident in doing this. The quality assurance provided by the moderator and EE is essential to the development of any HE course in an FE environment. It is, therefore, likely when a college is recruiting an EE for their course, they may be more likely to recruit someone with experience of FE in HE, or a willingness to learn about the sector.

WIDENING PARTICIPATION

There are many complexities surrounding the students that study HE in FE. Avis and Orr (2016) argue that "HE in FE tends to recruit students from the more disadvantaged sectors of the population" (p. 14). Most FE colleges delivering HE are likely to have lower entry requirements than their university counterparts and lower tuition fees. As a result, they are likely to attract students who would not ordinarily study at HE level and mature students. Consequently, it is also often the case that these students require more support to reach the required academic standards.

FE institutions – as with HE institutions – often operate an "open-door" policy for students, where they can contact their lecturers and this ethos generally continues through to HE provisions. The main student intake for HE courses in FE will be those students who have progressed through the levels at the institution, and, therefore, the students are familiar with the staff delivering HE courses. There is often an expectation by the student and the college that the same level of support will be provided by the lecturers, despite the sector within which the student is studying. This can often be reflected in the student work produced for assessment, where grades can often cluster around the lower end of the scale. This may be a challenge for a new EE: there is the responsibility to understand the parameters of this type of student and that they are unlikely to access the full range of marks available for assessment.

From a primary research perspective, the students who access HE in an FE setting are generally those that would not have applied to a university. Colleges are able to engage in widening-participation initiatives in a way that perhaps some universities are unable to do. Department for Business Innovation and Skills (2012, p. 12) suggests that HE students who study in FE are "more likely to have come from areas of low participation in higher education." FE colleges, therefore, have the scope and reach within local communities to offer learners who may not consider HE study the opportunity to do so. Tummons et al. (2013) discusses the importance of the locale of the college in terms of recruitment:

> FE colleges are strongly located in local communities, often with close links to local industry and they offer local opportunities that are so important to their students. The college is part of the community, drawing students from the community and returning them to work in the same community. (p. 32)

Most of these students would not move away to university: they live at home, benefit from lower tuition fees, require the support of small class sizes and thrive in this environment. They are likely to be from families where they are the first person to go to university and are from working-class backgrounds. Students who have progressed from a college into HE in an FE setting often feel supported by the environment. Tummons et al. (2013) suggests that "colleges have drawn significant numbers of students to HE programs because they are perceived by many students to be a more familiar and less threatening environment than a university" (p. 33). The EE, therefore, needs to be aware of this and understand the type of students engaging with the program. Often when students' marks are at the lower end of the scale, this may be a high-level personal achievement for this type of student.

RESOURCES

More recently, many FE colleges have invested in HE-only buildings, which support students in the separation between the FE and the HE setting. This appears to be a positive move and one which is a more attractive offer to students. However, in terms of resources it is unlikely that these institutions can be comparable to their HE counterparts. Unless FE receives more government funding and HE tuition fees raised substantially, it would be hard to see how this situation might improve. However, resources are not particularly a primary concern for the students studying HE in an FE institution. From a primary perspective, students place higher value on locality, employment opportunities, support, familiar environment, class sizes and the support they would receive than positions within league tables. When you consider the wider picture of HE in FE, there is the acknowledgment that the target audience is not the same as traditional HE institutions, and the environment supporting that target audience has additional challenges – all of which must be considered by the EE.

OVERVIEW: TEACHING TEAM IN FE INSTITUTION

The perception outside of the HE in FE environment is that perhaps students get a lesser experience, an experience that is less valuable and is of substandard quality. Dixon and Pilkington (2017) believe that college lecturers also come under scrutiny "regardless of their qualifications or competency, have struggled to be accepted on equal footing with their HEI counterparts and remain poor relations" (p. 2). However, in reality, the experience of HE in FE serves its students abundantly. Avis and Orr (2016) suggest positively that "HE in FE courses can and do transform lives by opening up fields of knowledge that may explain and enhance experience" (p. 14). HE in FE supports students to gain higher level qualifications, at a very poignant moment in time, where the employment market is competitive and, therefore, these students now stand an equal chance of success.

THE CHALLENGES FACING THE EE

We have mentioned the fluidity in the interpretation of what an EE actually does, but Jackson and Lund (2000) highlights certain key points that have remained consistent:

> Ever since the first half of the nineteenth century when the University of Durham invited scholars from Oxford to help set and mark examinations, external examiners have been the primary means of cross-referencing standards or outcomes of learning between HE institutions to different subjects. Although the specific duties and functions of external examiners vary between institutions they essentially provide a department or programme team with an independent and objective perspective on the assessment process and outcome standards, by comparing what they see with what they have seen in other institutions. Thus external examiners act as a type of benchmarking agent for an unstructured, unsystematic and largely implicit type of benchmarking process. (p. 31)

There are many significant points to this citation, which reflect the fact that as an EE there are many challenges to be faced, based upon the "unsystematic" and "unstructured" moderation process. In addition, the "independent perspective" is also a point to consider. Independent from what? The QAA provides a central resource point for guidance with regard to the establishment of consistent benchmarks throughout HE. There is a network of guidelines intended to assure the quality of HE in terms of assessment. The "independent perspective" then must be one that's aligned with the "external" aspect of "external examining." From this angle, one interpretation could be that the EE is independent to the institution's processes, and that there is room for subjectivity with regard to assessments and moderation within the institution. For instance, a lecturer is aware of the progress and achievements of each individual student, whereas the EE has little-to-no such awareness. However, for an EE of a HE course in an FE environment to approach the moderation in a fair and robust way, some consideration to the processes that the FE lecturer is required to follow should be given in order for the individual course team's moderation process to be understood (Watson et al., 2000).

For instance, FE courses are subject to the bureaucratic attention of Ofsted, alongside mainstream state schools, independent schools (including those affiliated with the Steiner curriculum) and early-years environments. HE courses do not fall under Ofsted's remit but are subjected to other benchmarks, such as the National Student Survey. The pressures, guidance and challenges imposed upon FE colleges from Ofsted are remarkably similar to those imposed upon schools. FE colleges are subjected to the same categories relating to perceived quality as schools: ranging from "inadequate" to "outstanding."

This is particularly challenging when it comes to external examining HE provision delivered within an FE environment. When an institution's main focus is on HE delivery, QAA benchmarks are aligned. This is an endeavor that HE lecturers are expected to adhere to in order that an opportunity for a student to engage with the HE experience is offered. But when a lecturer is required to move between the role of "HE lecturer" and "FE tutor" – often with barely minutes' adjustment – then the challenge is set for the EE not to be independent and base their guidance and observations on experience as a HE lecturer within a HE environment, but to be aware of the particular challenges that face these colleagues.

It is the inconsistency of external examining HE courses in FE institutions that was highlighted by the review of external examining, conducted in 2011. Key recommendations included "the commitment to increased consistency of practice across universities and colleges and the commitment to increased transparency for students" (Finch, 2011, p. 4). This brings in a new perspective: that of the student. As Jackson and Lund (2000) stated, the original purpose of external examining was to provide the "programme team" with "independent" observations on academic practices. But this review incorporates the significance of "transparency" for students. This reiterates the shifting sands upon which EEs often find themselves: and when that EE has frequently been accustomed to the practices of HE (wherein Ofsted has no remit), then the reviewing of HE courses within FE institutions becomes an even more fluid practice.

And yet, the EE is deemed to be a significant cog in the setting and maintaining of standards, "... an integral and essential part of institutional quality assurance" (QAA, 2018, p. 4). There is, potentially, conflict in respect of the establishment of comparable standards and the autonomy of each institution.

> Over 140 universities and colleges separately set and maintain their own standards, but at the same time there is a public expectation that qualifications awarded by one institution are broadly comparable with those awarded by all others. This tension is resolved in a number of ways, including – importantly – by the external examining system. (Finch, 2011, p. 5)

But how can comparative standards be assessed when FE institutions – most notably, the program teams – are subject to differing benchmarks, broad perceptions, research demands and resource disadvantages?

These challenges, in terms of the ones facing the teaching staff, are explored in the first part of this chapter. Primary research, however (based on remote discussions with participants of an EE digital forum), shows that there are a number of challenges facing the EE that are consistent across experiences, regardless of institution. The comparability of standards is one that can be challenging to ascertain, when the experiences of educational environments (in terms of HE and FE institutions) are difficult to homogenize. There are a number of hurdles that challenge the program team of a HE course in an FE environment, and these in turn potentially pose challenges to the EE from an equivalent discipline but from a HE environment (Lea & Simmons, 2012). These are: a general, and comparatively minimal support to engage in research; a comparatively smaller pool of higher-achieving students from which to recruit; comparatively higher demands on student services; comparatively poorer perceptions of academic standards; and comparatively higher demands on college lecturers in terms of teaching allocation.

COMPARATIVE SUPPORT IN RESEARCH

There is the general assumption (or the "public expectation" that Finch, 2011 points to) that individuals who lecture on an HE course are specialists in the discipline within which they are positioned. That "assumption" is one that is often encountered on a primary level when speaking to the parents of students, colleagues from industry who do not teach at a HE level and the students themselves. HE institutions differ wildly with regard to the provision and support of research opportunities to teaching staff, which in itself is cause for discussion, though not within this particular context. When HE institutions are judged upon contributions to the research excellence framework (REF) in terms of their positioning within the league table, it is clear why colleagues are expected (albeit encouraged to various degrees) to engage with research. Indeed, the REF makes clear in guidance documents that the focus is on "higher education institutions," rather than "higher education lecturers" or "researchers affiliated with higher education," which can diminish the motivation of lecturers on HE courses within FE institutions to engage in the process.

Herein lies a problem for the EE of a HE course within an FE institution when aligned with the expectation to ensure that comparable and objective standards are met: how can the output of the students within an FE environment produce work of a comparable standard to students within an HE environment, when lecturers teaching within those environments are subject to different opportunities, incentives and workloads? One could argue that, in this situation, the outcomes of the students are entirely dependent on the initiatives of the lecturers. From a primary research perspective, it has been surprising to note the lack of research opportunities afforded to lecturers on a HE course within an FE institution.

On a number of occasions, participants of informal discussions we have held on the subject have said that research is to be conducted *in addition* to the teaching workload, and the teaching workload already brings the lecturer up to allocation. Considering the workload already weighing heavy on the shoulders of program teams within this scenario, it is understandable why research quickly slips down the list of priorities. And yet, within HE institutions, if you're not proactive in research, then the requirements of your vocational criteria are considered unmet. As such, engaging with research duties is often integrated (again, with distinct variations) into the workload. It is a privilege for lecturers who are able to engage with such duties to then be able to feed back into their teaching, and facilitate innovative thinking within their students' learning experience. When the opportunities to engage with research are minimal or non-existent, then the teaching cannot be considered comparable – regardless of the student experience. As such, if a HE course is to be delivered, then the program team involved within that student experience should be encouraged to engage with research that enhances that experience, and differentiates the HE curriculum and expected outcome from that within FE.

During primary research for this chapter with EEs of HE courses within an FE institution as well as course teams within HE and FE environments, a consistent theme was highlighted with regard to research: the support given to researchers varied considerably, with comparatively less support and opportunity afforded to researchers within the FE environment. This has ramifications with regard to the student experience and the student "output" (in terms of the standard of work produced). One participant in the primary research remarked that there was a managerial assumption that supporting FE staff teaching on a HE courses to engage in research activities would impact *negatively* on staff retention, in that staff would leave as career opportunities were widened through research profiles and achievements. However, the participant highlighted that it was that very lack of support to research that impacts negatively on staff retention, and staff were leaving because they were unable to engage in the research duties that their colleagues on equivocal courses in HE institutions were not only engaging with but were actively encouraged to engage with.

This contradictory point can be best demonstrated by the REF 2021 document offering guidelines with regard to application. While it states that it invites applications from HE institutions, and colleges providing HE courses, applicants keen to submit to the REF should have dedicated time to engage with research – indeed, there are expected to research, or teach and research. Eligible staff

> are defined as academic staff with a contract of employment of 0.2 FTE or greater, on the payroll of the submitting institution on the census date, whose primary employment function is to undertake either "research only" or "teaching and research." Staff should have a substantive research connection with the submitting unit. (REF, 2019, p. 29)

However, the common structure of FE is one that is influenced significantly by Ofsted, and as a result, few staff are able to have that "substantive research connection." As such, the challenge for the EE of a HE provision with an FE environment is to ensure the student work and experience is comparable to those of others in the discipline, but bearing in mind that there is a highly disproportionate emphasis on staff's research activities.

COMPARATIVE RECRUITMENT OPPORTUNITIES

One impactful factor that can determine the variables of student outcomes is the pool from which an institution can successfully recruit from. The Universities and Colleges Admissions Service remains the central point of processing applications to HE courses, and in 1998, it reported that an increasing number of applicants were choosing institutions that were geographically advantageous, being situated close to their "home region of domicile": "This [trend] is particularly true for mature applicants, applicants from ethnic minorities and partly skilled and unskilled social classes" (Coleman & Viggars, 2000, p. 132).

Widening participation has been a key consideration of the UK education system, with a 2018 report from the Department for Education (DfE) using free school meals (FSM) as a way in which to quantify progress (or lack thereof) in the national intention to equalize opportunity. The report found that:

> An estimated 25.6% of pupils who were in receipt of Free School Meals (FSM) aged 15 in 2012/13 entered Higher Education by age 19 in 2016/17. This compares to 43.3% of non-FSM pupils. (Department for Education (DfE), 2018, p. 1)

This is a marked increase from the progress of pupils receiving FSM in 2005/2006, of which only 14.2% progressed onto HE. However, there is also a marked increase in the progress of pupils not in receipt of FSM – from 33.5% in 2005/2006 to 43.3%. As such, while there has been an increase in the number of pupils in receipt of FSM progressing to HE, *the gap between those pupils and their peers who are non-FSM pupils remains* (own emphasis).

The implications here mean that, while the provision of HE courses in FE institutions has been a key factor in the widening-participation intent, the demographic of students recruited onto the course will vary. We have traditionally observed this, when we compare the recruitment practice of Russell Group (or "red brick" or "elite") universities (with comparatively higher requirements in terms of entry-point tariffs) and former polytechnics: there is the perception that one is more prestigious than the other. Similarly, the report found that pupils from independent schools were more likely to be recruited by the "most selective" of HE institutions than those who had attended state schools (DfE, 2018).

It has been previously noted that EEs are required to moderate the comparability of student work with regards performance and awards given, with the EE required to draw upon their respective experiences at other HEIs. However, to refer to higher-education providers in such a sweeping manner – as many reports often do – disregards the strata within that, including the red bricks, the former polytechnics and the FE colleges. What this would imply is that there is a general assumption as to what a higher-education provider looks like (to parents, employers and prospective students) based on primary or secondary schooling experience, but which a consistent framework in reality *does not exist*, and it is a challenge for the EE of a HE course within an FE institution to reconcile the requirement to comparatively analyze a cohort's achievement against those of another (particularly those within the more "selective" universities). The caliber of students is inconsistent across HE institutions, and while the EE must be mindful of this when working with colleagues on a HE course in an FE environment, the challenge is set that the "outputs" and achievements of those students within an FE environment are comparable with those in a HE environment.

DISCUSSION

In 2001, there was a governmental shift of focus onto the creation of a fertile environment to facilitate the flourishing of degree courses in FE institutions.

> The growth of higher education in FE colleges is now at the centre of government policy to expand undergraduate education at levels below the first degree and to incorporate this provision as rungs in a new vocational ladder spanning compulsory and post-compulsory education. (Parry & Thompson, 2001, p. 1)

The latter citation is from a report produced by the now defunct Parry and Thompson (2001) highlight issues that, nearly two decades later, are still prevalent. For instance, the report calls for "strong forms of coordination … if a new framework for vocational progression" was to be realized (Parry & Thompson, 2001, p. 4). It highlights the lack of clarity (as acknowledged in the 1997 Dearing review of HE) about "the primary purpose of higher education offered by or in association with colleges of further education" (Parry & Thompson, 2001, p. 5). Nearly two decades later, the ambiguity relating to purpose and the variation in coordination in terms of the provision of HE within an FE environment remain not only prevalent but impactful on the student experience – which in turn, causes inconsistencies and challenges for the academic who has assumed the EE role on a HE provision within an FE college.

But the inconsistencies are not exclusive to the external examining of degree courses within this framework. If we refer back to the introduction of this chapter, we imagined the teaching-and-learning experience of a student at a Russell Group institution to that of a student at a former polytechnic – a marked contrast, even if we make this conclusion based on the student:staff ratio as specified in league tables. The challenge for an EE of a HE provision within an FE institution is to advise and collaborate with their FE team not from what they know through experience (which is often within a HE environment) but from what the FE team is able to deliver. And from personal experience – as an EE for a college undergraduate degree, a university degree and a postgraduate degree – the teaching-and-learning experience is absolutely variable with regard to the institutional input relating but not limited to staff support and resourcing.

CONCLUSION

We've seen the perspectives of a lecturer and an EE with regard to the delivery of a HE course within an FE institution and common themes can be identified in terms of the challenges posing both positions – whether it be a lecturer within FE, or the EE. The two subsections within this chapter view the challenges facing the EE through two contrasting lenses: that of the person looking in (the EE), and the person "looking out" via the perspective of the EE looking in (the lecturer). There are consistent issues that persist from both internal and external perspectives which entwine to make the key challenge of: what is "comparable" anyway? Not even the QAA's (2018) glossary provides a definition, despite the "comparableness" of courses being the underpinning to the role of the EE.

We started the chapter imagining the teaching-and-learning experiences of students within an elite university. Having explored the teaching-and-learning experiences of students within an FE environment but studying a HE provision, we can gain an understanding of the contrasts between both situations. As such, it seems only pertinent to end this chapter by arguing that the experience of external examining for a course of an elite university is in contrast to that of external examining for a course within an FE institution – a challenge that must be recognized in order for FE courses to fully optimize the opportunity of having the external guidance of an EE.

REFERENCES

Avis, J., & Orr, K. (2016). *HE in FE: Vocationalism, class and social justice*. Huddersfield: Huddersfield University.

Bloxham, S., & Price, M. (2015). External examining: Fit for purpose? *Studies in Higher Education, 40*(2), 195–211.

Coleman,R., & Viggars,L. (2000). Benchmarking Student Recruitment: The UCAS Institutional Planning Service. In N. Jackson & H.Lund (Eds.), *Benchmarking for Higher Education*. London: Open University Press.

Department for Business Innovation and Skills. (2012). *Understanding higher education in further education colleges*. BIS Research Paper Number 69, London.

Department for Education (dfe). (2018). *Widening participation in higher education, England, 2016/17 age cohort official statistics*. Department for Education.

Dixon, J., & Pilkington, R. (2017). Poor relations? Tensions and torment: A view of excellence in teaching and learning from the Cinderella sector. *Teaching in Higher Education, 22*(4), 437–450.

Finch, J. (2011). *Review of external examining arrangements in universities and colleges in the UK Final report and recommendations*. London: Universities UK.

Gale, K., Turner, R., & McKenzie, L. M. (2011). Communities of praxis? Scholarship and practice styles of the HE in FE professional. *Journal of Vocational Education & Training, 63*(2), 159–169. doi:10.1080/13636820.2011.572175

The Guardian. (2020). University league tables 2020 [Online]. Retrieved from https://www.theguardian.com/education/ng-interactive/2019/jun/07/university-league-tables-2020. Accessed on February 5, 2020.

Jackson, M., & Lund, H. (Eds.). (2000). *Benchmarking for higher education*. London: Open University Press.

Lea, J., & Simmons, J. (2012). Higher education in further education: Capturing and promoting HEness. *Research in Post-compulsory Education, 17*(2), 179–193. doi:10.1080/13596748.2012.673888

Lucas, L. (2006). *The research game in academic life*. London: Open University Press.

McGhee, P. (2003). *The academic quality handbook, enhancing higher education in universities and further education colleges*. Glasgow: Bell and Bain Ltd.

Ofsted. (2019a). Further education and skills inspection handbook. Ofsted. Retrieved from https://www.gov.uk/government/publications/further-education-and-skills-inspection-handbook-eif

Ofsted. (2019b). Education inspection framework [Online]. Retrieved from https://www.gov.uk/government/collections/education-inspection-framework?#guidance-for-education-providers. Accessed on January 5, 2020.

Ofsted.(2019c). Inspecting schools: Guide for maintained and academic schools [Online]. Retrieved from https://www.gov.uk/guidance/inspecting-schools-guide-for-maintained-and-academy-schools. Accessed on January 5, 2020.

Parry, G., Callender, C., Scott, P., & Temple, P. (2012). *Understanding higher education in further education colleges*. Department for Business, Innovation and Skills Research Paper Number 69, London.

Parry,G., & Thompson, A. (2001). *LSDA Reports: Higher Education in FE Colleges*. Learning and Skills Development Agency.

QAA. (2013a). Chapter B6: Assessment of students and the recognition of prior learning. In UK Quality Code for Higher Education. Part B: Ensuring and Enhancing Academic Quality. Retrieved from https://www.qaa.ac.uk/docs/qaa/quality-code/chapter-b6_-assessment-of-students-and-the-recognition-of-prior-learning.pdf?sfvrsn=9901f781_8

QAA. (2013b). Chapter B7: External examining. In UK Quality Code for Higher Education. Part B: Ensuring and Enhancing Academic Quality. Retrieved from https://www.qaa.ac.uk/docs/qaa/quality-code/chapter-b7_-external-examining.pdf?sfvrsn=2101f781_8

QAA. (2018). QAA glossary [Online]. Retrieved from https://www.qaa.ac.uk/search-results?indexCatalogue=global&searchQuery=Glossary&wordsMode=AllWords. Accessed on February 18, 2020.

Research Excellence Framework (REF). (2019). REF 2021 (ND) guidance on submissions. Retrieved from https://www.ref.ac.uk/publications/guidance-on-submissions-201901/

Tummons, J, Orr, K., & Atkins, L. (2013). *Teaching higher education in further education colleges*. London: Sage Publications.

Watson, J., Yeomans, D., Smith, D., Nelson, N., & Ainley, P. (2000) Higher education and diversity: Regional learning infrastructures and student progression in the post-dearing era. In I. McNay (Ed.), Higher education and communities (pp. 122–133). London: Open University Press.

PART II

CHALLENGES AND QUALITY ASSURANCE

CHAPTER 6

A STUDY OF THE EFFECTIVENESS OF THE EXTERNAL EXAMINING SYSTEM OF POSTGRADUATE (MBA) DISSERTATIONS AND THE MISMATCH BETWEEN EXPECTATIONS AND PRACTICE

Deepanjana Varshney

ABSTRACT

External examining imparts one of the pivotal means for ensuring the monitoring of the guidelines and standards within private autonomous universities and institutes. External examiners are considered independent individuals who can provide unbiased, objective evaluation, and informed comment on the student's quality of the project as compared to the standards. Hence, the role of the external examiner is vital and has a strong influence on institutional quality assurance. The qualitative research has primarily aimed to study the external examining practices involving a private university in India. Interviews were conducted mainly with the external appointed examiners; however, the internal faculty guides or supervisors were also made to participate in separate interviews. The results were coded following the content analysis framework. The research unraveled Pandora's box of the system bottlenecks and challenges concerning the expected and actual practices. Limitations, recommendations, and future research implications were discussed.

The Role of External Examining in Higher Education: Challenges and Best Practices
Innovations in Higher Education Teaching and Learning, Volume 38, 77–93

ISSN: 2055-3641/doi:10.1108/S2055-364120210000038006

Keywords: External examiner; faculty supervisor; dissertation; MBA program; private university; assessment; India; qualitative; interviews; controller of examination

INTRODUCTION

The external examination is a challenging process in which the evaluation is done by examiners to ensure unbiased evaluation and conformation conformance to the set academic standards formulated by the policy-makers of higher education.

The research aimed to understand the effectiveness of the external examining process concerning an Indian University. The objectives of the study were manifold:

- To analyze the effectiveness of the internal examining process.
- To evaluate the external examining process.
- To critically examine the collaboration between the external and internal examining systems and process.

The chapter has been categorized into the following distinct sections: the overview, a literature review covering examining systems and procedures over a period, the external examining, and role of examiner. The method consists of the description of the internal process flow (faculty guides or supervisors being allocated with students, internal examining process) followed by the external examining process and evaluation. It needs to be mentioned that the internal examiners are the same faculty/guides selected to assess the projects of other faculty/supervisors and vice versa. Though the primary participants of the qualitative study were the external examiners, but to obtain deep insights, the internal faculty guides/supervisors and the internal examiners were also interviewed.

Many systematic reviews and assessments have been carried out (Bloxham & Price, 2015). External examining has been taking place in some Asian Countries though the duties performed by the examiners varied (Ross, 2009). The Masters programs, more particularly, the MBA program has dissertations in the advanced semesters and is research oriented. It becomes imperative that the evaluation of postgraduate dissertations by expert examiners should be done because it will enhance the effectiveness of the Master's program as a whole. Holbrook, Bourke, Fairbairn, and Lovat (2007) aptly suggest that the dissertation should be examined and assessed by external assessors for strong validity and constructive feedback. Practical insights found in dissertations and reports provide significant understanding to less experienced supervisors. This research aims to unravel the challenges and issues faced by the external examiners and highlight their roles and responsibilities. The case of a private university would be taken to portray the different areas of conducting viva voce and interaction with the external and internal examiners. The final section of the chapter would outline critically the challenges, gaps, and perceptions of the external examiners from the sequence of the events. In-depth individual interviews were conducted with the selected external examiners and the internal faculty guides or supervisors in different phases of the research. Here, the MBA dissertations, which is a non-taught but research-based course has been analyzed in the context of external examining process.

The remarks given by both external and internal examiners in the dissertation reports impart insights on the strengths and the drawbacks of the reports and provide guidelines (Mafora & Lessing, 2014). The comments of the examiners after studying the reports can be considered valuable and informative.

LITERATURE REVIEW

A review of the literature demonstrates that there is a serious gap in the examiners' level of comprehension and usage of the concepts of academic standards (Bloxham & Price, 2015) except for the research of Colley and Silver (2005). Though there has been a satisfactory body of articles, white papers, and essays on the area of external examining; however, there has been a paucity of research in fathoming the loopholes in the external examining system (Attwood, 2010). Sadler (2011), on the contrary, had questioned the mechanism of measurement of the examiners' evaluation and had found that the objective mechanism methods of evaluation were missing. There was a framework sometime back that had been conveniently replicated by the new universities (Silver & Williams, 1996). Ironically, the current phase has witnessed a dilution of the expected academic standards due to the rampant mushrooming of higher education institutions, and a standard benchmark for consistent external examining seems to be missing.

The QAA (2009) report a few years back suggested that the external examination system should be open and comprehensible including streamlined steps in assisting external examiners to define roles and standards These views have been corroborated by the Universities UK (2011) report, which discusses similar suggestions, but the added one was related to the students' right to go through the reports. The literature demonstrates that the prescribed guidelines for external examiners are not strictly followed (Mafora & Lessing, 2014). Different theories have been presented regarding the lack of uniformity in the implementation of guidelines.

On the one hand, guidelines available for the examiners may not be adequately explained or familiar (Sankaran, Swepson, & Hill, 2005), and on the other hand, despite knowing the guidelines, they may not be followed due to various reasons (Mullins & Kiley, 2002). Furthermore, the guidelines may have been interpreted in different ways and contexts by a varied group of external examiners (Lessing, 2009). Perceptual biases color the external examiners' notion of the standards of the project or the entire experiences gained in the evaluation process. Such biases influence their ideas of how the reports should be (Johnston, 1997), even the outline recommended for writing reports is not adhered according to the guidelines of the university (Lovat, Holbrook, & Hazel, 2002). These contradictions led to the cascading effect of irrational remarks on the students' reports (Cantwell & Scevak, 2004). To summarize, the general areas pointed as important by the external examiners encompass the importance of the study, the literature, the methodology of the research, analysis, suggestions, and the presentation aspects. The crux of the problem lies in the different areas of emphasis given by the external examiners on these sections (Holbrook et al., 2007).

Earlier research shows that the examiners in reviewing the projects give serious attention to literature, format, grammar and language mistakes, the flow, and the background theory. Examiners' insights and critical comments on the intricacies of the research methods and data analysis sections were brief (Hansford & Maxwell, 1993). Additionally, Mullins and Kiley (2002) stressed the distinctive usage of theoretical models, well-developed rationale, and rigorous development of literature and data analysis methods as a reflection of good research reports. On the contrary, they described inferior reports having an unstructured presentation, vague theory development, faulty problem analysis, plagiarized sources, the unsystematic blending of theory and methods, and the shortcoming of assembling the different sections of the dissertation. Johnston (1997) found that external examiners focused on the documental presentation of the students' projects, but on the contrary, other research (Carter, 2008; Lovat et al., 2002) did not give much importance to these issues. External examiners also prefer to classify projects as low, average that can be acceptable, and the excellent ones (Mullins & Kiley, 2002). It becomes imperative that there is quality categorization done for the projects having a better evaluation process.

Colley and Silver (2005) had thrown light on the learning mechanisms of the external examiner, especially that the process is observational. The vital reasons for which academicians take the role of the external examiner from time to time are varied, including the intention to add value to the academic community, professional networking, and gaining insights on the systems and processes of other colleges and institutions (Hannan & Silver, 2004).

Ross (2009) elaborates that examiners come for the assessment with their subjective attributes, and it is understood that they know the academic guidelines and regulations.

Examiners expect independence in the evaluation process and tend to avoid restrictions of standards and the flow process (Warren-Piper, 1994). Hence, there is a trade-off between the flexibility arena of assessment and learning of external evaluation and the stated standards to be followed by the examiners (Sadler, 2011), and as a result, the examiner can denounce the rigid standards of the institution (Hawe, 2002).

ROLE OF THE EXTERNAL EXAMINER

Lately, the roles of the external examiner have become multifaceted with a combination of the academic, administrative, and more humane ones. The HEQC (1996) study summed up four crucial roles of the external examiner: additional examiner role, assessment of consistency level, judging the finesse, and a consultative role.

The Silver report (Silver, Stennett, & Williams, 1995) emphasized on the consultative role as a more effective means of evaluation. With the emergence of course modules and services software in present times, the examiner is almost virtually placed (Yorke, 2008). There has been serious criticism over the years apart from the individual assessment of the students' project reports, researchers have raised questions on the effectiveness in following the quality and standards of the external examining systems (Alderman, 2009; Harvey, 2002). The main thrust has been on the usage of clearly defined processes maintaining the standard guidelines stressing uniformity (Yorke, 2008) and perfection (Satchell & Pratt, 2010). The inevitable question arises on what defines standards and the eligibility of standard, setters; however, in reality, the external examiners are not able to work in such a constricting manner. They may have to comment or extend beyond their area of specialized knowledge.

Additionally, it has to be understood that the set of external examiners only have professional associations with some limited universities and institutions and are aware of their set patterns in examining procedures and may not have the requisite experience of different institutions (Colley & Silver, 2005). Research shows that external examiners are considered torch-bearers and regarded highly by the faculty guides (Bloxham & Boyd, 2012). Nevertheless, having blind-folded faith in the assessment capacity of the external examiner needs to be examined.

The research conducted for this purpose has primarily aimed at understanding the assessment literacy of the external examiners, keeping in mind the challenges they face throughout the examining process that may have affected their assessment standards and wisdom. In a way, this chapter is a humble effort to understand the objective criteria against the subjective biases that may impede the entire process of the external examining system. In the context of assessment literacy of the external examiners, there is scant research in higher education perspective (Medland, 2015). The assessment criteria perspective is missing in the examiners' and students' domain (Price, Carroll, O'Donovan, & Rust, 2011). Smith, Worsfold, Davies, Fisher, and McPhail (2013) have suitably described the importance of assessment awareness and literacy among students too, especially the students' thorough understanding of the objectives of conducting the external examination, the process involved, and the students' learning outcomes.

In the light of Holroyd (2000), where the expertise dimension and professional approaches are given weightage, the term assessment scholarship has gained immense importance. Assessment scholarship needs to be carved out and given thrust, and it is embedded in the assessment literature and applications. Ironically, there is a poor correlation between assessment theory and practice (Boud & Falchikov, 2007). According to Medland (2015), assessment literacy refers to the wide coverage of understanding of the assessment methods, acumen, and indisputable subject knowledge. Price, Rust, O'Donovan, and Handley (2012) have made valuable contributions to this perspective; the focus was made on acquired knowledge, skills, and competencies and also possessing an enriched stock of words and grammar sense.

METHODOLOGY

The University Process from Allocation to Assessment of the Dissertation

The external examining process, usually in the private universities, is according to the written guidelines set following the United Grants Commission (UGC) and the All India Council for Technical Education (AICTE) norms. The UGC is the statutory body established by the Indian Union government according to the UGC Act, 1956, under the flagship of the Ministry of Human Resource Development. AICTE is a national-level council monitoring only the technical education. AICTE is under the egis of the Department of Higher Education, Ministry of Human Resource Development. UGC, in contrast, has a more comprehensive role to play in the field of higher education, including both technical and non-technical programs and courses.

Some universities customize the UGC and AICTE guidelines as well as other similar bodies to formulate the policies without diluting the essential regulations. In the private university mentioned in the chapter, the students of the Master's program are assigned the faculty members of the university who are referred to as internal examiners or guides.

Context of the University, MBA Program and Internal Process

The private university started as a group of institutions in the 1960s in South India (Bengaluru) by an educator and is at present spread across five campuses and having around 20,000 students enrolled in various courses. It is a young university, operating as a private university from the last five years with a wide range of courses in Engineering, Computer Applications, Applied Sciences, Nursing, Pharmacy, Management, and EMBA programs. The MBA program has been started at the university around four years back and is an autonomous one. It is a two-year full-time program with specializations, namely, Marketing, HRM, Finance, and Analytics. There is the summer internship of 6–8 weeks after the completion of first two semesters. The research-based dissertations have to be completed by the students in the fourth or last semester.

The initial weeks following allotment of dissertations are spent on finalizing the area of research, the organization identification, and associated aspects of the research. The dissertation project is usually started at the beginning of the last and the fourth semester of the two-year Master (MBA) program. A session is conducted to familiarize on the guidelines of the proposed dissertation to be done by the students. This workshop is pivotal in the sense that it provides the expectations regarding the standards to be followed by the students over the period. The salient dimensions of the guidelines cover the required structure of the format of the dissertation with particular emphasis on literature and gap analysis, research methods and analysis, and suggestions for future research implications. The faculty guides plan the workshop agenda and conduct the workshop together. A faculty guide is the university's internal faculty member who is assigned certain number of students under him. He guides the projects of the specific number of students assigned under him.

The allotted students meet up with the guides on a fixed day in the week and discuss on the progress of their dissertations. The guides sign weekly reports with relevant critical remarks, and the students are supposed to improve upon the comments. The weekly report forms not only incorporate the attendance details but also the areas of progress related to topic selection, literature review, methods, and analysis and the extent of the progress of the students week wise. As per the standard operating procedures, in the middle of the semester (after approximately 8–9 weeks), an internal viva voce has to be conducted by the internal examiners. The internal viva voce is essentially a follow-up on the work-in-progress of the dissertation and is conducted by any two internal examiners (internal faculty members other than the concerned faculty guides) out of three names suggested by the faculty guide. Since the viva voce is internally done and it amounts to a work-in-progress presentation, no plagiarism certificate is required at this phase. The student makes a detailed presentation, and the internal examiners go through the rough draft of the dissertation project. The remarks of the internal examiners are noted down by the guide and the student. The completion of the dissertation project is done following the suggestions. There is a dissertation evaluation form of 100 marks based on specific parameters previously marked by the guide (50 marks), and the remaining marks (50) are assessed by the internal examiners.

Furthermore, as per the guidelines, the controller of examinations (COE) instructs the dissertation coordinator to finalize the dates of the external viva voce immediately after the last date of the semester-end examinations. This viva voce process applies to those students who have cleared all subject examinations, including the third semester. Detained students (students who are not allowed to appear for examinations due to dismal performance or low attendance for the end semester examinations), as well as the students with subject arrears, are not allowed to proceed for this stage One external examiner can be assigned a maximum of 10 students, and the viva voce should be rigorously conducted and should take the entire day and a maximum of three days is scheduled for each external examiner. The guide faculty members are supposed to propose six to seven names of external examiners to the university's examination controller office. The names are provided by the faculty guides and are usually sourced from academic and other professional network in the same city. On nominating the external examiners, the guide has to ensure that the respective individual has done his/her Ph.D. from a reputed university, has a minimum of 10 years of academic and research experience, and is presently employed as an Associate Professor or Professor position in the current institution.

The areas on which the external examiner has to give his/her comments are:

- Whether the recommendation of the thesis can be made, if so, with comments.
- Whether the examiner recommends resubmission of the thesis after revision/modifications?

For such cases (details suggesting specific improvements to be provided)

- Whether the examiner recommends rejection of the thesis, reasons to be provided.
- Whether the dissertation is worthy of distinction with remarks.

Two weeks are given to the external examiners to submit their detailed feedback on the assigned dissertations; reminders are sent in between to speed up the process. During this period, the concerned examiner's availability for the viva voce is asked and confirmed. An external examiner's availability on the viva voce dates is crucial, and in case the examiner declines to be present on the available dates, then a new examiner has to be appointed within this time. The viva voce day consists of both the respective external and the internal examiners attending throughout the process with the assigned students presenting their research and submitting the hard-bound copies of the dissertation for examination. Marks are given and signed by both the examiners in the evaluation sheet.

Fig. 1 is the flowchart of the dissertation evaluation process:

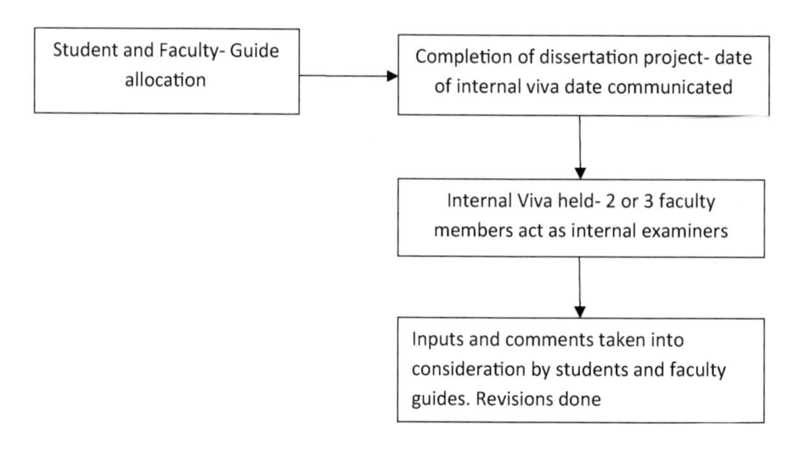

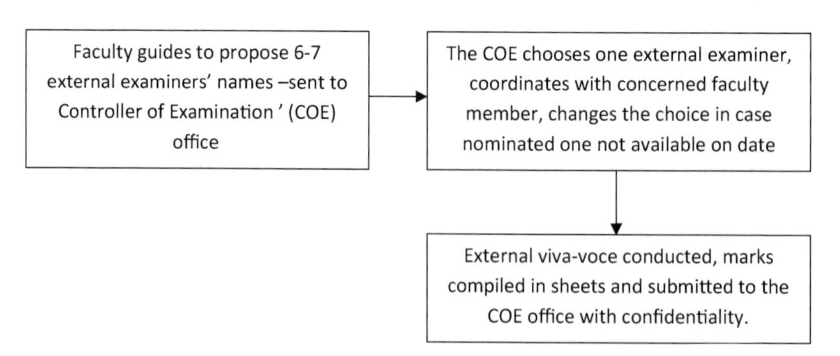

Fig. 1. Flowchart of the Dissertation Evaluation Process. *Source*: Author.

METHOD

Participants

A set of semi-structured telephonic interviews were conducted to give participants autonomy to be imaginative and original, as suggested by past research (Longhurst, 2016). The participants were given information about the research and requested their participation through informed consent. The participants attended the interview but were free to opt out at any moment from the interview process. Before the meetings, the researcher and the participant had an explicit talk about the ethical considerations and the anonymous aspects of the study so that the participant felt at ease and settled down during the actual process of the interview. Even after the completion of the interview process, the participant was given the scope to assess the interview, ask questions and add value by providing suitable inputs.

As the coding categories were created were directly created from the responses obtained, a conventional content analysis was done using a deductive and inductive approach following the iterative approach (Kondracki, Wellman, & Amundson, 2002). Responses were categorized under different codes. These codes represented an appropriate response to understand the number of times a reply containing certain information was given, and the number of circumstances mentioned in totality. More coding schemes were generated as the transcripts were scanned, and initial codes were created based on the interviews conducted utilizing a constant comparison to oversee the differences and commonalities in the interview sessions.

The qualitative study was conducted with informed consent and participation was voluntary. Participants had the scope to opt out from the study anytime. After the interviews were conducted, the responses were also shared with the particular participants, in case they wanted any modification.

The first phase of the research involved the informal, candid interviews of the internal faculty guides and the detailed study of selected projects (between eight to ten). Notes were taken from the selected projects based on the guidelines and the standards set by the university, the study of the selected projects based on the parameters, and the weekly reports and internal evaluation sheets of the faculty guides.

The second phase of the research has aimed to understand through qualitative studies the external examiners' perception of the examining process. In-depth, one-to-one interviews were conducted with five external examiners to understand the challenges and issues faced by them throughout the examining process. Furthermore, some informal interviews were conducted with the faculty guides and the internal examiners to understand their challenges and feedback. Some responses of the faculty guides are provided below:

The participants were asked the interview questions and the responses were recorded, coded, and examined. The similar responses were categorized and below are the salient responses:

Faculty guide 1:

> The allocation of students is done without keeping in mind the functional specialisation … as a result, sometimes I find guiding and examining difficult.

Faculty guide 2:

Students plagiarise sometimes … but only things come out at the end in the plagiarism check.

Faculty guide 3:

There is a disconnect between what I am doing with my students and how other faculty guides are handling and moving ahead … sometimes I feel whether I am stricter or more lenient.

Faculty guide 4:

Students should be let off officially to do the field project but keep on getting complaints about academic pressure from them.

Faculty guide 5:

I don't know whether it should be taken as a point, but I can see some external examiners are more lenient with the students if the concerned faculty guide is lucky enough, but sometimes the external examiner can be extremely rigid and even average and above-average students suffer the ordeal. How to solve this uneven assessment cases?

The research followed the perspectives of Medland (2015) and has aimed to understand the comparative importance of assessment proficiency over subject acumen. Two dimensions of the skills were discussed, namely subject acumen and assessment proficiency. However, the primary deciding factor has usually been the subject proficiency factor. This practice has been corroborated (Finch Review, 2011) with time; however, the assessment criteria have been found to have a more practical basis even though the subject criteria hold more significance in the selection process of the external examiners. The post-structuralist assessment approach can be considered more relevant and customized and associated with the existing cultural domain (Shay, 2005). Previous research (Bloxham & Boyd, 2012) has emphasized on the role of assessment attributes over the subject expertise dimensions. In the present research, personal interviews have been conducted after the examination process. The private university concerned gave the ethical clearance but requested anonymity. The views of the individuals involved in the process were taken into consideration and the participation was voluntary. The projects and evaluation sheets were investigated to collect pertinent data for this research. Necessary measures were taken to ensure the rights and privacy of both the selected internal and external examiners.

The areas discussed during the interviews were as follows:

1. Financial remuneration.
2. Time adequacy for assessment.
3. Assessment criteria and marks.
4. Satisfaction with faculty guide performance with students' projects.
5. General issues/challenges faced as an external examiner.
6. Preparation level before coming for viva voce after project assessment.

The interviews of the selected external examiners revealed the following details and some excerpts are given as follows:

External examiner 1:

Though I am coming as an external examiner here for the last three years, considering the payment they give and months taken to credit is really disheartening. The response had been corroborated by most of the other participants too.

External examiner 2:

Insufficient time is given to assess the project; I have other assignments too and cannot give single-minded devotion. They are in a hurry to fix the external viva date also.

Two of the participants voiced the same issue.

External examiner 3:

The division of marks as per the guidelines of the University is 50% for internal faculty guide and 50% for the external examiner, but this should not be the case. For more objective assessment, the external examiner should be allotted more percentage of marks.

External examiner 4:

Sometimes, students are outstanding in their project development part that I see in the assessment of the hard copy but when I eventually take the viva-voce, they are not able to defend the contents of research done; it is really surprising.

The satisfaction level with faculty guides, as expressed by the participants, is mixed. Few of them are in general satisfied with the quality of the project, but some of them complained about inferior work done.

One of the external examiners had revealed:

If the student has finished a project of poor quality then I will surely blame the faculty guide for not pointing out the drawbacks at the initial stages when I have to assess in the final Viva, I am in a dilemma. In addition too, there is a psychological pressure on me when the faculty guide persuades for better marks.

Regarding preparation before coming for the viva voce, three examiners had pointed out clearly:

Despite asking for the guidelines of the particular university related to the dissertation, they refused point-blank, so I only had the project emailed to me and later straight came for viva.

RESULTS

Table 1 presents the general overview of the results with the coding scheme: coding category, code description, example, the total amount of codes within the respective group, and the corresponding percentage. It has to be mentioned that because the coding process was continuing, some codes were adjusted during codification.

DISCUSSION

The research has raised some significant questions on the effectiveness of the external examining process and system as per the university guidelines. It observed

Table 1. Coding Categories and Descriptions.

Coding Category	Codes	Description	Example Quote	Total
Internal factors	Allocation issues	The allocation of the postgraduate students to the internal faculty to act as a guide or supervisor	"I have students allocated whose functional areas are different from mine; it becomes difficult to supervise …."	74
	Ambiguity	The lack of clarity on examining and assessment. Low uniformity	I have students under me where I have to follow the guidelines … at the same time, I am in charge of internal examining some other supervisor's allocated students … somewhere in both the roles there is a lack of coherence."	62
	Internal examining –Severity and leniency	The perceptual biases of faculty guide or supervisor from one another	"I am moderately strict, but when another internal or external comes to examine … either, he is too strict or too lenient." "I think there should be some workshops for internal and external examiners to reduce the rating biases."	43
External Examining	Financial	The remuneration paid by the university to the external examiner as already set by the guidelines	"I am not satisfied with the money given for the examining work … have complained the program head but it has been futile. I guess revision is a long drawn process."	61
	Weightage of marks	The marks allocated for dissertation as per the university guidelines	"I have complained about the rationale behind the marks distribution … have been told it has been noted, but till date, there was no modification done."	40
	Time factor	The time given by the university to the appointed examiner from the time of project evaluation to the final assessment	"I think abruptly external examiners are contacted (15 days or a month before) and offered the assignment in tight-rope schedule … reaching out should be done 2–3 months in advance … even we have our engagements."	32
	Communication	The communication from various levels of the university members related to effective external examining	"Everything transpires orally; the student evaluation sheets are sent. However, the instructions and guidelines are not provided despite requests. I have been told it is internal."	28
	Expectations of Standards	The standards of evaluation expected from the external examiner	"This is an unpredictable issue … sometimes the faculty supervisor tells me I am quite strict as compared to others."	25
	Clarity	The clarity of the process	"I am afraid … clarity and definite system-driven approaches are less."	18

that criterion-based assessment was not implemented in the entire process. When interviewed, different external examiners revealed different perceived criteria. Even if the criteria were the same, for example, language or grammar, one examiner stated he overlooked minor errors as the subject was a technical one, while someone else clearly stressed that he dislikes assessing spelling/grammar errors in any percentage. It becomes imperative that a criterion-referenced assessment was the need of the hour, and to enforce this, there has to be a proper rubric of scores range with suitable examples on which the examiners are briefed. It is, in fact, the same construct that has been suggested by Bloxham and Boyd (2012). That brings the process to the salient purpose of the system, that is, projects having the same quality standards should be given similar grades. This system can be validated as open, fair, and objective. This comparison is more popular as it compares students against each other (Hudson, Bloxham, den Outer, & Price, 2017).

Furthermore, it was found that the feedback or evaluation of the external examiner has not been cross-checked. The internal examiner at this stage screens the students' projects and gives his comments and feedback to be implemented by the students for external examining process. Hence, the question of validity remains and the possibility of subjective biases cannot be dismissed. There was another vital issue that cropped up from the interviews and an investigation of randomly selected dissertation projects, and that was the central tendency factor. Most of the projects were evaluated categorizing the students within the safety net, few were assessed as outstanding and very few as poor, and no student was failed.

Another point that needs to be pointed out was the difference between the external examiner's and the internal faculty guide/examiner's scores.

It was a debatable issue whether a pure academician would be the appropriate external examiner or an industry person without a Ph.D. or a combination of both. The faculty guides opined that academic experience was necessary for the external examiners, otherwise performing the external examiners' role becomes a challenge.

Nevertheless, there are other perspectives that a non-academic external examiner can bring to the process. In a way, it suffices to say that somewhere down the line, the essential elements of impartiality, the independent voice had been diluted in voicing the project approval process. The selection of the external examiner has been sound and more or less scientific, but in contrast, the entire assessment and evaluation could have been made more objective. Some degree of latitude was seen in the study of the projects as evaluated by the external examiners; some examiners have explicitly expressed this: "I do not expect the quality of the MBA dissertation to be like the doctorate thesis ... it is only a learning process." The same insights that MBA dissertation was a learning cycle have been demonstrated in previous research (Johnston, 1997; Kiley & Mullins, 2004). External examiners also positively appraise dissertations that deeply discuss and justify the results from a practical perspective. The research also reflects that there are some common attributes that the evaluators want from the dissertation projects (Holbrook, Bourke, Lovat, & Fairbairn, 2008) so that the external examining system is standardized irrespective of area (Lovat, Holbrook, & Bourke, 2008), national origin (Pitkethly & Prosser, 1995), the degree (Bourke & Holbrook, 2013), and the background experience of the examiners (Kiley and Mullins, 2004). Another interesting finding from the research was that the suggestions and the feedback points were not consistent. This was due to the perceptual dimensions playing a significant role; some external examiners had suggested immediate rejections or elaborate revisions, while others approved the projects with minor revisions or no revision at all. This finding is in contrast to previous research (Holbrook et al., 2008). The research of Golding, Sharmini, and Lazarovitch (2014) has concisely presented the external examiners' expectations from the dissertations emphasizing consistency, pass through, evaluation based on first or second chapter, evaluation as a layman reader and an academician, picking on errors, flow of the thesis concerning the background literature, reach out with good research, and discussion of the relevance of the findings. Following the present research, some of the aspects were found to match but not all, for example, external examiners, in this case, evaluated all the chapters thoroughly and although some gave separate comments orally and wrote on the gaps, some examiners in the research turned a blind eye to the errors in the projects and some rigorously scanned for spelling and grammatical errors.

CONCLUSIONS, LIMITATIONS, AND FUTURE RESEARCH IMPLICATIONS

The research aimed to understand the effectiveness of the external examining system and process in an Indian context. It was found that there was some disconnect between the internal examining and the external examining process of the university. External examiners are also subject to the perceptual limitations that this research highlighted. Hence, there were some inconsistencies observed.

Limitations

One weakness of this qualitative research is the absence of interviews conducted to delve into the students' perception of the examining process. Future studies should include selected, serious, and diligent students to participate and present an untapped angle of the external examining process, the areas they feel the internal examining process and guidance has missed out, and dimensions of assessment criteria that need deeper preparation from the faculty guide's behalf to hone their skills. Publishing quality dissertations were also a sidelined area as understood in the interviews conducted, as the primary objective was to ensure that the students were obtaining satisfactory grades in the dissertation projects; however, there should be mandatory instructions given to the faculty guides to publish the good research in cited journals when the post-external examining process is completed.

Recommendations

The process can be streamlined with more professionalism whereby the internal guides could follow some workshops to reduce rating errors, and at the same time external examiners should be briefed with the university guidelines. A virtual session of briefing of the external examiners can be organized by the COE office to clarify areas of doubt. Once the external examiner has assessed a student's project another blind review should be undertaken to gauge its validity. Administrative issues like disbursement of the payment should be taken care of promptly because any lateness tarnishes the reputation of the university in the long run. For efficient metrics, a 360-degree feedback form on the quality of the faculty guide's inputs in the dissertation can be done by the external examiner, the assigned students, and the head of the department.

Similarly, feedback should be sought on the system bottlenecks from each internal faculty guide. The insights and suggestions have to be meticulously reviewed to modify the process and the methods.

Future Research Implications

The research highlights a stark reality between expectations and standards in the domain of external examining, and comparative empirical studies need to be conducted between universities to depict the prevailing situations of the universities. Secondly, longitudinal studies related to the entire examining process can be represented adequately. Thirdly, the external examiners' evaluations concerning guidelines provided should also be evaluated, and a transparent system of sharing guidelines should be enforced to alleviate the challenges in external examining. Hence, there should be more relevant research to be conducted to gauge the external examiners' perceptions about the institution support and more particularly departmental assistance.

REFERENCES

Alderman, G. (2009). Defining and measuring academic standards: A British perspective. *Higher Education Management and Policy*, *21*(3), 11–22.

Attwood, R. (2010, August 12). Nip and tuck for externals? A radical facelift is required. *Times Higher Educational Supplement*. Retrieved from https://www.timeshighereducation.com/news/nip-and-tuck-for-externals-a-radical-facelift-is-required/412961.article

Bloxham, S., & Boyd, P. (2012). Accountability in grading student work: Securing academic standards in a twenty-first century quality assurance context. *British Educational Research Journal*, *38*(4), 615–634. doi:10.1080/01411926.2011

Bloxham, S., & Price, M. (2015). External examining: Fit for purpose? *Studies in Higher Education*, *40*(2), 195–211.

Boud, D., & Falchikov, N. (2007). *Rethinking assessment in higher education: Learning for the longer term*. London: Routledge.

Bourke, S., & Holbrook, A. P. (2013). Examining PhD and research masters theses. *Assessment & Evaluation in Higher Education*, *38*(4), 407–416. doi:10.1080/02602938.2011.638738

Cantwell, R. H., & Scevak, J. (2004, November). Discrepancies between the 'ideal' and 'passable' doctorate: Supervisor thinking on doctoral standards [Paper presentation]. Annual conference of the Australian Association for Research in Education (AARE), Melbourne, Australia.

Carter, S. (2008). Examining the doctoral thesis: A discussion. Innovations in Education and Teaching International, *45*(4), 365–374.

Colley, H., & Silver, H. (2005). *External examiners and the benchmarking of standards*. York: Higher Education Academy.

Finch Review. (2011). *Review of external examining arrangements in universities and colleges in the UK: Final report and recommendations.* A report commissioned by Universities UK and GuildHE. Retrieved from www.universitiesuk.ac.uk/highereducation/Documents/2011/ReviewOfExternalExaminingArrangements.pdf

Golding, C., Sharmini, S., & Lazarovitch, A. (2014). What examiners do: What thesis students should know. *Assessment & Evaluation in Higher Education, 39*(5), 563–576.

Hannan, A., & Silver, H. (2004). Enquiry into the nature of external examining: Final report. Retrieved from http://www.heacademy.ac.uk/resources.asp?process=full_record§ion= generic &id= 376

Hansford, B. C., & Maxwell, T. W. (1993). A master's degree program: Structural components and examiners' comments. *Higher Education Research Development, 12*(2), 171–187.

Harvey, L. (2002). Evaluation for what? *Teaching in Higher Education, 7*(3), 246–263.

Hawe, E. (2002). Assessment in a pre-service teacher education programme: The rhetoric and the practice of standards-based assessment. *Asia Pacific Journal of Teacher Education, 30*(1), 93–106.

HEQC. (1996). *Strengthening external examining.* London: Higher Education Quality Council.

Holbrook, A., Bourke, S., Fairbairn, S., & Lovat, T. (2007). Examiner comments on the literature review in PhD theses. *Studies in Higher Education, 32*(3), 337–356.

Holbrook, A., Bourke, S., Lovat, T., & Fairbairn, H. (2008). Consistency and inconsistency in PhD thesis examination. *Australian Journal of Education, 52*(1), 36–48.

Holroyd, C. (2000). Are assessors professional? Student assessment and the professionalism of academics. *Active Learning in Higher Education, 1*(1), 28–44.

Hudson, J., Bloxham, S., den Outer, B., & Price, M. (2017). Conceptual acrobatics: Talking about assessment standards in the transparency era. *Studies in Higher Education, 42*(7), 1309–1323.

Johnston, S. (1997). Examining the examiners: An analysis of examiners' reports on doctoral theses. *Studies in Higher Education, 22*(3), 333–347.

Kiley, M., & Mullins, G. (2004). Examining the examiners: How inexperienced examiners approach the assessment of research theses. *International Journal of Educational Research, 41*(2), 121–135.

Kondracki, N. L., Wellman, N. S., & Amundson, D. R. (2002). Content analysis: Review of methods and their applications in nutrition education. *Journal of Nutrition Education and Behavior, 34,* 224–230. http://dx.doi.org/10.1016/S1499-4046(06)60097-3

Lessing, A. C. (2009). The examination of research for dissertations and theses. *Acta Academica, 41*(1), 255–272.

Longhurst, R. (2016). Semi-structured interviews and focus groups. In N. Clifford, M. Cope, T. Gillespie, & S. French (Eds.), *Key methods in geography* (3rd ed., pp. 143–156). New York, NY: SAGE.

Lovat, T., Holbrook, A., & Bourke, S. (2008). Ways of knowing in doctoral examination: How well is the doctoral regime? *Educational Research Review, 3*(1), 66–76.

Lovat, T., Holbrook, A., & Hazel, G. (2002). What qualities are rare in examiners' reports?. Retrieved from https://pdfs.semanticscholar.org/3166/c28a021dd1be85fc62f64073a048ea7f5af7.pdf?_ga= 2.53870952.1380733078.1582013142-1566385041.1582013142

Mafora, P., & Lessing, A. C. (2014). The voice of the external examiner in Master's dissertations. *South African Journal of Higher Education, 28*(4), 1295–1314. https://doi.org/10.20853/28-4-391

Medland, E. (2015). Examining the assessment literacy of external examiners. *London Review of Education, 13*(3), 21–33.

Mullins, G., & Kiley, M. (2002). It's a PhD, not a Nobel Prize: How experienced examiners assess research theses. *Studies in Higher Education, 27*(4), 369–386.

Pitkethly, A., & Prosser, M. (1995). Examiners' comments on the international context of PhD theses. In K. Beattie & C. McNaught (Eds.), *Research into higher education* (pp. 129–136). Melbourne: HERDSA.

Price, M., Carroll, J., O'Donovan, B., & Rust, C. (2011). If I was going there I wouldn't start from here: A critical commentary on current assessment practice. *Assessment & Evaluation in Higher Education, 36*(4), 479–492.

Price, M., Rust, C., O'Donovan, B., & Handley, K. (2012). *Assessment literacy: The foundation for improving student learning.* Oxford: The Oxford Centre for Staff and Learning Development.

QAA. (2009). *Thematic enquiries into concerns about academic standards in higher education in England.* Gloucester: QAA.

Ross, V. (2009). External music examiners: Micro–macro tasks in quality assurance practices. *Music Education Research*, *11*(4), 473–484.

Sadler, D. R. (2011). Academic freedom, achievement standards and professional identity. *Quality in Higher Education*, *17*(1), 85–100.

Sankaran, S., Swepson, S., & Hill, H. (2005). Do research thesis examiners need training? Practitioner stories. *The Qualitative Report*, *10*(4), 817–835.

Satchell, S., & Pratt, J. (2010). The dubiety of double marking. *Higher Education Review*, *42*(2), 59–62.

Shay, S. (2005). The assessment of complex tasks: A double reading. *Studies in Higher Education*, *30*(6), 663–679.

Silver, H., Stennett, R., & Williams, R. (1995). *The external examiner system: possible futures (The Silver Report)*. London: Higher Education Quality Council.

Silver, H., & Williams, S. (1996). Academic standards and the external examiner system. In J. Brennan, M. Frazer, R. Middleburst, H. Silver & R. Williams (Eds.), *Changing conceptions of academic standards* (pp. 27–48). London: Quality Support Centre,Open University.

Smith, C. D., Worsfold, K., Davies, L., Fisher, R., & McPhail, R. (2013). Assessment literacy and student learning: The case for explicitly developing students "assessment literacy." *Assessment & Evaluation in Higher Education*, *38*(1), 44–60.

Universities UK. (2011). *Review of external examiner arrangements in universities and colleges in the UK: Final Report and Recommendations*. London: Universities, UK.

Warren-Piper, D. (1994). *Are professors professional?* London: Jessica Kingsley.

Yorke, M. (2008). *Grading student achievement in higher education*. London: Routledge.

CHAPTER 7

EXTERNAL EXAMINING THE PROFESSIONAL DOCTORATE AS DISTINCT FROM THE TRADITIONAL PhD: DIFFERENTIATING AND DEVELOPING POLICY AND PRACTICE

Dionisia Tzavara and Victoria L. O'Donnell

ABSTRACT

Professional Doctorates (PDs) have been added to the curriculum of many universities worldwide, as an alternative to the traditional Doctor of Philosophy (PhD). PDs are more focused on practice-based knowledge that advances professional practice and contributes to society, industry and the economy. The dominance of the PhD as the typical higher degree by research has led universities to develop frameworks for their PDs which are very similar to the PhD framework. This includes the assessment of the PD, which in many cases follows the same process and is based on the same criteria as for the PhD. This similarity in the assessment of the two types of doctorates creates challenges for external examiners (EEs), who are invited to evaluate the contribution of the PD within frameworks which are tailored around the PhD. Here, the authors focus the investigation on the Doctorate in Business Administration and conduct a

The Role of External Examining in Higher Education: Challenges and Best Practices
Innovations in Higher Education Teaching and Learning, Volume 38, 95–121

ISSN: 2055-3641/doi:10.1108/S2055-364120210000038007

review and analysis of institutional documents from universities in England in an attempt to understand the similarities and differences between the examination process of the PD and the PhD and the extent to which the examination process of the PD supports the evaluation of the practice-based contribution that is at its heart. Through this review and analysis, the authors identify the challenges that exist for EEs who are called to assess PDs, and make recommendations which will support EEs to evaluate the contribution of the PD.

Keywords: Higher education; assessment guidelines; policy and regulations; Professional Doctorates; doctoral education; research degrees; practice-based research; Doctor of Business Administration; external examiners; viva voce examinations

DISTINGUISHING THE PROFESSIONAL DOCTORATE FROM THE PHD: WHAT ARE THE KEY CONSIDERATIONS FOR EXTERNAL EXAMINERS?

Many universities offer Professional Doctorates (PDs) (Banerjee & Morley, 2013; Costley & Lester, 2010; Kot & Hendel, 2012; Servage, 2009), developed to be distinct from traditional PhDs. PDs represent universities' response to the changing needs of industry, economy and society. Traditional PhDs have been criticized for their lack of relevance to professionals seeking to support the advancement of their career by developing knowledge and skills that will equip them to solve complex, real world and work-based problems (Banerjee & Morley, 2013; Poole, 2018). To address these criticisms, PDs are centered around the "production of 'knowledge-in-context' and the application of research to the social, political and economic contexts" (Kot & Hendel, 2012, p. 7). The PD generates independent research that is context specific, "conducted outside of the academy, in the workplace or professional field" (Servage, 2009, p. 769). PD programs are differentiated from traditional PhDs using words like *professional practice*, *applied research*, *applied knowledge* or *actionable knowledge* (Banerjee & Morley, 2013; Poole, 2018).

Following the growth of PDs, some early discourses questioned whether the work undertaken for a PD represents research at all. Lester's (2004) conceptualization of the PD focused on the centrality of academic research as a unifying feature of traditional PhDs which, he argued, distinguishes them from PDs whose focus is on what he referred to instead as "development projects" (p. 757) whose contribution is to professional or organizational practice, and is therefore different from "research."

However, contemporary national frameworks, descriptors and guidance relating to research and doctoral learning, specifically, provide definitions and understandings of research that are broad and flexible enough to encompass the work of a PD, without having to define it as anything other than research. For example, the Research Excellence Framework 2014 Assessment Framework and Guidance on Submissions, defines research as "a process of investigation leading to new insights, effectively shared" (REF 02.2011, 2011, p. 48). The Dublin Descriptors, which were extended in 2004 to include attributes of doctoral (as well as bachelor and master's) students, includes a definition of "research" in its glossary, which explicitly states that:

> The word is used in an inclusive way to accommodate the range of activities that support original and innovative work in the whole range of academic, professional and technological fields … it is not used in any limited or restricted sense, or relating solely to a traditional "scientific method." (Joint Quality Initiative, 2004, p. 3)

The UK Quality Code for Higher Education's Doctoral Degree Characteristics Statement identifies professional and practice-based (or practitioner) doctorates as one of three overarching categories of doctoral degrees, which can "… advance professional practice or use practice as a legitimate research method" (Quality Assurance Agency, 2015, p. 9).

The qualifications framework in the UK provides a single descriptor for doctoral degrees which does not differentiate traditional PhDs from PDs, and which acknowledges that both "original research and advanced scholarship" of sufficient quality are equally acceptable. The Dublin Descriptors articulate the knowledge and understanding, the ability to apply knowledge and understanding, the judgments, the communication skills and the learning skills that are expected of doctoral students. These encompass both traditional PhDs and PDs across Europe and do not differentiate between them. The Dublin Descriptors are incorporated within the UK Quality Code for Higher Education's Frameworks for Higher Education Qualifications (Quality Assurance Agency, 2014).

This acceptance of the broader range of ways research can be enacted allows the focus to shift from the question of whether PDs should be assessed as research at all, to the question of how research conducted within a PD should be assessed. Given the deliberate and intended differences between the PD and the traditional PhD, the assessment of PDs should recognize their distinction from PhDs in terms of the nature of knowledge they produce, their products, the types of graduates they produce and their expected contribution. The significance of these differentiating features for the viva voce examination are discussed here.

The Nature of Knowledge

Gibbons et al. (1994) argue that there are two distinct modes of knowledge: Mode 1 and Mode 2. Mode 1 knowledge is traditionally developed within the academy, where knowledge and understanding for their own sakes are the focus, and the knowledge is highly theoretical. In contrast, Mode 2 knowledge is developed within the context of practice, where the focus is on how the knowledge can solve real-world (probably workplace) problems. Mode 1 knowledge is disciplinary, while Mode 2 knowledge extends across and beyond disciplinary boundaries. The legitimacy of Mode 1 knowledge is established through its suitability for publication in peer-reviewed journals or academic conferences, while the legitimacy of Mode 2 knowledge is established through links with industry.

Lester (2004, 2012) argues that what should be central to PDs is workplace knowledge developed within and through practice, and he distinguishes this from research carried out in the workplace, but separate from everyday workplace practice. Lester has developed a typology of workplace practice to demonstrate this, within which four types of workplace knowledge generating activities are identified. These are "A: practice as research," "B: research within practice," "C: research for practice" and "D: synthesis." He argues that type A and type B activities can lead to significant knowledge generation with "relevance far beyond the immediate context" (Lester, 2012, p. 278). This type of knowledge may be different to traditional Mode 1 knowledge, yet still has the potential to meet the required attributes of a doctoral student according to the Dublin Descriptors, since it "[includes] a systematic understanding of their field of study and mastery of the methods of research associated with that field" (Joint Quality Initiative, 2004, p. 4).

Logically, then, we might expect that the external examiner (EE) for a PD would be drawn from the relevant industry or professional context so that such judgments about the knowledge produced and its impact can be made. In the field of engineering, it is common practice for the examination to be conducted by a panel of three examiners, with two externals (one academic and one from industry) (Barnes, 2011). Where universities' criteria for the appointment of doctoral EEs do not suggest or allow this, the challenge for the lone academic EE lies in evaluating the value or significance of the knowledge that the student has produced, to a workplace or an industry of which they may have little direct knowledge or experience and across disciplinary boundaries to workplaces generally. The professional doctoral candidate is likely to be disadvantaged if the knowledge produced is evaluated against the criteria traditionally used for Mode 1 knowledge, when their focus has been on the production of Mode 2 knowledge.

The End Product

The award of a PhD is usually based on submission of a thesis or dissertation (the product), review of the thesis by examiners and the outcome of a viva voce examination. Many universities apply this model of assessment to the award of a PD, despite the alternative "products" that could allow a professional doctoral student to demonstrate their learning, development, knowledge and contribution. For example, more practically focused outputs (e.g. policy or strategic documents, portfolios, books, pieces of art, creative artifacts, curriculum innovation, manuals, guidelines or a collection of related projects) accompanied by a narrative piece of critical and contextual writing with details of the methodological approach taken would allow the work of the PD and its contribution to be presented and evaluated (Barnes, 2011; Costley, 2013; Lunt, 2011; Lycouris, 2011). The production of a portfolio rather than a thesis should be a key distinguishing feature of a PD (Bourner, Bowden, & Laing, 2001; Scott, Brown, Lunt, & Thorne, 2004). Yet the most common and popular PD programs globally continue to rely on the traditional thesis or dissertation as their product. In their review of Australian Doctor of Business Administration (DBA) programs, Sarros, Willis, Fisher, and Storen

(2005) did not find a single instance of a university requiring anything other than a thesis. Where universities' regulations and guidelines continue to require or refer to the product of a PD as a thesis, the ability of the student to demonstrate Mode 2 knowledge and the contribution of their learning and development to practice could be limited.

The Types of Graduates

In their discussion of universities' approaches to the support of research degrees, Boud and Lee (2005) argue that postgraduate research degrees should be conceptualized as peer learning, theorized and situated within a communities of practice framework (Lave & Wenger, 1991; Wenger, 1998). They argue that the learning which takes place in the context of a PhD is about the student becoming a peer to their supervisor, and thus about becoming an academic. Essentially, the process of undertaking a PhD represents movement from peripheral to full participation in the academic community of practice; a PhD is a license to be a researcher, and this is reflected in the way that the PhD is assessed.

This powerful discourse of peer learning applied to the PhD itself should lead us to consider what it means for the PD. Professional doctoral students' trajectories are not inbound toward becoming full participants in the community of academia – their primary communities are professional or industrial and external to the university. Most professional doctoral students are undertaking their program on a part-time basis, while maintaining their professional careers (Taylor, 2008). The student's intention is to facilitate the development of that career through the PD and to become "practitioner-scholars" (Pina, MacLennan, Moran, & Hafford, 2016) or "researching professionals" (Schildkraut & Stafford, 2015) rather than academic researchers.

The learning is not intended to lead to becoming an academic, so the assessment of that learning should not be about assessing the extent to which the student has become an academic; instead it should focus on the extent to which the student has become an influential member of their professional community.

The Contribution

While traditional criteria such as theoretical strength and methodological rigor are generally used to evaluate PhDs' contributions, Johnson (2005) expressed concerns about the appropriateness of such criteria for PDs, given the kinds of differences already discussed here (Banerjee & Morley, 2013). Poole (2018) notes that the Doctoral Degree Characteristics document (Quality Assurance Agency, 2015) includes the statement that "all doctoral candidates are required to make an original contribution to knowledge." However, since the nature of knowledge differs between PhDs and PDs, any evaluation of the contribution of that knowledge should take account of such differences.

The focus within a PD on work and on workplace knowledge production means that EEs of PDs should be assessing the original contribution that is made to high-level practice, rather than just to an academic field or discipline through a research output. This requires consideration of the contribution to or impact on the relevant industry and professional community, not just to a field of enquiry or to the academic community. The Dublin Descriptors specify that a doctoral student is "expected to be able to promote, with academic and professional contexts, technological, social or cultural advancement" (Joint Quality Initiative, 2004, p. 4). Methods for promoting such advancements, and the evaluation of their effectiveness, will differ within and between professional contexts. It is important that the assessment of this contribution by the examiner takes account of the specifics of the professional context relevant to the individual student.

Professional doctoral students are expected to develop a high level of "reflexivity" (Banerjee & Morley, 2013). The examiners should therefore explore the advanced professional development of the professional doctoral candidate, and the extent to which this has had a demonstrable impact on their colleagues. In terms of assessment, this necessitates more generic criteria with a greater emphasis on soft skills, horizontal learning and work-based knowledge (Bernstein, 1999; Eraut, 2004). As indicated already, all of this suggests that EEs from the relevant professional context should be central to the assessment of a PD to adequately assess its contribution to practice.

The Challenges for External Examiners

According to the Quality Assurance Agency (2013) Quality Code, the assessment procedures of research degrees offered in the UK must "include input from an external examiner" (p. 25). The role of the examiners is crucial in ensuring that academic standards are applied to the assessment, which are in accordance with the "national higher education qualification descriptions for doctoral [...] degrees in the national higher education qualification frameworks" (p. 25) and that the standards of the programs are, where relevant, equivalent to international expectations (p. 9). EEs have the dual role of both assessing the doctoral thesis and assuring that the standards of the thesis are comparable across the sector. As such, doctoral EEs are an integral element of the quality assurance process. This second role is especially challenging for EEs of PDs, in particular, when there is an absence of specific guidance about their assessment and marking criteria and when there is variability in the guidance that different institutions offer.

Since "[m]ost institutions that award professional doctorates (PDs) have introduced their PDs alongside regulations, systems and mindsets designated for PhDs" (Costley, 2013, p. 7), this presents a particular challenge from the perspective of the EE examining a PD thesis, working with institutional guidance around the conduct and criteria for the viva voce examination that is often identical to that which is given for a traditional PhD (Banerjee & Morley, 2013; Poole, 2018; Sarros et al., 2005), all of which may impact upon the outcome for the student. The lack of specific guidance for EEs of PD programs leads EEs to evaluate the contribution of PDs on the traditional criteria that are used for PhDs' "theoretical strength and methodological rigor" (Banerjee & Morley, 2013, p. 176). Lack of distinct definition of the learning outcomes of the PD as well as lack of understanding of the candidate's working context creates significant challenges for examiners, external as well as internal (Johnson, 2005). In relation to the DBA, Sarros et al. (2005) argue that

> in some instances the information provided to examiners of DBA theses was either unavailable or limited, or did not articulate clearly the differences between a DBA and a PhD and how these differences are to be addressed when examining a DBA thesis. (p. 151)

Relative to EEs, professional doctoral internal examiners are usually closely connected to the program – they are members of the university and often of the program team, and in many cases they are supervising other candidates of the same PD program – hence they have a better understanding of the practice-based nature of the program, the program requirements and the expectations for the thesis. For this reason, the challenges of examining a PD thesis are more significant for EEs than they are for internal examiners. For this reason, we have more clearly differentiated the roles of internal examiners and EEs, elucidating the quality assurance elements of the external's role which are in addition to the roles of "assessor" that both examiners fulfill.

HOW ARE THESE DIFFERENT CONSIDERATIONS EMBEDDED IN INSTITUTIONAL REGULATIONS AND PRACTICE GUIDANCE?

Universities alone determine the knowledge content and purposes of PhD learning, through institutional guidance and regulations for PhDs, including assessment regulations and learning outcomes. The topics of individual PhD projects may be linked to industry or contextual knowledge gaps, and certain PhD projects may be sponsored by commercial organizations, but these would still be assessed in line with institutional policy for all PhDs. In contrast, the development of PDs, their purposes, processes and products has been determined in response to the knowledge, interests and alliances of those undertaking them, of other stakeholders and of their professional communities (Costley, 2013). Therefore, it is reasonable to expect that the aims, learning outcomes and assessment criteria for PDs should also be set in conjunction with these others, and not by the university community alone. Yet "[m]ost institutions that award Professional Doctorates (PDs) have introduced their PDs alongside regulations, systems and mindsets designed for PhDs" (Costley, 2013, p. 1).

Based on the differences discussed already, it is reasonable to expect that institutions offering PDs will have developed a range of acceptable and appropriate aims, outcomes and assessment criteria within their own regulatory frameworks to encompass PDs as well as traditional PhDs. These could incorporate alternative examination processes where appropriate, and assessment criteria aligned with the different expectations for knowledge, product, graduate attributes and contribution associated with the PD, while still aligning with nationally recognized frameworks and descriptors for doctoral level qualifications. We would also expect clear accompanying guidance for the examination of a PD, addressing these issues and written with the non-academic EE in mind.

Review of Institutional Documents: The Scoping and Data Collection Process

To explore the extent to which university practices reflect these differences, we conducted a review and analysis of relevant institutional documents from UK universities. With different processes for higher education quality review in Scotland and Wales, we chose to focus our review on English universities, where we were able to identify more than 80 universities offering over 250 PD programs. These programs were mainly in the fields of Business and Management, Education, Psychology, Engineering, Health and Law. From our initial literature review and institutional scoping, we identified that the DBA is one of the most commonly occurring PDs available. Since its appearance in the USA in the 1950s the DBA has become "one of the main types of doctorate that have emerged …" (Poole, 2018, p. 211), and a body of literature specific to this particular type of PD continues to grow (e.g. Banerjee & Morley, 2013; Davies, 2016; Kortt, Pervan, & Hogan, 2016; MacLennan, Pina, & Gibbons, 2018; Neumann & Goldstein, 2002; Perry & Cavaye, 2004; Pina et al., 2016; Sarros et al., 2005). Other examples of commonly available PD programs included the Doctor of Education, Doctor of Clinical Psychology, Doctor in Health and Social Care, Doctor of Engineering (with various specializations).

For the scale and scope of our review to allow for meaningful comparisons across the sector, and for the volume of data to be manageable, we chose to focus our attention specifically on DBA documentation. In our initial review, we identified 28 universities offering a DBA program (see Appendix 1). The initial review did not include universities which offered a DBA in the past but were not enrolling students at the time of the review. Also, of the 28 universities identified in the initial review two were excluded because the information available was unreliable (significantly out-of-date or inconsistent between different sources). Thus, 26 institutions were included in the final review.

Before scrutinizing the documents, we reviewed the websites of the 26 universities to get a sense of how they describe their DBA programs. On their webpages, these universities described their program as *practice-based, applied, with a strong focus on real-world issues, designed for senior professionals, seeking to advance professional knowledge and practice* and they placed an emphasis on impacting the candidate's own professional practice and making a contribution to the candidate's organization. On their websites, several of these 26 universities made an explicit distinction between the DBA and the traditional PhD. For example, according to Aston University (n.d.) "a PhD degree is tailored toward producing academics, as a DBA is customized for future executives," while according to Liverpool John Moores University (2020a), "In contrast to a PhD, a DBA requires a contribution to both theory and practice. Candidates on the DBA are therefore required to demonstrate that they make an impact on the development of a profession and/or an organization" (see Appendix 2 for full details).

Having established that universities were highlighting the practice-based focus of the DBA and explicitly articulating differences between the DBA and the PhD, we collected and reviewed their policies and regulations to investigate the extent to which these were also reflected in their examination processes and criteria for assessment. Our data were collected between December 2019 and January 2020. We reviewed 82 postgraduate research degree regulation and guidance documents and webpages, all of which are included in the reference list (see also Appendix 1). There were only a couple of cases where we found separate policy and framework documents for the DBA. In other cases, we found separate documents for PDs, and the DBA was subsumed within these. We refer to the DBA/PDs below to indicate that in many cases the policy documents were common for all PDs, including the DBA. Most of the universities had common documents covering all types of doctorates and PDs were subsumed within these.

We focused on the research phase of the award, and the taught phase was outside of the scope of our investigation. In the regulations and guidance documents, we looked for information relating to the DBA/PD examination process. More specifically, we focused on the following six elements that emerged from the review of the literature above, and were key themes in the policy documents that we reviewed:

(i) Whether there were separate regulation and guidance documents for the DBA/PDs.
(ii) The requirements for the award, as these were captured in the regulations.
(iii) The product of the research phase.
(iv) The examination process.
(v) Criteria for the appointment of EEs.
(vi) Examination outcomes.

Within the remainder of this chapter, we provide a review and analysis of these universities' policy and practice documents, with a focus on how differences between DBAs and PhDs are articulated and reflected, and how differences in examination processes are presented for DBA EEs.

REVIEW AND ANALYSIS OF INSTITUTIONAL DOCUMENTS: THE FINDINGS

Separate Policy Documents for the DBA/PD

Of the 26 universities, 19 had common policy documents containing the framework and regulations for both types of doctorates (PhD and DBA/PDs). Where such common policy documents existed, some had separate sections for the DBA/PDs, or when there were no separate sections there was a specific mention of the DBA/PDs. However, we also found cases where there was no specific mention of the DBA/PDs and where the regulations were to be applied to all doctoral awards without differences.

We only found two cases where there were separate framework documents for the DBA; despite having a separate framework for the DBA, the University of Reading still had a common *Code of Practice for Postgraduate Students* (University of Reading, 2019a) and common *Rules for Submission of Theses for Research Degrees* (University of Reading, 2019d) which applied to all types of doctorate. Nevertheless, it had separate guides for examiners for the DBA (University of Reading, 2019b) and for research degrees (University of Reading, 2019c). Sheffield Hallam had one document with DBA regulations (Sheffield Hallam University, 2017b) and another document with PhD and MPhil regulations (Sheffield Hallam University, 2017a).

Of the remaining five universities, the first one had a common *Research Student Assessment Policies and Procedures Handbook* (University of Central Lancashire, 2019b) for both types of doctorates and additional *Academic Regulations for PDs* (University of Central Lancashire, 2019a). The second included PDs in its general framework for awarding doctorates (Nottingham Trent University, 2019a, 2019b) and there was a separate chapter in the *University Quality Handbook* dedicated to PDs (Nottingham Trent University, 2019c). The third had a common *Research Degrees Handbook* (University of Plymouth, 2018) for both types of doctorate and an additional *Regulatory Framework for Professional Doctorates* (University of Plymouth, 2013). The fourth had a common *Research Degrees Operational Handbook* (University of Portsmouth, 2019d) for both types of doctoral awards. In addition, there were separate policy documents for higher degrees by research (University of Portsmouth, 2019c) and for PDs (University of Portsmouth, 2019c) and also separate documents outlining the examination arrangements for higher degrees by research (University of Portsmouth, 2019a) and PDs (University of Portsmouth, 2019b). The fifth had a common *Code of Practice for Postgraduate Research* (Teesside University, 2018a), a common *General Framework for Higher Degrees by Research* (Teesside University, 2018b), common *General Submission and Examination Regulations for the Award of Higher Degrees by Research* (Teesside University, 2018c) and separate *Professional Doctorate Assessment Regulations* (Teesside University, 2018d).

Even in cases where we found separate documents outlining the framework for the DBA/PDs, the framework included in the document was not necessarily different from the one for the PhD. This lack of separate documents, and in several cases lack of specific mention of the DBA/PD in the regulations, presents a challenge for EEs who are called to evaluate the research output of the DBA within a framework which differentiates very little between the PhD and the DBA. As will be shown below in more detail, the common policy documents allow for little differentiation between the PhD and the DBA in terms of the criteria for the award, the choice of the EEs, the examination process and in some cases about the recommendations that the EEs can make about the conferment or not of the award.

Requirements for the Conferment of the Award

We looked at the criteria for the conferment of the award. In some policy documents, these were referred to as assessment criteria for the research component (e.g. Liverpool John Moores University, 2020b; University of Derby, 2019; University of Salford, 2019a); in other cases, they were called the requirements for the award (e.g. Aston University, 2019; Leeds Beckett University, 2019); in others still they were called the award descriptor (e.g. Chester University, 2019;

University of Winchester, 2019). In general, what we looked for in the regulations was a description of what successful candidates should achieve in order to receive the award, however this was expressed.

There were eight cases where we did not find any evidence in the regulations of different criteria for the PhD and the DBA/PDs. Also, we found two cases where the requirements for the DBA/PD were distinguished from those for the PhD, but where there was very little information about the different criteria for awarding the DBA/PD.

Of the remaining universities, most of the frameworks made some distinction between the criteria for awarding a PhD and those for the DBA/PD, but the differences were minor, and they did not provide detail of the criteria against which the DBA/PD should be assessed. One example comes from the University of Derby (see Table 1) where the regulations do not provide additional information to explain how the application of the research to the professional context in terms of its contribution, the end product or the graduate's skills should be addressed.

Another example where minor differences can be found between the requirements for the PhD and those for PDs comes from Leeds Beckett University (see Table 1). In this case, in the criteria for awarding the doctorates, and the differences between the PhD and the PD seem to be related to the conditions of admission of the student to the program. A PhD student may be exempted from completing "an approved programme of research training" while the PD student will not. The initial taught element must also include "contextual" study for the professional doctoral student. In this case, the differentiation between the criteria for the research phase seems to be simply the addition of the words "practice and/or" in the case of the PD's contribution, which captures the practice-based nature of the program.

A further example also demonstrates little difference in the assessment criteria between the PhD and the DBA/PD, which comes from the University of Reading (see Table 1). Here, PD students are expected to demonstrate the same learning outcomes as PhD students, with the additional requirement to demonstrate "an understanding of how research informs professional practice and knowledge." In this case, the criteria for awarding the DBA emphasized the research meriting publication. This was the case for many institutions (e.g. University of Hertfordshire, University of Northumbria, University of Reading and Staffordshire University). The contribution to the academic field is very relevant for candidates who will seek a career in academia, but not necessarily for senior practitioners and for the advancement of professional practice, as discussed earlier. These institutions do not explore what is expected of a professional doctoral candidate in terms of a high-level contribution to practice.

We only found three cases where there was considerable differentiation in the criteria for awarding the degree between PhD and DBA/PD. These were the regulations of Anglia Ruskin University, Nottingham Trent University and Sheffield Hallam University, where the criteria for the awards provided enough information to differentiate the PD from the traditional PhD award in terms of the nature of knowledge, the end product, the types of graduates and the expected contribution (see Tables 2 and 3).

Table 1. Requirements for the Confinement of the Award – Limited Differentiation.

"Common to all these routes is academic recognition based on the successful conduct of supervised research culminating (variously as specified for the individual routes or awards) in the production of either a research thesis; a critical review accompanied by creative works; or publications accompanied by a critical review.

The primary aims across all these awards are to enable students to:

- through research training develop a range of skills in research;
- undertake work learning to an original contribution in a field of enquiry;
- engage in academic research which promotes innovative thinking and creativity.

1.3 And in the Professional or Practice-based doctorates, additionally, to:

-critically reflect on and evaluate the process and outcomes of their research and apply this deeper understanding, including from the outcomes of their independent research, *within their profession or field of practice*." (University of Derby, 2019, pp. 2–3)

"A Doctor of Philosophy (PhD) is awarded to a candidate who has satisfactorily *completed, or been exempted from*, an approved programme of research training; has investigated or critically studied an appropriate topic resulting in a significant contribution *to knowledge*; and has presented a satisfactory thesis. The candidate is required to defend the thesis by oral examination.

A Professional Doctorate is awarded to a candidate who has satisfactorily *completed* an approved programme of research training *and contextual study*. The candidate will also have investigated or critically studied an approved topic *or topics* which make a significant contribution *to practice and/or knowledge*, and presented a satisfactory thesis. The candidate is required to defend the thesis by oral examination." (Leeds Becket University, 2019, p. 3)

"For the PhD the candidate must demonstrate each of the following:

(a) the creation and interpretation of new knowledge, through original research or other advanced scholarship, of a quality to satisfy peer review, to extend the forefront of the discipline, and to merit publication in an appropriate form.
(b) a systematic acquisition and understanding of a substantial body of knowledge which is at the forefront of an academic discipline or area of professional practice.
(c) The general ability to conceptualise, design and implement a project for the generation of new knowledge, applications or understanding at the forefront of the discipline, and the ability to adjust the project design in the light of unforeseen problems.
(d) a comprehensive understanding of techniques applicable to their own research or advanced scholarship." (University of Reading, 2019c, p. 5)

"For the DBA the candidate must demonstrate each of the following:

(a), (b), (c) and (d) same as above and in addition.
(b) An understanding of how research informs professional practice and knowledge." (University of Reading, 2019b, p. 4)

With these notable exceptions, the general lack of meaningful differentiation in the assessment criteria of the research output for the DBA/PD creates a major challenge for EEs who are called to evaluate it using the same criteria that they would for a PhD. Without differentiated criteria, it is difficult for EEs to evaluate the practice-based, context specific, workplace knowledge that is at the heart of the DBA/PD. Inevitably, because the PhD is the traditional research degree that universities have offered for many years, academics are more familiar with assessing PhD research. Differentiation in the assessment criteria would help examiners to focus on the professional value of the research and on the advancement of professional knowledge. Its absence presents a risk for DBA/PD students who

Table 2. Requirements for the Confinement of the Award – Adequate Differentiation: the PhD.

"A PhD shall be awarded to a candidate who:

a. having critically investigated an evaluated an appropriate topic resulting in an independent and original contribution to knowledge,
b. demonstrated an understanding of research methods appropriate to the chosen field, and
c. has presented and defended a thesis by oral examination to the satisfaction of the examiners." (Anglia Ruskin University, 2019a, p. 20)

"Holders of a PhD will have demonstrated the creation and interpretation of new knowledge, through original research or other advanced scholarship, of a quality to satisfy peer review, *extend the forefront of the discipline, and merit publication*. They will systematically acquire and understand a substantial body of knowledge which is at the forefront of *an academic discipline*. Holders will be able to conceptualise, design and implement a project for the generation *of new knowledge, applications or understanding at the forefront of the discipline*, and to adjust the project design in the light of unforeseen problems. They have a detailed understanding of applicable methods and techniques for research and advanced academic inquiry.

Holders of a PhD are able to make informed judgements on complex issues *in a specialist field*, often in the absence of compete data. They are able to communicate ideas and conclusions clearly to specialist and non-specialist audiences, and to defend they thesis orally to the satisfaction of the examiners." (Nottingham Trent University, 2019a, p. 9)

"PhD award objectives

The PhD will be awarded to a candidate who, having critically investigated and evaluated an approved topic, resulting in an independent and original contribution to knowledge, and *demonstrated an understanding of research methods appropriate to the chosen field*, has presented and defended a thesis by oral examination to the satisfaction of the examiners." (Sheffield Hallam University, 2017a, p. 3)

Table 3. Requirements for the Confinement of the Award – Adequate Differentiation: the DBA/PD.

"Successful candidates for the award of Professional Doctorate will be expected to demonstrate:

(a) the systematic acquisition and critical understanding of a substantial body of knowledge that is at the forefront of the academic discipline and area of professional practice;
(b) the ability to reflect on and examine critically their own professional activity;
(c) the ability to conduct research in accordance with academic and professional ethical standards;
(d) the creation and interpretation of new knowledge through original research or other advanced scholarship which is of a quality to satisfy peer review, extend the forefront of the discipline, and merit publication;
(e) the ability to ingrate theoretical and professional-practical perspectives, knowledge and understanding in such a way as to generate mutual critique, and reformulation of theory and of professional practice;
(f) the ability to conceptualise, design and implement a project for the generation of new knowledge, applications or understanding which are at the forefront of the discipline or area of professional practice, and to adjust the project design in the light of unforeseen problems;
(g) a critical and contextually appropriate application of the techniques for original research, effective communication, critical and independent reasoning appropriate to advance academic enquiry; the qualities and transferable skills necessary for employment requiring exercise of personal responsibility and unpredictable situations, and in professional/institutional or equivalent environments." (Anglia Ruskin University, 2019a, p. 118)

Table 3. *(Continued)*

"Holders of a Professional Doctorate will have demonstrated the creation and interpretation of new knowledge *in a particular professional field that will contribute to the enhancement of professional practice and practitioners*, through original research or other advanced scholarship. They will systematically acquire and understand a substantial body of knowledge which is at the forefront of *a professional discipline*. Holders will be able to conceptualise, design and implement a project for the generation *of new professional knowledge, applications or understanding at the forefront of practice*, and to adjust the project design in the light of unforeseen problems. They have a detailed understanding of applicable methods and techniques for research and advanced academic inquiry. Holders of a Professional Doctorate are able to make informed judgements on complex issues *in a professional field*, often in the absence of compete data. They are able to communicate ideas and conclusions clearly to specialist and non-specialist audiences. *They will have undertaken research that has direct relevance to their own professional interest, working life or that of an organisation.* They are able to defend they thesis orally to the satisfaction of the examiners." (Nottingham Trent University, 2019a, p. 9)
"The specific objectives of the DBA are to: (a) provide an opportunity to make an independent and original contribution to knowledge *and to the practice of management and the professions*; (b) *provide a sound research training and development to enable candidates to complete their research successfully and to continue to contribute to knowledge*; (c) *build a rich community of reflective practitioners*; (d) *contribute to the enhancement of management in the regions and beyond*; (e) *contribute to business success in the region and beyond*." (Sheffield Hallam University, 2017b, p. 3)

have conducted research that has workplace, industry or practical value, but are evaluated on the basis of contributing to a discipline and to scholarly knowledge.

Product of the Research Phase

Turning to the product of the research phase, we reviewed how the regulations described this, whether the requirement for the DBA/PD was to produce a thesis at the end of this phase, or whether some other type of product was also an option. We found that most of the universities required DBA/PD candidates to produce a thesis as the product of the research phase. The regulations for 19 of the universities that we reviewed described the product of the research as a thesis.

Of the remaining seven universities, three sets of regulations required candidates to produce a *thesis or practice-based materials* (University of Central Lancashire), *thesis or portfolio* (University of Coventry) and a *thesis or appropriate form of submitted material* (Liverpool John Moores University). These three "products" applied both to PD and PhD candidates in these institutions. We could not find additional information about the precise nature of these alternative products in relation to the practice-based nature of the DBA/PD. A fourth, Teesside University, called the product of the research phase "Advanced Independent Work (AIW)," which sets it apart from the traditional PhD thesis. However, in the *Assessment Regulations for Professional Doctorate Awards* (Teesside University, 2018d) it was written that "[t]he AIW part of Professional Doctorate Awards is intended to reflect the principles underpinning the assessment of Higher Degrees by Research (e.g. PhD)" (p. 25), which means that despite any differences in the product being assessed, the same underlying criteria are in place for its assessment.

We identified three institutions with significant differences in the product of the research phase for the DBA/PD. Aston University regulations require PD candidates to submit "a thesis or portfolio," Northumbria University regulations state that PD candidates may submit "a thesis or equivalent" and Staffordshire University regulations required PD candidates to submit a "thesis, portfolio or equivalent." More specifically, the regulations of these three universities can be found in Table 4.

Table 4. Product of the Research Phase.

"ii The portfolio material will demonstrate a substantial engagement with professional practice over a period of time; the portfolio must contain a body of evidence, which might include published work or innovative practice. iii The portfolio will include both an overriding line of argument and a critical commentary which sets the material in a theoretical and professional context. iv The portfolio must focus on an area/theme of direct relevance to the student's professional area of work, and aim to disseminate new knowledge and practice throughout the profession to aid its development. v The portfolio, taken as a whole, will make an original contribution to knowledge and professional practice. vi The nature and indicative components of a portfolio will be specified at the outset as part of the programme approval process, such as to enable the candidate to demonstrate (at the final examination) that the outcomes expected of doctoral candidates have been met. Details of assessment including the minimum number of articles, the minimum length of articles will be specified at the time the programme is approved. A minimum of two published articles and a covering paper outlining the overall line of argument will be required." (Aston University, 2019, p. 22)
"[w]here a non-standard equivalent to a thesis such as a portfolio is submitted (this option normally applies to Professional Doctorate programmes only), rather than a Thesis, the following is relevant: […] The submission will always contain a critical commentary of between 15,000–20,000 words (depending on the requirements of the specific programme on which the student is enrolled). The critical commentary sets the material in a theoretical and professional context; elaborates the overriding line of argument, discussion of the research philosophies, methodology and evidence of data collection which are included in the portfolio; and demonstrates the original contribution made by the portfolio to theory and (in the case of Professional Doctorate programmes) professional practice." (Northumbria University, 2018, p. 19)
According to the document the following are examples of what could be included in the non-standard equivalent to the thesis, and they explicitly include alternatives to peer-reviewed academic journals:
"Published journal and conference papers, book chapters or books; Strategic Organisational Reports; Strategic Policy Documents; Evaluation Reports; Web work; Videos of practice interventions; Innovative methods of developing professional practice; Feedback on interventions, developments and professional practice; Student's own self-development evidence, contributions and reflections on professional practice; Reflective diary extracts." (Northumbria University, 2018, pp. 19–20)
"[s]uccessful completion of the research component will involve a candidate working on one or a linked series of research projects or studies. The format of the final assessment shall be agreed as part of course approval and stated in the approved course specification. Some of the credits for the research component may be derived from practice based work. In some cases, the research component will be examined by a research thesis. In other cases, the work to be submitted may be more closely related to professional practice and candidates may submit a work-based research project in the form of a portfolio or report. The work to be submitted could include a permanent record (video, photographic record, CD_ROM, DVD_ROM) of the practical component of the work, if this has been agreed as part of course approval and stated in the course specification." (Staffordshire University, 2018, p. 20)

It is important to note that in the case of Aston University, despite the differentiation in the product of the research phase, the requirement for published articles to be produced as evidence of contribution is still in place. However, perhaps articles published in industry publications could be acceptable as contributions to professional practice.

We expected that DBA/PD students would have the option of producing an alternative product at the end of the research phase, but our research suggests that very few universities allow for this. As the regulations of Aston and Northumbria Universities and the University of Staffordshire suggest, this alternative product would allow students to demonstrate Mode 2 knowledge and the contribution of their learning and development to practice, the profession and to the specific context of their research.

Examination Process

In terms of the examination process, we were interested to see whether the examination of the DBA/PD included an oral examination – the viva voce – or whether alternative forms of examination were in place. Across all the universities, the examination process included an initial evaluation of the thesis (or alternative product) and an oral examination for both types of doctorate (PhD and DBA/PD). This uniformity in the examination process probably stems from the nature of the product. Since in most cases, the product of the research for a DBA/PD student is still a thesis, there seems little scope for differentiation in the examination process. What is not clear is whether these examination arrangements allow EEs to evaluate the level of "reflexivity" that DBA/PD students are expected to develop, and the extent to which they have demonstrated development of their professional practice and an impact on their organization and on their colleagues. For example, the submission of a reflexive log, a journal, workplace project reports, organizational change implementation plans or other alternative products might warrant a different type of assessment. A presentation or demonstration, a panel discussion, a workplace visit or meetings with the student's colleagues or co-workers might be considered more appropriate ways for PD students to demonstrate their professional development and to assess the impact of the students' work on the organizational context. These could be implemented instead of, or in addition to, a traditional viva voce.

Criteria for the Appointment of Examiners

We did not find any evidence in the documents of 22 of the universities that we reviewed, of different criteria for the selection of the examiners for the oral examination (viva voce) for DBA/PDs versus the traditional PhD. Among these 22 universities, the frameworks of two universities did refer to the professional experience of the examiners, but this was for both types of doctorates and was not specifically in relation to the DBA/PD. Rather, the regulations mentioned that when relevant or practicable or applicable, examiners should have or may have relevant professional experience. Also, one university allowed for the possibility of appointing non-academic EEs, but this again was both for PhD and

PDs. Some of the university regulations referred to examiners having appropriate specialization, but this specialization was in relation to the topic of the research within the broader academic field, and was not related to the professional nature of the DBA/PDs.

The frameworks of just four universities made specific requirements for appointing examiners for the oral examination for the DBA/PD. According to the framework of Anglia Ruskin University (2019b, p. 63) "in an examination for a Professional Doctorate the examining team shall have experience of examining at least one Professional Doctorate candidate."

This does not imply any experience or expertise in the candidate's professional context, only in the examination of PDs generally.

Coventry University (2019) regulations stated "in the case of Professional Doctorate Candidates or a doctorate by alternate format based on creative practice, the examination panel may also include an experienced practitioner in the relevant field" (p. 8). This allows for, but does not require, the inclusion of a relevant practitioner as an EE. In contrast, Teesside University's (2018c) general examination regulations set a requirement for a professional expert on the panel. It said

> a candidate shall be examined by at least two, and normally not more than three, examiners of whom at least one shall be an External Examiner, and in the case of M. Prof. or D. Prof., at least one of whom shall have an up-to-date professional expertise. (p. 14)

Teeside University's (2018d) Professional Doctorate Assessment Regulations said that

> a student shall be examined by at least two, and normally, not more than three examiners [*except where 6.6.6, Appointment of an Additional External Examiner, applies*], of which at least one of whom shall be an External Examiner, and at least one of whom shall have up-to-date professional expertise. (p. 31)

Finally, according to the framework of the University of Winchester (2019) "in the case of Professional Doctorates: at least one of the two examiners shall have relevant professional experience" (p. 13).

We expected that universities would appoint EEs for the DBA/PD who would bring the professional expertise and industry knowledge relevant to make judgments about the value of its contribution to the specific work context of the research and to professional practice. Without this professional expertise, the challenge for EEs is to evaluate the significance of the contribution of the DBA/PD to an industry or workplace context with which they may not be familiar. If the expertise of the examination panel is disciplinary, but practice-based expertise is missing, then the risk is that examiners will focus on evaluating Mode 1 knowledge, the highly theoretical disciplinary knowledge that is traditionally the focus of the academy. The focus of PDs is on the development of Mode 2 knowledge, or the intersection of Mode 1 and Mode 2 knowledge, which is where the theoretical becomes applied, where disciplinary boundaries are crossed and where knowledge is practice-based with an emphasis on solving contextualized real-world problems. This should be the PD examiners' focus, but it requires the appointment of industry professionals to the examination panel.

Examination Outcomes

One issue that caught our attention as we reviewed these regulations was that the regulations of five universities suggested that among the viva voce examination outcomes for the DBA/PD was an option for the examiners to recommend the candidate for the award of the MPhil. According to the regulations of these five universities, if the examination panel feels that the candidate does not meet the requirements for the DBA/PD, the panel can recommend the candidate for the award of the MPhil, with or without amendments to the thesis, provided the thesis meets the institutional standards for the MPhil award. The fact that the examination panel may award a DBA/PD student the same compensation award as would be given to a PhD student (the MPhil) makes it difficult for examiners to differentiate the kind of knowledge and contribution that the DBA/PD is expected to generate and to make a clear decision about whether they are evaluating Mode 1 or Mode 2 knowledge. Given that the DBA/PD is expected to advance professional knowledge, we would expect that the compensation award for the DBA/PD would be different than that for the PhD, and would instead be an award which reflects the practice-based, workplace contribution of the DBA/PD.

DISCUSSION AND CONCLUSIONS

Based on our findings, only a small number of the universities reviewed have separate policy documents for the DBA/PD and even in cases where separate documents do exist, the differentiation between the frameworks for the PhD and DBA/PD is minimal. Perhaps the overarching statements and frameworks that have been developed to encompass all doctoral level study and attributes create a false impression that there is no need to consider any differences between PhDs and PDs when it comes to their assessment. As a result, the majority of the universities have similar or identical criteria for awarding the two types of doctorate, the examination process for both types of doctorate is a two-stage process consisting of a preliminary evaluation of the end product and an oral examination (the viva voce). The end product of the research phase of the DBA/PD is in most cases a thesis, following the requirements of the PhD – and there are even some universities which offer the same compensation award both to PhD students and DBA/PD students – and candidates are required to demonstrate the same or similar skills upon completion of the research. Examiners are appointed on the basis of the same criteria, with very few exceptions where professional/industry experience may be brought into the examination. In one university, there was a requirement that the EE for a PD should have experience of examining PDs before. As we have seen, the university where the EE has examined a PD before is unlikely to have differentiated the assessment process for the PD from a PhD in terms of the nature of knowledge, the product, the types of graduate being developed, and the contribution made. This creates a circularity, because prior experience of examining a PD does not guarantee prior experience of examining a PD *in a way that is distinct from examining a PhD*. It falls to the institutions themselves to issue clear guidance and training for EEs on the differentiation of approaches to be taken. Without this, EEs will be unable to do anything except apply their experience of PhDs to the examination of PDs, and subsequently apply that same experience to yet another institution, perpetuating an acceptance of the same approach across the sector.

This lack of differentiation of the framework for the DBA/PD from that of the PhD presents several challenges for EEs who are called to evaluate the value of the practice-based PD within a framework that is very similar to that of the PhD. For example, the similarity of the assessment criteria limits the ability of EEs to evaluate the practical contribution to practice and to professional knowledge that should be the outcome of the DBA/PD (unless the professional community in question is the academic community itself, as is the case for some educationally focused PDs). Also, although one would expect that the examination panel for a DBA/PD examination would consist of academic as well as professional experts, the evidence suggests that only in a few cases this is required or mentioned in the policy frameworks. Despite the emphasis that universities put on the practical nature of the DBA and on advancement of professional practice for the candidates and professional knowledge in context, our research shows that the examination process for the research phase of the award does not bring out this nature of the program.

One factor which limits the PD student's ability to demonstrate the kind of learning and development that they have engaged in is the expectation that they produce a thesis at the end of the research phase. In very few cases do students have the option of submitting an alternative end product which may be better suited to a practice-based contribution. Another limitation is the traditional viva voce examination which gives limited opportunities for EEs to evaluate the level of "reflexivity" that DBA/PD students are expected to develop and the extent to which they have demonstrated development of their professional skills and practice and the impact that their research makes on their organization and peers.

Recommendations

Our research therefore confirms what Banerjee and Morley (2013) wrote in their study that "[d]espite the espoused focus on practice, DBA theses still tend to be assessed by their theoretical and empirical attributes" (p. 188). There is a long way to go before universities can say that they have developed appropriate frameworks for the DBA/PD that reflect the doctoral level of the award as well as its practical, applied, real-world, industry focused nature. We recommend that universities consider how doctoral level criteria can be "translated" and adapted to suit the practice-based nature of the DBA/PD, and that they develop frameworks that will bring practice-based experience into the examination team and examination process in a way that will support the practice-based nature of the program and will not compromise its academic rigor. Given the emphasis that the DBA/PDs place on the development of professional knowledge and on knowledge that is created and relevant "in context," we recommend that universities find ways to bring workplace/industry expertise into the examination process. Also, that they should think carefully about what the end product of the research phase should be in order to allow the candidates to demonstrate the professional development and the contribution to professional practice that the DBA promises. Universities should re-think the examination process and agree a process that will allow for the evaluation of the DBA/PD student's professional development and their development into practitioner scholars.

Further Research

We recognize that we only used information that was publicly available on the universities' websites and that additional guidance documents may exist on password protected university intranet pages. However, if additional guidance does exist then it should still be reflected in the overarching framework documents, and available to potential DBA/PD candidates who seek to make an informed decision about selecting their program of study. This is very important for the positioning of the DBA and for the sustainability of the program and of PDs in general. Also, our study is focusing on DBA programs offered by universities in England. It would be useful to do a similar investigation beyond England to include DBA programs in the UK and other countries. Also, it would be interesting to expand the scope of the investigation beyond the DBA program and to explore the challenges associated with examining other PDs where the end product of the research phase may not be the traditional thesis. One example would be the dissertation in practice which is required by some EdD programs in the USA (Fowler, 2017).

REFERENCES

Anglia Ruskin University. (2019a). Research degree regulations. Retrieved from https://web.anglia.ac.uk/anet/academic/public/research_degree_regs.pdf. Accessed on January 10, 2020.

Anglia Ruskin University. (2019b). Research degree regulations, Summary of amendments, Section A9, The examiners. Retrieved from https://web.anglia.ac.uk/anet/academic/public/research_regs_sa9_alt.pdf. Accessed on January 10, 2020.

Aston University. (2019). General regulations for degrees by research and thesis. Retrieved fromhttps://www2.aston.ac.uk/current-students/graduate-school/documents/regulations/new/au-gsmc-18-1701-a-general-regulations-for-degrees-by-research-and-thesis-2019-20-final.pdf. Accessed on January 10, 2020.

Aston University. (n.d.). Our Executive Doctor of Business Administration. Retrieved from https://studyonline.aston.ac.uk/programmes/executive-doctor-business-administration-dba. Accessed on January 26, 2020.

Banerjee, S., & Morley, C. (2013). Professional Doctorates in management: Toward a practice-based approach to doctoral education. *Academy of Management Learning & Education*, *12*(2), 173–193.

Barnes, T. (2011). The engineering doctorate. In T. Fell, K. Flint, & I. Haines (Eds.), *Professional Doctorates in the UK* (pp. 35–39). Staffordshire: UK Council for Graduate Education.

Bernstein, B. (1999). Vertical and horizontal discourses: An essay. *British Journal of Sociology of Education*, *20*(2), 157–173.

Boud, D., & Lee, A. (2005). 'Peer learning' as pedagogic discourse for research education. *Studies in Higher Education*, *30*(5), 501–516.

Bourner, T., Bowden, R., & Laing, S. (2001). Professional Doctorates in England. *Studies in Higher Education*, *26*(1), 65–83.

Chester University. (2019). Quality and standards manual, handbook G – Postgraduate research degrees. Retrieved from https://www1.chester.ac.uk/social-responsibility/academic-quality-support-services/academic-regulatory-information/quality-and. Accessed on January 10, 2020.

Costley, C. (2013). Evaluation of the current status and knowledge contributions of Professional Doctorates. *Quality in Higher Education*, *19*(1), 7–27.

Costley, C., & Lester, S. (2010). Work-based doctorates: Professional extension at highest levels. *Studies in Higher Education*, *37*(3), 257–269.

Coventry University. (2019). Postgraduate research examination and award policy. Retrieved from https://livecoventryac.sharepoint.com/:w:/s/all.documents/EaqYbYOxm4tJorsLyK5qhPIBGFrH9XD4km7RlypdRQnyNQ?rtime=Dmx55tox10g. Accessed on January 10, 2020.

Davies, J. (2016). DBA impact statements as self-research methods: PhD plus or practitioner frolic? In *Proceedings of the 15th European conference on research methodology for business and management studies* (pp. 91–98). Reading: Academic Conferences and Publishing International Ltd. Retrieved from http://eprints.hud.ac.uk/id/eprint/29244/. Accessed on January 19, 2020.

De Montford University. (n.d.). Doctor of Business Administration DBA. Retrieved from https://www.dmu.ac.uk/study/courses/postgraduate-courses/dba/doctor-of-business-administration-dba.aspx. Accessed on January 26, 2020.

Eraut, M. (2004). Informal learning in the workplace. *Studies in Continuing Education*, *26*(2), 247–273.

Fowler, D. J. (2017). Through a professor's lens. In V.A. Storey (Ed.), *Exploring the impact of the dissertation in practice* (pp. 17–30). Charlotte, NC: Information Age Publishing.

Gibbons, M., Limoges, C., Nowotny, H., Schwartzman, S., Scott, P., & Trow, M. (1994). *The new production of knowledge: The dynamics of science and research in contemporary societies*. London: Sage.

Johnson, D. (2005). Assessment matters: Some issues concerning the supervision and assessment of work-based doctorates. *Innovations in Education and Teaching International*, *42*(1), 87–92.

Joint Quality Initiative. (2004). Shared 'Dublin' descriptors for the bachelor's, master's and doctoral awards. Retrieved from http://www.aqu.cat/doc/doc_24496811_1.pdf. Accessed on February 19, 2020.

Kortt, M. A., Pervan, S. J., & Hogan, O. (2016). The rise and fall of the Australian DBA. *Education and Training*, *58*(4), 390–408.

Kot, F. C., & Hendel, D. D. (2012). Emergence and growth of Professional Doctorates in the United States, United Kingdom, Canada and Australia: A comparative analysis. *Studies in Higher Education*, *37*(3), 345–364.

Lave, J., & Wenger, E. (1991). *Situated learning: Legitimate peripheral participation*. Cambridge: Cambridge University Press.

Leeds Becket University. (2019). Academic regulations research awards. Retrieved from https://www.leedsbeckett.ac.uk/-/media/files/academic-regs-new/2019/11-research-awards-1920.pdf?la=en. Accessed on January 12, 2020.

Lester, S. (2004). Conceptualizing the practitioner doctorate. *Studies in Higher Education*, *29*(6), 757–770.

Lester, S. (2012). Creating original knowledge in and for the workplace: Evidence from a practitioner doctorate. *Studies in Continuing Education*, *34*(3), 267–280.

Liverpool John Moores University. (2020a). DBA Doctorate in Business Administration. Retrieved from https://www.ljmu.ac.uk/study/courses/postgraduates/doctorate-in-business-administration. Accessed on January 26, 2020.

Liverpool John Moores University. (2020b). Policy and procedure for the examination of research degrees. Retrieved from https://www.ljmu.ac.uk/the-doctoral-academy/policies/policy-and-procedures-for-the-examination-of-research-degrees. Accessed on January 12, 2020.

Lunt, I. (2011). The D. Clin. Psy. In T. Fell, K. Flint, & I. Haines (Eds.), *Professional Doctorates in the UK* (pp. 45–48). Staffordshire: UK Council for Graduate Education.

Lycouris, S. (2011). Practice-led doctorates in the arts, design and architecture. In T. Fell, K. Flint, & I. Haines (Eds.), *Professional Doctorates in the UK* (pp. 62–70). Staffordshire: UK Council for Graduate Education.

MacLennan, H., Pina, A., & Gibbons, S. (2018). Content analysis of DBA and PhD dissertations in business. *Journal of Education for Business*, *93*(4), 149–154.

Neumann, R., & Goldstein, M. (2002). Issues in the ongoing development of Professional Doctorates: The DBA example. *Journal of Institutional Research*, *11*(1), 23–37.

Northumbria University. (2018). Academic regulations for research awards. Retrieved from https://northumbria-cdn.azureedge.net/-/media/corporate-website/new-sitecore-gallery/services/academic-registry/documents/academic-support/2018-academic-regulations-for-research-awards.pdf. Accessed on January 12, 2020.

Nottingham Trent University. (2019a). Quality handbook, Part B: Award frameworks, Section 4: Postgraduate taught & research awards. Retrieved from http://www4.ntu.ac.uk/adq/document_uploads/quality_handbook/2019/sections/4-pg-taught-and-research-awards.pdf. Accessed on January 12, 2020.

Nottingham Trent University. (2019b). Quality handbook, Part C: Assuring and enhancing quality, Section 11: Research degrees. Retrieved from http://www4.ntu.ac.uk/adq/document_uploads/quality_handbook/2019/sections/11-research-degrees.pdf. Accessed on January 12, 2020.

Nottingham Trent University. (2019c). Quality handbook, Part E: Regulations, Section 16E: Professional Doctorate degrees. Retrieved from http://www4.ntu.ac.uk/adq/document_uploads/quality_handbook/2019/sections/16e-professional-doctorate-degrees.pdf. Accessed on January 12, 2020.

Perry, C., & Cavaye, A. (2004). Australian universities examination criteria for DBA dissertations. *International Journal of Organisational Behaviour*, *7*(5), 411–421.

Pina, A. A., MacLennan, H. L., Moran, K. A., & Hafford, P. F. (2016). The D.B.A. vs. Ph.D. in the U.S. business and management programs: Different by degrees?*Journal for Excellence in Business Education*, *4*(1), 6–19.

Poole, B. (2018). Doctorateness and the DBA: What next? *Higher Education, Skills and Work-based Learning*, *8*(2), 211–223.

Quality Assurance Agency. (2013). UK Quality Code for higher education: Part B: Assuring and enhancing academic quality. Chapter 11: Research degrees. Retrieved from https://www.qaa.ac.uk/docs/qaa/quality-code/chapter-b11_-research-degrees.pdf. Accessed on July 03, 2020.

Quality Assurance Agency. (2014). UK Quality Code for higher education: Part A: Setting and maintaining academic standards: The frameworks for higher education qualifications of UK degree-awarding bodies. Retrieved from https://www.qaa.ac.uk/quality-code/UK-Quality-Code-for-Higher-Education-2013-18. Accessed on February 19, 2020.

Quality Assurance Agency. (2015). Characteristics statement: Doctoral degree. Retrieved from https://www.qaa.ac.uk/docs/qaa/quality-code/doctoral-degree-characteristics-15.pdf. Accessed on February 19, 2020.

REF 02.2011. (2011). Research excellence framework 2014: Assessment framework and guidance on submissions. Retrieved from http://www.ref.ac.uk/2014/pubs/2011-02/. Accessed on February 19, 2020.

Sarros, J. C., Willis, R. J., Fisher, R., & Storen, A. (2005). DBA examination procedures and protocols. *Journal of Higher Education Policy and Management*, *27*(2), 151–172.

Schildkraut, J., & Stafford, M. C. (2015). Researching professionals or professional researchers? A comparison of Professional Doctorate and PhD programs in criminology and criminal justice. *American Journal of Criminal Justice*, *40*(1), 183–198.

Scott, D., Brown, A., Lunt, I., & Thorne, L. (2004). *Professional Doctorates: Integrating academic and professional knowledge*. Berkshire: Open University Press.

Servage, L. (2009). Alternative and Professional Doctorate programs: What is driving the demand? *Studies in Higher Education*, *34*(7), 765–767.

Sheffield Hallam University. (2017a). *Regulations for the awards of the university's degrees of Master of Philosophy and Doctor of Philosophy*. Retrieved from https://students.shu.ac.uk/regulations/research_degrees/1718/MPhil%20and%20PhD%20Regulations%202017-18.pdf. Accessed on January 13, 2020.

Sheffield Hallam University. (2017b). Regulations for the award of Doctorate in Business Administration. Retrieved from https://students.shu.ac.uk/regulations/research_degrees/1718/Doctorate%20in%20Business%20Administraton%20Regulations%202017-18.pdf. Accessed on January 13, 2020.

Staffordshire University. (2018). Framework and Regulations for Professional Doctorates 2018-19. Retrieved from https://www.staffs.ac.uk/legal/policies/professional-doctorate-framework.jsp. Accessed on January 14, 2020.

Taylor, J. (2008). Quality and standards: The challenge of the Professional Doctorate. *Higher Education in Europe*, *33*(1), 65–87.

Teesside University. (2018a). Code of practice for postgraduate research. Retrieved from https://www.tees.ac.uk/docs/DocRepo/Research/Code%20of%20Practice%20for%20PG%20Research.pdf. Accessed on January 16, 2020.
Teesside University. (2018b). General framework for higher degrees by research. Retrieved from https://www.tees.ac.uk/docs/DocRepo/Research/RDC-A.pdf. Accessed on January 16, 2020.
Teesside University. (2018c). General submission and examination regulations for the award of higher degrees by research. Retrieved from https://www.tees.ac.uk/docs/DocRepo/Research/RDC-E.pdf. Accessed on January 16, 2020.
Teesside University. (2018d). Assessment regulations Professional Doctorate awards. Retrieved from https://www.tees.ac.uk/docs/DocRepo/student%20regulations/Assessment%20special/Professional%20Doctorate%20Assessment%20Regulations.pdf. Accessed on January 16, 2020.
Teesside University. (2020). Business Administration (DBA) Doctorate. Retrieved from https://www.tees.ac.uk/postgraduate_courses/Business_Accounting_Marketing_&_Enterprise/Doctorate_Business_Administration_(DBA).cfm. Accessed on January 26, 2020.
University of Bradford. (n.d.). Executive Doctor of Business Administration (DBA). Retrieved from https://www.bradford.ac.uk/courses/pg/dba/. Accessed on January 26, 2020.
University of Central Lancashire. (2019a). Academic regulations for Professional Doctorates. Retrieved from https://www.uclan.ac.uk/study_here/assets/academic_regulations_for_professional_doctorates_2021.pdf. Accessed on January 10, 2020.
University of Central Lancashire. (2019b). Research student assessment policies and procedures handbook. Retrieved from https://www.uclan.ac.uk/study_here/assets/research_student_assessment_policies_and_procedures_handbook_2021.pdf. Accessed on January 10, 2020.
University of Central Lancashire. (n.d.). Doctor of Business Administration DBA. Retrieved from https://www.uclan.ac.uk/courses/doctor_business_administration.php. Accessed on January 26, 2020.
University of Derby. (2019). Regulations for postgraduate research students (PGR) working towards the awards of Master of Philosophy (MPhil) and Doctor of Philosophy and independent research by thesis forming a part of professional or practice-based doctoral awards. Retrieved from https://www.derby.ac.uk/media/derbyacuk/assets/departments/the-registry/academic-regulations-2018-aug/PGR-REGULATIONS-Oct-2019.pdf. Accessed on January 12, 2020.
University of Plymouth. (2013). Regulatory framework for Professional Doctorates. Retrieved from https://www.plymouth.ac.uk/uploads/production/document/path/15/15331/Regulatory_Framework_for_Professional_Doctorates.pdf. Accessed on January 12, 2020.
University of Plymouth. (2018). Research degrees handbook. Retrieved from https://www.plymouth.ac.uk/uploads/production/document/path/2/2240/Research_Degrees_Handbook_2018.pdf. Accessed on January 12, 2020.
University of Portsmouth. (2019a). Examination arrangements higher degrees by research. Retrieved from http://www2.port.ac.uk/accesstoinformation/policies/academicregistry/filetodownload,163754,en.pdf. Accessed on January 12, 2020.
University of Portsmouth. (2019b). Examination arrangements Professional Doctorates. Retrieved from http://www2.port.ac.uk/accesstoinformation/policies/academicregistry/filetodownload,163764,en.pdf. Accessed on January 12, 2020.
University of Portsmouth. (2019c). Regulations for higher degrees by research. Retrieved from-http://policies.docstore.port.ac.uk/policy-115.pdf?_ga=2.90637850.1806976853.1578847403-917307125.1571834428. Accessed on January 12, 2020.
University of Portsmouth. (2019d). Research degrees operational handbook. Retrieved from http://www2.port.ac.uk/departments/services/academicregistry/qmd/researchdegrees/usefulinformation/RDRegulationsPoliciesandDocumentation/filetodownload,195943,en.pdf. Accessed on January 19, 2020.
University of Reading. (2019a). Code of practice on research students. Retrieved from http://www.reading.ac.uk/web/files/qualitysupport/pgr_Code_of_Practice_October.pdf. Accessed on January 13, 2020.
University of Reading. (2019b). Guide for examiners of Doctor of Business Administration (DBA). Retrieved from http://www.reading.ac.uk/web/files/graduateschool/pgr_guide_for_examiners_for_DBA_sept2019.pdf. Accessed on January 13, 2020.
University of Reading. (2019c). Guide for examiners of research degrees (PhD, MPhil, LLM). Retrieved from http://www.reading.ac.uk/web/files/graduateschool/pgr_guide_for_examiners_of_research_degrees_FINAL_Sept2019.pdf. Accessed on January 13, 2020.

University of Reading. (2019d). Rules for submission of theses for research degrees. Retrieved from http://www.reading.ac.uk/web/files/graduateschool/1_pgr_rules_for_submission_of_theses.pdf. Accessed on January 13, 2020.

University of Reading. (n.d.). Doctor of Business Administration (DBA). Retrieved from https://www.henley.ac.uk/postgraduate-research/course/doctor-of-business-administration. Accessed on January 26, 2020.

University of Salford. (2019). Academic regulations for research awards. Retrieved from http://www.salford.ac.uk/__data/assets/pdf_file/0006/1818186/AcademicRegulationsResearch201920.pdf. Accessed on January 22, 2020.

University of Salford. (2020). Doctor of Business Administration (The Salford DBA). Retrieved from-https://beta.salford.ac.uk/courses/postgraduate-researchdoctorate/doctor-business-administration-salford-dba. Accessed on January 26, 2020.

University of Winchester. (2019). Academic regulations for postgraduate research programmes. Retrieved from https://winchester.ac.uk/about-us/leadership-and-governance/policies-and-procedures/?download=true&id=402. Accessed on January 16, 2020.

University of Worchester. (n.d.). Doctor of Business Administration DBA. Retrieved from https://www.worcester.ac.uk/courses/doctor-of-business-administration-dba. Accessed on January 26, 2020.

Wenger, E. (1998). *Communities of practice: Learning, meaning and identity.*Cambridge: Cambridge University Press.

APPENDIX 1: UNIVERSITIES AND POLICY DOCUMENTS

Anglia Ruskin University	Research Degree Regulations Research Degree Regulations, Summary of Amendments, Part A Research Degree Regulations, Summary of Amendments, Part C(a) Research Degree Regulations, Summary of Amendments, Section A9, The Examiners Research Degree Regulations, Summary of Amendments, Section A10, The Thesis Research Degree Regulations, Summary of Amendments, Section A11, First Examination Research Degree Regulations, Summary of Amendments, Section A12, Re-examination
Aston University	General Regulations for Degrees by Research and Thesis General Regulations for the Presentation of the Theses
Birmingham City University	Research Degrees Handbook Academic Regulations: Assessment, Progression and Award Academic Regulations: Assessment, Progression and Award Second Edition
University of Bradford	Regulation 10: Regulations for Research Degrees Ordinance 6 & 8: Ordinance Governing the Degrees of Doctor or Philosophy, Master of Philosophy and Professional Doctorates
University of Central Lancashire	Academic Regulations for Postgraduate Research Degrees Academic Regulations for Professional Doctorates Research Student Assessment Policies and Procedures Handbook Student Handbook for Postgraduate Research The Code of Practice Relating to the Supervision, Examination and Administration of Research Degrees
Chester University	Quality and Standards Manual, Handbook G – Postgraduate Research Degrees
Coventry University	Academic and General Regulations 2019–2020 Examination of Research Degrees: Guidance Notes for Examiners Postgraduate Research Examination and Award Policy
Cranfield University	Managing Research Students Research Students' Handbook
De Montfort University	Code of Practice for Research Degree Students
University of Derby	Regulations for Postgraduate Research Students (PGR) working towards the awards of Master of Philosophy (MPhil) and Doctor of Philosophy and Independent Research by Thesis forming a part of Professional or Practice-based Doctoral awards
University of Hertfordshire	Doctoral College Handbook Research Degrees – General Institutional Regulations
Leeds Beckett University	Quality Manual for Research Degree Programmes Academic Regulations Research Awards
Liverpool John Moores University	Academic Regulations for Research Degrees DBA Doctorate in Business Administration Policy and Procedure for the Examination of Research Degrees Policy for the Presentation of Research Theses.
University of Northampton	The University of Northampton Academic Regulations and Student Code of Conduct
Northumbria University	Academic Regulations for Research Awards Handbook of Student Regulations – Research Awards

Nottingham Trent University	Quality Handbook, Part B: Award Frameworks, Section 4: Postgraduate Taught & Research Awards
	Quality Handbook, Part C: Assuring and Enhancing Quality, Section 11: Research Degrees
	Quality Handbook, Part E: Regulations, Section 16D: Master and Doctor of Philosophy
	Quality Handbook, Part E: Regulations, Section 16E: Professional Doctorate Degrees
University of Plymouth	Regulatory Framework for Professional Doctorates
	Research Degrees Handbook
	Academic Regulations, Section E: Awards
University of Portsmouth	Examination Arrangements Professional Doctorates
	Awards of the University of Portsmouth
	Examination Arrangements Higher Degrees by Research
	Examination Arrangements Professional Doctorates
	Regulations for Higher Degrees by Research
	Regulations for Professional Doctorates
	Research Degrees Operational Handbook
University of Reading	Code of Practice on Research Students
	Guide for Examiners of Doctor of Business Administration (DBA)
	Guide for Examiners of Research Degrees (PhD, MPhil, LLM)
	Rules for Submission of Theses for Research Degrees
University of Salford	Academic Regulations for Research Awards
	Code of Practice for the Conduct of Postgraduate Research Degree Programmes
Sheffield Hallam University	Regulations for the Awards of the University's Degrees of Master of Philosophy and Doctor of Philosophy
	Regulations for the Award of Doctorate in Business Administration
University of Southampton	Code of Practice for Research Degree Candidature and Supervision
	Different types of Doctoral Programmes
	Guidance for Examiners of Postgraduate Research Awards
	Postgraduate Research Examining Team: Guidance for Faculties
	Regulations for Research Degrees
	Examination and Examiners
	Guidelines for Doctoral Degrees
Staffordshire University	Framework and Regulations for Professional Doctorates 2018-2019
	PhD Regulations Supervised Research 2019
Teesside University	Code of Practice for Postgraduate Research
	General Framework for Higher Degrees by Research
	General Submission and Examination Regulations for the Award of Higher Degrees by Research
	Assessment Regulations Professional Doctorate Awards
University of Warwick	PGR Guidance
	Reg. 38 Research Degrees
University of West of England	Postgraduate Research Degree Programmes Code of Practice
	Postgraduate Research Degrees – Guidelines for Examiners
	Academic Regulations 2019–2020 Volume 2 – Postgraduate Research Programmes of study
	Graduate School Handbook Part 2 – Postgraduate Qualification Descriptors
	Graduate School Handbook Part 14 – Final Assessment
University of Winchester	Academic Regulations for Postgraduate Research Programmes
University of Worcester	Research Degrees Regulatory Framework

APPENDIX 2: DBA VERSUS PHD

Aston University (n.d.)	"For example, a PhD degree is tailored toward producing academics, as a DBA is customized for future executives"
University of Bradford (n.d.)	"The programme is as academically rigorous as a PhD, but is specifically designed for executives, professionals and senior managers who seek to combine the best of academic knowledge with the best of practitioner knowledge in order to push forward the boundaries of understanding contemporary and rapidly transforming business and management challenges"
University of Central Lancashire (n.d.)	"The DBA is regarded as being the same status as the more commonly known PhD and permits you to use the title of 'Dr.' upon satisfactory completion"
De Montford University (n.d.)	"Unlike a PhD programme, the DBA is a peer-based experience and focuses on research that emerges from a field of practice to draw in academic knowledge, and also includes a 12-week Executive Company Project"
Liverpool John Moores University (2020b)	"Equivalent to a PhD, the DBA is ideal for those who would like a doctoral level qualification whilst remaining in their chosen professional career. [...] In contrast to a PhD, a DBA requires a contribution to both theory and practice. Candidates on the DBA are therefore required to demonstrate that they make an impact on the development of a profession and/or an organization"
University of Reading (n.d.)	"DBA and PhDs – Equal but Different. The DBA has both rigour and relevance as it contributes to theory and practice in business and management. The DBA typically focuses on research "in" organisations rather than research "on" organisations. It is more likely to involve cross-disciplinary work and mixed methods and contribute to developing students' own practice and development"
University of Salford (2020)	"Whilst equivalent to a PhD, the part-time delivery and commercial focus of the DBA make it far more relevant to high-level business professionals"
Teesside University (2020)	"The DBA is a Professional Doctorate equivalent to a PhD but with a strong focus on applied research"
University of Worcester (n.d.)	"The PD award is distinct from the PhD award in the following respects: There is a considerable weighting given to a taught component which comprises an integral and key part of the programme, and the assessment of the taught component contributes directly towards the final award; The thesis produced by Professional Doctorate students will make an original contribution to knowledge within the relevant area or areas of professional practice; The benefits of the DBA are both organisational and personal"

CHAPTER 8

EXTERNAL EXAMINING POLICIES AT THE UNIVERSITY OF MAURITIUS

Fareeda Khodabocus and Henri Li Kam Wah

ABSTRACT

The primary roles of external examiners at the University of Mauritius (UoM) are to assist the university in ensuring that degrees awarded meet international standards, that assessment is valid, and that procedures and arrangements for assessment, examinations, and determination of awards are sound and conducted rigorously, fairly, reliably, and consistently. External examiners come from a wide range of highly reputed institutions across the globe and the UoM has a set of external examining policies that act as a guide to external examiners. At the end of their visit, the external examiners submit their signed reports to the Vice-Chancellor. The reports, which include their concerns, are circulated to all administrators and academic staff for their review and analysis. Analysis of the external examiners' reports (UoM, 2016–2019) reveal that 28% of the UoM external examiners come from the UK, 39% were from South Africa, and the remaining 33% from Australia, India, and other European countries. Overall, 98% of external examiners have rated the UoM programs as average and above compared to institutions where they had experience of external examining. The contributions of external examiners are highly valued in the continued growth of the new vision of the institution aspiring to be a research-engaged and entrepreneurial institution.

Keywords: Academic standards; appointment; assessment; award; benchmarking; continuous improvement; external examining; good practices; monitoring; role

---

The Role of External Examining in Higher Education: Challenges and Best Practices
Innovations in Higher Education Teaching and Learning, Volume 38, 123–138

ISSN: 2055-3641/doi:10.1108/S2055-364120210000038008

INTRODUCTION

The external examining system in many higher education institutions (HEIs) is considered as a vital function in the attainment of high academic standards nowadays and achieving high standards or excellence in teaching and learning is aimed at by comparison and benchmarking quality indicators of one's institution with best practices of leading HEIs in the same disciplines (Henderson-Smart, Winning, Gerzina, King, & Hyde, 2006; Jackson, 2001). The key elements of any Teaching and Learning Quality Assurance Framework are the curriculum design, assessment methods, approval, monitoring, and review (Henderson-Smart et al., 2006; QAA, 2000–2018). In the UK and at the University of Mauritius (UoM), the external examining system plays an essential part in institutional quality assurance for program monitoring and in the attainment of high academic standards (QAA, 2000–2018; UoM, 2020). The QAA Code of Practice for External Examining (QAA, 2008–2018) has been subject to many revisions since its inception, given the various factors that have influenced changes in the teaching and learning landscape over decades. Research by Becket and Brookes (2006), Alderman (2009), and HERANA (2011–2018) indicate that universities, including the UoM, have increasingly been faced with many challenges, such as expansion in student population, increasing competition, more expectations from learners, internationalization, and accreditation. These, among others, have driven HEIs to review their quality assurance policies and procedures for more rigor, transparency, and accountability. The need to continue to improve and maintain high quality of academic standards, have over time, called for systematic measurement, monitoring, and benchmarking of performance indicators with the best-in-class HEIs (Coates, 2010; Jackson, Parks, Harrison, & Stebbings, 2000; Yorke, 2002). The external examining system is thus seen as one way of enabling benchmarking of standards in many international HEIs. Furthermore, Becket and Brookes (2006) and QAA (2000–2018) argue that the external examining system will continue to be perceived as "the principal means for the maintenance of nationally comparable standards within autonomous higher education institutions". The aims of this chapter, therefore, are to:

1. provide a critical literature review on current external examining policies and how they have evolved over the past decade;
2. evaluate the extent to which the external examining system has been effective in maintaining and comparing academic standards across faculties/center of the UoM, through a desk-study evaluation of the undergraduate and Master's degree external examiners' reports of the three most recent years at the UoM; and
3. consider the implications of the results with reference to existing practices, new developments, external reviews, and their impact on future strategies.

Institutional Context

The UoM is a public tertiary education institution, set up in 1965 and is governed by its Act established in 1971 and Statutes, revised in 1991 and 2013. Over the years, it has gradually evolved from a developmental university into a full-fledged one and is presently regarded as the largest and most reputed public tertiary education provider in the country. The external examining system at the UoM is incorporated in the Statutes of the UoM (Amendment) 2013 (UoM, 2013) Section 24, Powers and Function of the Senate clause (e) which reads as follows:

> To appoint, after consultation, with the Boards of Faculties or Units concerned, and with such duties and under such conditions as the Senate may determine, one or more external examiners for award courses.

Following the setting up of the Quality Assurance Office in 2002, the external examining policies for the institution were adapted from the UK QAA Code of Practice for External Examining for undergraduate and postgraduate programs and were updated, wherever applicable, to align with subsequent revisions of the Code (QAA, 2000–2018; UoM, 2020). Heads of departments, program coordinators, and administrative officers of faculties/center ensure that all newly appointed external examiners familiarize themselves with the university's regulations and Quality Assurance Framework upon their appointment. The external examining process applies to all of the university's provision at both undergraduate and postgraduate degree levels, including those within its partner or affiliated institutions leading to the UoM degree awards. Prevailing practice is that for the taught programs the external examiners visit the institution over a one-week period, whereas for MPhil/PhD and Masters by Research, the reports/dissertations are sent abroad for assessment/examination to external assessors/examiners. It is noteworthy that the external quality audit panel set up by the Tertiary Education Commission (TEC, 2012) commended the UoM external examining system stating that:

> The UoM has clear and user-friendly compendium of guidelines/policy papers/procedures pertaining to examinations; clear guidelines exist relating to the recruitment and appointment of the external examiners including for dissertations and theses; appropriate security measures are in place to protect the integrity of all aspects related to examinations and for the certification of degree awards at the UoM. (p. 60)

The UoM offers programs covering a wide range of disciplines in the field of law and management, engineering, sciences, medicine, agriculture, social sciences and humanities, digital technologies, and lifelong learning. It offered 170 undergraduate and 53 postgraduate programs in the academic year 2019/2020. Its student intake and number of programs have been increasing yearly over the past decade (HERANA, 2011–2018). As at 2019/2020, the overall student population stands at 9,791 (headcount), with 225 students enrolled in MPhil/PhD research programs. New programs are mounted every year, and existing ones are revised to address the changing needs of the job market, entailing extensive consultation with stakeholders from both the public and private sectors.

Driven to innovate, one of the strategies of the UoM, over the past five years, has been to internationalize its curricula and to ensure that its programs are developed in accordance with the professional standards of the subject disciplines that the twenty-first-century job market demands. The UoM thus sought accreditation for several of its programs namely the BSc (Hons) Chemistry and BSc (Hons) Actuarial Science which became accredited respectively with the Royal

Society of Chemistry and the Institute and Faculty of Actuaries in the UK. The BEng (Hons) programs of the Faculty of Engineering are currently undergoing the accreditation process with the Engineering Council of South Africa (ECSA). The UoM is further developing collaboration with international institutions to design dual programs with a view to attracting more international students on the campus. The UoM faculties and center thus are continuously engaged to work in collaboration with its external stakeholders to ensure the quality and relevance of their provisions and to remain competitive on the job market.

METHODOLOGY

This work draws from a desk-based review of external examiners' reports for the period of 2016–2019 for undergraduate degree and Masters programs. A total of 209 reports were scrutinized, and the research includes a literature review, including an evaluation of the changes which have occurred in the external examining arrangements, mostly in the UK, for the period from 2004 to 2018 (QAA, 2000–2018). The existing provision of external examining arrangements in the UoM context will be discussed. They will focus on: the role of the external examiner and criteria for appointment, information provided to the external examiner, that is, examination policies, external examiners' report, responsibilities for action to be taken on the external examiner's report, good practices emanating thereof, and areas for improvement. New developments emerging from the external examining system in combination with outcomes of the latest external reviews will be highlighted, and recommendations will be made in the light of institution vision to be a research-engaged and entrepreneurial university.

LITERATURE REVIEW

Research by Harvey (2004–2020) and Bloxham and Price (2015) reveals that the external examining system is prevalent in the UK, and several countries such as Ireland, New Zealand, Denmark, India, Hong Kong, and South Africa make use or have used the external examining system. The UoM has, in the past, appointed and still appoints external examiners from these countries, and also Australia, Canada, USA, Scandinavian, and the Sub-Saharan countries such as Botswana, Kenya, among others.

Latest reviews in the QAA Code of Practice for External Examining (Bloxham & Price, 2015; HEA, 2015; QAA, 2000–2018) reveal that the external examiner operates in the presence of the following guidelines: the framework for higher education qualifications at the national level, the subject benchmark statements, professional standards at the discipline level, institutional assessment regulations, grade descriptors, and specified program and learning outcomes. Bloxham and Price (2015) further indicate that external examiners draw from a combination of their own experience as well as documented statements of above standards to do their work correctly. The external examining system is thus seen as one of the leading quality assurance mechanisms that directly evaluates student output, and is very highly regarded in the UK as an accountability measure where rigor and fairness of assessment of the academic standards are monitored. External examiners are appointed to provide their advice on whether threshold academic standards have been achieved in programs to which they have been assigned and on good practices and opportunities to enhance the quality of the programs.

Threshold academic standards will be an area of study in this chapter and are viewed as "the level of achievement that a student has to reach to gain an academic award" (QAA, 2008–2018) and in the determination of equivalence between two awards, the threshold academic standards must be somewhat similar by comparison. Students contribute largely to the achievement of the academic standards and, therefore, the threshold academic standards are linked to a large extent to students' achievement. At the end of their assessment and evaluation, the external examiners provide a report detailing what they have observed of the degree-awarding body's assessment processes, and students' work, and they will make recommendations for further improvement to the university. Faculties and departments highly value these reports for quality improvement initiatives.

Coates (2010), Olabanji and Abayomi (2013), and QAA (2000–2018) reveal a strong link between external examining, accountability, and achievable academic outcomes. Coates (2010) and Olabanji and Abayomi (2013) further argue that accountability of institutions focuses on the results that institutions achieve and is, therefore, directly related to program learning outcomes and students' achievements. In the UK, discussions have been ongoing over the past decade, with several meetings conducted by the professional and regulatory bodies comprising of academics and registered professionals, to review existing arrangements for external examining processes. The QAA Code of Practice for External Examining has thus been revised in 2004, 2011, and 2018. The effectiveness of these revisions has been assessed by the Higher Education Academy (HEA) (Universities UK, 2011). Outcomes of the 2011 reviews reveal that the UK external examining system has been working well, and the main recommendations for improvement were on the selection and appointment of external examiners, more professional induction and training in their tasks, and more transparency and trust such as to enable students to have access to the external examiners' reports.

In universities where programs are being taught to high numbers of students, Bloxham and Price (2015) indicate that there will always be a variance in the teaching and assessment methods, student experience, degree of achievement, but overall minimum threshold standards must be achieved wherever the programs are taught. In the UK, these minimum thresholds are, in principle, determined at subject level statements of the QAA (2008–2018) which set out expectations about degrees in a range of subject areas. They describe what gives a discipline its coherence and identity and what can be expected of a graduate in terms of skills and competencies (HEA, 2015; Houghton, 2002; Jackson, 2001; Jackson et al., 2000). Benchmark statements exist for both undergraduate and MSc degrees and the programs' learning outcomes are mapped against those benchmarking statements. Knowledge of these statements assists the external examiners in their tasks for safeguarding, maintaining, and comparing standards. Hannan and

Silver (2006) further advocate, following a series of interviews undertaken with external examiners, that the success of external examining is based on a combination of knowledge in external examining, experience in the process itself, and expertise and scholarship in the subject under scrutiny. The question which arises here is what happens in the absence of the benchmarking statements? According to the authors' point of view and Jackson et al. (2000), the external examiners' evaluations will then be based on the program learning outcomes and competencies embedded at the curriculum design, but despite same was practised at UoM, the third cycle quality audit report (TEC, 2018) of the UoM recommended that:

> the UoM develops a graduate profile document that takes into account desired graduate attributes and that its programmes are responsive to national and regional needs. The Panel is of the view that a graduate profile document is crucial in informing curriculum design as it outlines the various knowledge, skills (critical, problem-solving, communication amongst others) and competences graduates are expected to develop by the end of their studies. The finalisation and approval of such a document will help inform the development, management, and review of programmes. (p. 54)

As evidenced by the above recommendation, the subject benchmark statement is still needed at the UoM. Analysis by Jackson (2002) and Henderson-Smart et al. (2006) reveal that the subject benchmark statement is a policy document in the public domain which provides a set of reference points for standards at subject level, derived from the program learning outcomes, and leading to improvements in teaching, assessment, curriculum design and ultimately student learning. Yorke (1996) and Jackson (2002) further argue that these statements are for guidance only and are not prescriptive, but they must continuously be enhanced through new research knowledge in the subject area and professional exchanges and benchmarking.

SELECTION AND APPOINTMENT OF EXTERNAL EXAMINER

Two broad characteristics identified by Joyner (2003) that demarcate the choice of an external examiner are: they should be sufficiently well experienced in the subject to make a good knowledge contribution to the award, and they should be experts of sufficient wisdom and humanity to influence the examination process professionally for further progress. Joyner (2003) further states that institutions must have well-documented policies regarding what they expect from the external examiner as well as proper regulations to facilitate the external examining process. External examiners at the UoM are identified by the program coordinators/heads of department at departmental level and subsequently approved by faculty/center board, teaching and research committee, and Senate. The curriculum vitae of the proposed external examiners are duly scrutinized at faculty board/Senate prior to approval. External examiners must be competent and experienced in the field covered by the subject area; they must be professionally qualified at least to the level of qualification being examined and, where appropriate, meet the criteria set out by professional accrediting bodies for professional disciplines such as medicine or engineering. To some extent, they are expected to be acquainted with the latest developments in the design and delivery of the curriculum as well as student enhancement in the subject discipline.

For more than two decades, external examiners in UK universities (Harvey, 2004–2020) and at the UoM have been appointed for up to a three or four-year period, with a one-year allowable extension, subject to valid reasons provided by the department/center. This enabled them to provide a sustainable contribution as supported by Becket and Brookes (2006) to the enhancement of standards and sharing good practices in the module or program. The reasons being that, in many HEIs (Becket & Brookes, 2006), the faculties undertake an annual review of their programs in relation to the university's objectives. The reviews consider feedback from students and external examiners as well as internal data on student recruitment and progression to make changes to the programs. Given the fast-changing rate of skill needs on the job market nowadays, the UoM Senate reviewed the tenure of the external examiner to two years, renewable for another two years, if the knowledge content of the subject has not changed drastically. The external examiners must not have any conflict of interest and most are only appointed to evaluate one program. However, in instances where modules are more complex, have more students, and/or include a clinical component, more than one external examiner is appointed.

After the appointment, external examiners are directed to all the online relevant information pertaining to their future visits, such as student regulations, examination policies, quality assurance documents pertaining to external examining, and relevant guidelines. The visits of the external examiners are typically conducted over the course of one week.

ROLE OF THE EXTERNAL EXAMINER

The responsibility to clarify the role of the external examiner with regard to standards lies with the individual institution. QAA (2008–2018) regulates that external examiners will operate in the presence of a set of internal and external reference documents. Internal reference points include institutional assessment and examination regulations, program specifications, whereas external reference points comprise national qualifications framework, benchmarking statements, and professional body's requirements (Bloxham & Price, 2015). At the UoM, as in many other institutions where the external examining process is in force (Becket & Brookes, 2006), the external examiners are called upon to comment on draft examination papers, model answers, and marking schemes prepared by the institutional examiners. They are expected to ensure that questions are appropriate to the course objectives and learning outcomes, worded clearly, are non-duplicative in nature, sufficiently challenging, and pertinent. Their recommendations are addressed in the revised examination papers, model answers, and marking schemes and in case of non-acceptance by the internal examiners, the external examiners are informed of the underlying reasons. The external examiners also assist in the mounting of new programs of study and provide their advice for the revision of existing ones.

On the first day of their visit to the UoM, the external examiners are provided with all or samples of the project reports/dissertations and marking sheets filled in by supervisors and second examiners/assessors. This provides them with an in-depth insight into the quality of research work undertaken by the students in their final years. In case there are any intellectual property rights issues that may emanate from students' dissertations or project work, the external examiners are required to sign a contract, mandating that any student transgressions of which they are made aware are kept confidential for a period of three years. The external examiners also discuss with the program team on the schedules of students who will interact with them through interviews, oral, or poster presentations. External examiners are expected to review and arbitrate cases where the supervisor and the second examiner/assessor's mark differ by 10% or more. They are also provided with all or samples of students' examination scripts together with the marking schemes, outline model answers, list of student names with their UoM identification numbers, and any other material which may be relevant for external examining of the program concerned. If a sample of scripts is selected, this would include scripts with first-class marks/distinctions, marks from lower and upper-second class divisions, borderline marks, third class marks, and failed marks. If needed, the external examiners are also provided with a 12-page guideline for the processing of examination results summarizing all rules pertaining to marking, moderation, resits, retakes, and handling of borderline cases. If more information on students' assignments and coursework are required, the UoM regulations make provisions for students to keep a portfolio of their assessed work together with feedback provided by their lecturers during their programs of study. The portfolio can be accessed upon preliminary arrangements made with the program team. Evaluation of the external examiners' role by Clements (2005), Hannan and Silver (2006), and Bloxham and Price (2015) indicates that their role consists mainly to: review that there are consistency and rigor in the assessment, marking, and moderation of the students' work to achieve the expected outcomes; provide comparability of the students' performance and standard of awards with standards of similar institutions they have experience with; highlight pockets of good practice; provide recommendations for improvement in weaker areas; ensure that the proceedings are conducted appropriately in line with the institution policies and regulations; and that the threshold for passing the students has been set correctly. External examiners have the option to see all the assessments or samples of assessments subject to preliminary discussion and arrangements with the departmental program coordinator. Quite common but becoming rarer nowadays as advocated by Hannan and Silver (2006), external examiners can only modify marks if they have seen the assessment markings for all students of a particular component (e.g. module) under examination or as further argued by Harvey (2004–2020), the external examiner may act exceptionally as the second marker if there is insufficient expertise in the discipline for full moderation subject to prior agreement.

For the professional undergraduate programs such as medicine and engineering, the external examiners will also consider the professional and regulatory body requirements. With recent developments, where seven flagship programs of the Faculty of Engineering have embarked on accreditation with the ECSA, the remit of the external examiner has been reviewed to include for the assessment of the exit level outcomes of the programs.

All programs of study at the UoM are now designed to be outcome based. During early 2019, more than 100 programs at the UoM were converted to the learner-centered credit system (LCCS), which is based on the European credit transfer system (ECTS). Pursuant to this, the appointed external examiners have also been called to review the Year 1 programs to ensure that they have oversight of the academic standards of not only the final years but on the preliminary years of the programs as well.

The external examiners are members of the respective faculty/center examination boards, and they are convened to provide views on the outcomes of their reviews, borderline cases, recommendations, and areas for improvement as well as observations during their visit. All suggestions and comments made by the external examiners during their visits are also covered in their official report to the Vice-Chancellor. Besides and in view of good practice sharing during their visits, external examiners can be called to conduct workshops/talks in their field of expertise for the benefit of staff and students if time allows.

To conclude, the external examiner's role is to provide an informed and objective external view on performance both within modules and the entire program of study (Becket & Brookes, 2006). Although it is more likely that their role will be more concerned with the outputs of the educational process, nowadays, they are also being called to provide their inputs at all the three levels of the Examinations Quality Assurance Framework, namely the input–process–output as confirmed by Becket and Brookes (2006).

EXTERNAL EXAMINERS' REPORTS

The external examiners' reports are crucial as they provide an opportunity to formalize the points made during their visits, and Hannan and Silver (2006) further stressed that external examiners expect their reports to be acknowledged, considered, and acted upon. However as specified by Becket and Brookes (2006), since the potential for enhancement initiatives is likely to vary across different departments or institutions, most universities provide the external examiner with a proforma that has to be completed, and these tend to be similar in UK-based universities (Clements, 2005). The UoM external examiners' report form covers the following areas: the standards of the structure, organization, design, and marking of all examination papers, dissertations, and other forms of assessments in relation to comparable courses/programs in other institutions; the student performance; the quality of delivery of the course/module(s) through students' works; the strengths and weaknesses of students' performance; strengths and weaknesses of the program; and comparability with programs of study at other institutions they had experience with, to which the external examiners provide an overall rating on a five-point Likert scale: 1. considerably below average; 2. slightly below average; 3. average; 4. slightly above average; and 5. considerably above average. The external examiners also comment on whether the course is adequately resourced and are invited to make further insightful comments, which can enable departments to consider for improvement. The UoM proforma/ template has recently been revised in 2019 to align with recent revision of the QAA Code of Practice for External Examining (QAA, 2008–2018) to enable the external examiners to comment on whether the learning outcomes of the courses align with the program learning outcomes and whether the assessment methods deployed during the delivery of the program were appropriate.

In a nutshell, external examiners are expected to provide their views on whether the overall program and course/module learning outcomes have been achieved; whether the program contents are in line with international standards; and whether courses/modules under examination have been adequately assessed through the use of appropriate tools. Where weaknesses are identified, they will share, if applicable, the best practices from within their institutions or their experience with other universities. One or two weeks after their visit, the external examiners submit their reports, which include their recommendations, to the Vice-Chancellor, who will circulate same to the internal stakeholders as per institutional procedures for external examination. Compared to what happens for most UK universities, following the recent revision of the UK QAA Code of Practice for External Examining (QAA, 2008–2018), external examiners' reports at the UoM are not made available to the public as the university is still at an early stage of the implementation of the outcome-based learning (OBL) concept. However, it is deemed that pertinent comments from the external examiners are valuable for the achievement of the OBL. Faculties/center are expected to revert back to the external examiners within six months upon receipt of their reports on any actions taken in response to recommendations made.

It is noteworthy that the external examiners' reports, together with feedback reports of the faculties/center are also made available to external audit panels of the UoM. Action is also taken by the examinations committee on any recommendations pertaining to the improvement of the examination process. The UoM thus relies to a large extent on the voice of external examiners for continuous improvement, and further research is needed to ensure that their recommendations are used effectively for both quality assurance and enhancement.

FINDINGS AND DISCUSSION

External examiners' distribution by country and their ratings of programs for the period 2016–2019 are shown in Tables 1 and 2.

The overall analysis of the data reveals that 28% of the UoM external examiners come from the UK, out of which 50% rated the UoM programs as above average, and 39% were from South Africa, out of which 69% rated the programs as above average. The remaining 33% from Australia, India, and other European countries all rated the institution's programs as average and above compared to institutions where they had experience of external examining. It is to be highlighted that overall 98% of external examiners have rated the UoM programs as average and above for the past three years. It is noteworthy that nearly all external

Table 1. Distribution of External Examiners by Country (2016–2019). UoM External Examiners Reports for the Period of 2016–2019.

	2016–2017	2017–2018	2018–2019	Total	%
United Kingdom	29	16	14	59	28
South Africa	28	28	26	82	39
Australia	5	8	5	18	9
India	17	14	13	44	21
Other European Countries	1	3	2	6	3
Total	80	69	60	209	100

Table 2. Ratings of External Examiners by Country (2016–2019). UoM External Examiners Reports for the Period of 2016–2019.

	CAAV	SAAV	AV	BAV	SBAV	Total	% ≥ SAAV
United Kingdom	3	23	24	2	–	52	50
South Africa	8	48	23	2	–	81	69
Australia	1	10	4	–	–	15	73
India	9	34	5	–	–	48	90
Other European Countries	1	3	1	–	–	5	80
Total	22	118	57	4	0	201	
%	11	59	28	2	0	100	

Note: CAAV: considerably above average; SAAV: slightly above average; AV: average; BAV: below average; and SBAV: slightly below average.

examiners for our partner and affiliated institutions are from India due to their program specificities (e.g. Asian languages).

The external examining system at the UoM has been functioning satisfactorily so far. The primary roles and responsibilities of the external examiners are to ensure: that examination papers for modules and programs are designed appropriately to address the respective learning outcomes, and that the model answers and marking schemes are adequate; assessment, in all its aspects, is conducted fairly and there is consistency in the marking within components of the programs; assessment and examination processes in place are well documented, transparent, and the arrangements associated with the establishment of the awards are sound and up to international standards; program contents are of appropriate academic standards (and professional standards where relevant); and students' performance demonstrate that they are well taught, assessed, and examined compared with standards from other international institutions. For almost four decades of existence since the creation of the UoM in 1965, most external examiners came from the UK. However, during the past decade, there has been an increase in student numbers, creation of new faculties, and an increasing number of programs. As a result, cost-cutting strategies were adopted, and faculties/departments were recommended to appoint their external examiners from regional countries, wherever applicable. This resulted in departments recruiting their external examiners, mostly from South Africa, India, and Australia. The shift in recruitment could also be attributed to the UoM participating in an important benchmarking project with eight flagship universities of the African continent, namely the Higher Education Research Advocacy Network for Africa (HERANA, 2011–2018) in which the authors participated, professional engineering programs embarking on accreditation with the ECSA as well as the need for increasing collaboration with countries of the Southern African Development Community.

GOOD PRACTICES

The following two good practices emanating from the UoM external examining process were commended by the external quality audit panels of the UoM (TEC, 2012, 2018).

Standards of the Structure, Organization, Design, and Marking of Examination Papers

One main good practice identified from the UoM external examining process is attributed to the well-structured and design of examination papers and assessment section of the external examiners' reports. Over the years, external examiners have continuously commended: that the standards of examination questions set were consistent with the level of course; that the structure of the courses and subjects were appropriate for the levels of the degree; the careful design of assessed work and the diligence that went into its careful assessment; the availability of appropriate marking schemes and assessment rubrics for the final year dissertations; and that the markings were rigorous, fair, and consistent with proper annotations used to demarcate between examiners and moderators. Other frequent observations were: good representation of domain-specific knowledge and competencies for programs, excellent design projects and group presentations, broad range of learning styles, and a variety of assessments are used by departments to assess learning outcomes in line with prevailing international standards. The quality of teaching is generally well commended through the evaluation of the student achievements and documentation provided, although many external examiners would indicate that they have not been into the lecture rooms to provide their comments.

Oral/Poster Presentation as a Good Practice to Evaluate Students' Achievement in Projects/Dissertations

The second good practice identified relates to the students' research undertakings, which are usually of nine months' duration during their final year of their programs. The submission of this vital piece of work is supported by well-laid regulations and guidelines, submission rules, and assessment. External examiners are provided with all the students' dissertations during their visits. A decade ago, it was common practice for all the students to defend their research dissertations through a viva in the presence of the external examiners. Given that the student numbers have been on the increase, oral presentations are nowadays undertaken in the presence of the internal examiners and/or moderators in many departments and are considered as an essential aspect of the evaluation of the research skills and competencies of learners. Only a selected number of students will be subjected to a viva by the external examiners. In the engineering discipline, final year students are given the additional opportunity to present a poster following well-set guidelines after their oral presentations, and they have a minimum of five minutes of interaction with the external examiner. This also enables the external examiner to discuss any further gaps identified in the process of reviewing other works of the students. It provides the external examiner with a better opportunity to arbitrate between the internal examiners and moderators' markings and to evaluate whether the competencies and program learning outcomes have been achieved. It is noteworthy that the second cycle quality audit panel commended this process in 2012. As a best practice at the UoM, it is deemed vital for external examiners to interact with students and to assess whether they have achieved expected program outcomes compared to performance with students of similar disciplines from universities that the external examiners have experience of. The high standards cumulated over the years was supported by a well-established system of external examining and enabled the maintenance and comparability of academic standards at the UoM as revealed by the quality audit report (TEC, 2012) which also encouraged faculties/departments to accredit their programs for better accountability, mobility, recognition, and for the institution to remain competitive.

AREAS FOR IMPROVEMENT

In August 2019, the UoM embarked on a new credit system framework embracing the outcome-based concept, namely, the LCCS framework, which is aligned with the ECTS for most of its programs. In support of this transition, and to ensure a more rigorous external examining quality assurance process, the UoM Senate strengthened its policy as from the academic year 2019/2020 to ensure that external examiners have oversight on all the years of the programs that are based on the new LCCS framework. The aim was to enhance the concept of the OBL in its curricula in support of the academic development of learners in line with international trends. Further, the proforma for the external examiners' report has been amended, and future external examiners will be expected to look into the achievement of the learning outcomes more closely and to evaluate whether module learning outcomes align with the program learning outcomes through well-designed assessment methods. However, as mentioned in the literature review, in order to assess the learning outcome, the minimum threshold outcomes to be achieved have to be defined in the programs. Taking the recommendations of the external quality audit report further, TEC (2018) stipulates that academics must develop graduate profiles delineating the various knowledge, skills (critical, problem-solving, communication among others), and competences graduates are expected to develop by the end of their studies. TEC (2018) thus recommended that faculties/departments must:

> give serious consideration to moving beyond reliance on the external examiner system which inhibits other forms of innovation and improvement in programme monitoring and evaluation and to seek a benchmarking strategy for its curriculum and programmes, and through strategic partnerships for a targeted external examining system which would focus on academic standards and quality. (p. 55)

Departments thus must develop a strategy to benchmark their programs as part of departmental/faculty research to enhance teaching and research in disciplines and departments.

CONCLUSIONS

The external examining system has been a robust mechanism used so far at the UoM to promote and ensure the high quality of its programs. Results indicate that the external examining system is working well and compares well against standards in the UK, South Africa, and Australia, among others. Pockets of excellence have emerged as good practices over the years of implementation of external examining of the UoM programs. Accreditation and implementation of the LCCS are now high on the UoM agenda. There are strong academic arguments for coupling the external examining system with newer forms of quality assurance, such as accreditation (Coates, 2010; Stensaker, Brant, & Solum, 2008). To remain accountable, competitive, and to consolidate its leading role as the main tertiary education provider in the country (HERANA, 2011–2018; TEC, 2018), the UoM external examining system must be strengthened, and research must be furthered into areas as recommended by TEC (2018) such as the graduate profiles and benchmarking which can assist the institution in the enhancement of academic standards.

RECOMMENDATIONS

In line with this study, the authors support the recommendation from the quality audit report (TEC, 2018), which encourages the benchmarking of academic and administrative processes with internationally comparable standards as follows:

> For the UoM to be internationally comparable, it is advised to seek a benchmarking strategy for its curriculum and programmes, and through strategic partnerships for a targeted external examining system which would focus on academic standards and quality. In this case, much of the work could be done virtually and significantly reduce, but not eliminate, travel costs related to the system. (p. 55)

Given the high cost of professional accreditation, the external examining system, as provided per UoM (2013) Statutes, will continue to play a significant role in the maintenance and comparability of academic standards of programs. To the authors' opinion, to implement the above recommendations, the role of the external examiners must be enlarged to include their contribution to research in teaching and learning, and the term of the external examiners must perhaps be extended above two years to enable a longitudinal contribution in the advancement of standards. Minimum academic thresholds must be implemented at every discipline level in line with the UoM vision to be a research-engaged and entrepreneurial institution. This study calls for faculties/departments to be more proactive and research-oriented through collaborative benchmarking in their quest to improve academic standards.

ACKNOWLEDGMENTS

The authors wish to acknowledge the support provided by the Vice-Chancellor and the Pro-Vice-Chancellor (Academia) of the UoM for this work.

REFERENCES

Alderman, G. (2009). Defining and measuring academic standards: A British perspective. *Higher Education Management and Policy*, *21*(3), 9–22.

Becket, N., & Brookes, M. (2006). Evaluating quality management in university departments. *Quality Assurance in Education*, *14*(2), 123–142. https://doi.org/10.1108/09684880610662015

Bloxham, S., & Price, M. (2015). External examining: fit for purpose? *Studies in Higher Education*, *40*(2), 195–221. https://doi.org/10.1080/03075079.2013.823931

Clements, A. (2005). Strengths and weaknesses of the external examiner mechanism. In *Proceedings Frontiers in Education 35th Annual Conference, Indianapolis, USA. F2D-19-T1A-24*. https://doi.org/10.1109/FIE.2005.1612048

Coates, H. (2010). Defining and monitoring academic standards in Australian higher education. *Higher Education Management and Policy*, *22*(1), 1–17.

Hannan, A., & Silver, H. (2006). On being an external examiner. *Studies in Higher Education*, *31*(1), 57–69. https://doi.org/10.1080/03075070500392300

Harvey, L. (2004–2020). Analytic quality glossary. Quality Research International. Retrieved from http://www.qualityresearchinternational.com/glossary/externalexaminer.htm

HEA. (2015). *A review of external examining arrangements across the UK*. Report to the UK higher education funding bodies by the Higher Education Academy. Retrieved from http://www.hefce.ac.uk/pubs/rereports/Year/2015/externalexam/Title,104316,en.html

Henderson-Smart, C., Winning, T., Gerzina, T., King, S., & Hyde, S. (2006). Benchmarking learning and teaching: Developing a method. *Quality Assurance in Education*, *14*(2), 143–155. https://doi.org/10.1108/09684880610662024

HERANA. (2011–2018). Research universities in Africa. Higher Education Advocacy Network for Africa. Retrieved from https://www.africanminds.co.za/research-universities-in-africa/

Houghton, W. (2002). Using QAA subject benchmark information: An academic teacher's perspective. *Quality Assurance in Education*, *10*(3), 172–186. https://doi.org/10.1108/09684880210435930

Jackson, N. (2001). Benchmarking in UK HE: An overview. *Quality Assurance in Education*, *9*(4), 218–235. https://doi.org/10.1108/09684880110411955

Jackson, N. (2002). Growing knowledge about QAA subject benchmarking. *Quality Assurance in Education*, *10*(3), 139–154. https://doi.org/10.1108/09684880210435912

Jackson, N., Parks, G., Harrison, M., & Stebbings, C. (2000). Making the benchmarks explicit through programme specification. *Quality Assurance in Education*, *8*(4), 190–202. https://doi.org/10.1108/09684880010356174

Joyner, R. W. (2003). The selection of external examiners for research degrees. *Quality Assurance in Education*, *11*(2), 123–127. https://doi.org/10.1108/09684880310471551

Olabanji, O., & Abayomi, A. (2013). Accreditation and quality assurance in Nigerian universities. *Journal of Education and Practice*, *4*(8), 34–41. Retrieved from www.iiste.org

QAA. (2000–2018). Quality code for higher education. External examining. Gloucester: Quality Assurance Agency

Stensaker, B., Brant, E., & Solum, N. H. (2008). Changing systems of external examination. *Quality Assurance in Education*, *16*(3), 211–223. https://doi.org/10.1108/09684880810886231

TEC. (2012). Report of the *second cycle quality audit* (QA) of the University of Mauritius. Mauritius: Tertiary Education Commission. Retrieved from http://www.tec.mu/pdf_downloads/pubrep/UoMAuditReport200213.pdf

TEC. (2018). *Report of the third cycle quality audit (QA) of the University of Mauritius*. Mauritius: Tertiary Education Commission. Retrieved from http://www.tec.mu/pdf_downloads/pubrep/UoM_Audit_Report_Final_041218.pdf

Universities UK. (2011). *Review of external examining arrangements in universities and colleges in the UK*. Final report and recommendations. Retrieved from https://www.universitiesuk.ac.uk/policy-and-analysis/reports/Documents/2011/review-of-external-examining-arrangements.pdf

UoM. (2013). Statutes of the University of Mauritius. Retrieved from http://www.uom.ac.mu/index.php/about-us/governance/act-statutes

UoM. (2016–2019). University of Mauritius external examiners reports.

UoM. (2020). External examining of undergraduate and postgraduate taught programmes. University of Mauritius Quality Assurance Framework. http://www.uom.ac.mu/images/FILES/Quality Assurance/ExternalExamining

Yorke, M. (1996). The use of external examiners in art and design. *Quality Assurance in Education*, *4*(2), 4–11. https://doi.org/10.1108/09684889610116003

Yorke, M. (2002). Subject benchmarking and the assessment of student learning. *Quality Assurance in Education*, *10*(3), 155–171. https://doi.org/10.1108/09684880210435921

CHAPTER 9

BENCHMARKING: A COMPARATIVE CASE STUDY ANALYSIS OF QUALITY ASSURANCE ACROSS THE PRIVATE AND UNIVERSITY SECTOR IN THE UK

Kay Maddox-Daines

ABSTRACT

This study compares quality assurance across two case studies in the UK; a commercial organization operating in the private sector and a university. Case Study A is a private education organization specializing in the delivery of business and management programs. Case Study B is a university that delivers courses across four academic schools and through a number of partnerships. The business school offers a range of undergraduate and postgraduate degrees in business management, economics, accounting, events, tourism, marketing, entrepreneurialism, and human resources.

Semi-structured interviews were conducted with 11 organizational members from across the two organizations including 8 academics/tutors, 6 of whom are also employed as external examiners and/or external quality assurers (EQAs).

The study compares the remit of both EQA working on behalf of awarding bodies and external examiners working on behalf of universities. The EQA role is conceptualized as an "arbiter of standards" whereas the external examiner is more likely to be considered as "critical friend." This variance in conception

The Role of External Examining in Higher Education: Challenges and Best Practices
Innovations in Higher Education Teaching and Learning, Volume 38, 139–158

ISSN: 2055-3641/doi:10.1108/S2055-364120210000038009

has important implications for the way the process of quality assurance is conducted and utilized in support of program and institutional development.

The research finds that one of the most significant differences between quality assurance processes in Case Studies A and B is the way in which student feedback is collected and utilized to support and enhance the process of review. This chapter provides recommendations designed to capitalize on the value of the quality assurance process through greater alignment of teaching and assessment strategy and policies and procedures in practice.

Keywords: Quality assurance; external examining; business; awarding body; higher education; professional body

INTRODUCTION

This study seeks to advance knowledge of internal and external quality assurance practices across higher institutions of learning. It seeks to further understanding of quality assurance in practice through a comparative analysis of higher education courses delivered across the private education and university sector in the UK. It endeavors to provide a benchmarking perspective of shared practice. Specifically, this research focuses on the delivery of business and management courses.

There are different terms used to describe the role of an organization that awards recognition of learning outcomes (through skills, knowledge, or competence) following an assessment and quality assurance process. For example, organizations can be registered charities, chartered institutes or commercial organizations (Federation of Awarding Bodies, 2019). Private sector organizations specializing in the delivery of professional courses are approved by awarding bodies and operate as registered delivery centers. Many awarding bodies (over 160 in the UK) are regulated by one of the public regulators governing qualifications in England (e.g., OFQUAL, SQA).

This study compares quality assurance across two case studies in the UK; a commercial organization operating in the private sector and a university. Case Study A is a private education organization specializing in the delivery of business and management programs, namely marketing, human resources, accountancy, health and safety and management courses that are accredited to their respective awarding bodies. The organization was established in 2007 and in that time has grown from an initial cohort of 30 to over 2,000 students. The organization is increasingly delivering professionally accredited programs in-house to large multi-national organizations. The finance, student support, and sales and marketing teams are employed and based in London. All academic staff, including quality assurance specialists, work as consultants and are paid on a day or evening rate. The quality unit consists of two full-time equivalents (FTEs). The organization has been recognized for its rigorous quality assurance checks, achieving a top-quality rating from the representative awarding bodies and the international standard ISO9001:2015 in respect of its systems and processes.

Case Study B is a university that has grown exponentially since inception with a thriving academic community of just over 5,000 students. Courses are delivered across four academic schools and a number of partnerships. The business school is recognized for its community impact and through its connections with regional business provides real world learning opportunities for students in a rapidly expanding city economy. The business school delivers a range of undergraduate and postgraduate degrees in business management, economics, accounting, events, tourism, marketing, entrepreneurialism, and human resources. In addition, the school works in partnership with a number of other institutions in the UK through the accreditation of degree programs. As with other universities, Case Study B has a dedicated quality unit of 6FTEs which oversee all aspects of quality assurance in the institution including a quality officer that specializes in the recruitment and management of external examiners.

The Private Higher Education System

Privately funded higher education in the UK is diverse and complex, covering a wide range of institutions, many of which have particular specialisms (e.g., law, pharmacy, business). The majority tend to be providers operating as for-profit organizations (Hunt & Boliver, 2019). The number of private education providers offering higher and professional education in the UK continues to grow with a 20% increase noted by Shury, Adams, Barnes, Huntley Hewitt, and Oozeerally (2016) over the last six years. Private providers tend to be small with only a handful having more than 2,000 students (Middlehurst & Fielden, 2011). Over half of these providers offer business and administration courses (Hughes, Porter, Jones, & Sheen, 2013), many of which are officially accredited business and management programs (Hunt & Boliver, 2019). The tendency to specialize in the delivery of one subject area is common across the private sector (Hunt & Boliver, 2019). Courses are delivered in a variety of formats, in the workplace, combined face to face and distance learning (blended), face-to-face and online learning.

External validation is required in the absence of own degree/professional qualification awarding powers. This requires a specific (commercial) arrangement with an external institution that holds degree awarding powers or professional associations that can license the teaching of courses such as the Chartered Institute of Personnel and Development (CIPD) for human resources professionals or Bar Licensing Course for Barristers (Hughes et al., 2013). The principal commercial partnerships are led by post 92 institutions, and older universities outside the Russell Group. Professional bodies, however, account for over 40% of the validating/accrediting involvement (Hunt & Boliver, 2019).

The UK HE System

Rapid marketization of higher education has seen increased university autonomy whilst public funding for teaching has been reduced with the gap being met through the introduction of tuition fees for students (Hunt & Boliver, 2019). Additionally, external factors such as globalization and information technology have had a big impact on the sector with a change in the distribution of national and international students (impacted by visa entry regulations) (Xu & Zhu, 2019).

The standard of professionalism in the sector has increased and many academics now adhere to the UK Professional Standards Framework for teaching in higher education. Yet, there is ongoing challenge to incorporate even more innovative and flexible curricula delivery (Ramsden, 2003). Bachan (2015) argues that universities are struggling to cope with the swift-changing landscape. During this corresponding period, there has been an increase in the proportion of "good" honors degrees awarded (first-class honors or upper second). Indeed, evidence suggests that 27% of students obtained a first-class honors degree in 2016/2017, up from 16% in 2010/2011 and 78% now obtain an upper degree (first or 2:1), up from 67% in 2010/2011 (Bachan, 2015). Additionally, the Office for Students (OFS) became operational in April 2018 following the closure of the Office for Fair Access (OFFA) and Higher Education Funding Council for England (HEFCE), moving university focus from the lens of the institution to the interest of students (Dandridge, 2019).

PURPOSE OF THIS STUDY

Aims

This study aims to provide a comparison of good practice across the private and university sectors, therefore offering a benchmarking perspective of varying quality assurance practices

Research Objectives

- To explore internal and external quality assurance practice in a private sector education organization specializing in the delivery of business and management programs at levels 5 and 7.
- To explore internal and external quality assurance practice in a university business school delivering programs across levels 4 to 7.
- To undertake a comparative analysis of internal and external quality assurance practices in a private sector education organization specializing in the delivery of business and management programs and a university business school.
- To evaluate varying internal and external practices across the private and university sectors in order to identify good practice.

LITERATURE REVIEW

Quality assurance is an umbrella term that covers a multitude of activities (Williams, 2010). Its purpose can range from critical friend to compliance. A key aspect of external quality assurance is to stimulate change and improvement in teaching and learning and yet, it appears that little is written in support of this focus (Stensaker, Langfeldt, Hervey, Huisman, & Westerheijden, 2011). Instead, the impact of quality assurance is largely discussed in relation to structural, organizational, and managerial processes (Stensaker et al., 2011). Indeed, quality assurance processes appear in some cases to be limited to outcomes and performance measures, which may suffice quality assurance but are rather less helpful in supporting a review of pedagogical quality (Brady & Bates, 2016).

Essentially, quality assurance refers to the business of making judgments against defined criteria (Filippakou & Tapper, 2008). This can be achieved through external scrutiny and review (Bloxham & Price, 2015) or as Cheung and Tsui (2010, p. 10) argue, "external interference." External quality assurance provides institutions with the means to demonstrate accountability which is essential to staff and students funding sources, approving authorities and the wider community.

Awarding Body External Quality Assurance

Private education organizations are generally far smaller than universities and offer specialisms in singular academic fields (D'Angelo, 2017). Hunt and Boliver (2019) argue that less than one in five private providers are registered with the English regulator, the OFS, although the largest and most significant institutions will. To become accredited centers must adhere to a standard-based quality model and awarding bodies insist on the existence of certain policies, structures, and practices (Martin, 2016). Indeed, centers are required to comply with awarding body directives and to allow access to any information required so that the awarding body can check for compliance (Institute of Leadership and Management (ILM), 2018). Hunt and Boliver (2019) contend that only 40% of private providers guarantee the quality of their provision via some form of oversight or validating arrangement, either with a professional body or a university. However, all providers who are contracted to deliver awarding body qualifications are subject to external quality assurance (EQA) visits and checks in order to ensure programs and qualifications are standardized across centers (CIPD, 2019).

The process of accreditation provides a set of standards from which centers can assess their progress in both reaching and maintaining quality. By reaching such standards, a center is able to guarantee the quality of their provision and to benchmark their achievement against peers (Wolff, 2009). Makhaul (2019) argues that the accreditation check is not an external audit, rather, its aim is to provide an assurance that an educational institution fulfills mandatory standards. The EQA review will focus on qualification delivery, assessment, learner achievement, and learner satisfaction. The role of the EQA is to assure that national standards are being maintained and that learner achievement and performance is assessed in accordance with qualification specifications and regulatory requirements (CIPD, 2019). External quality assurance ensures that learners know what is expected of them to meet assessment requirements and that the center has appropriate resources (including staff) to support effective delivery. An EQA is contracted (sometimes on a self-employed basis) to ensure that the center has in place robust processes (meaning rigorous and consistent) that evidence the quality and consistency of assessor judgments through sound internal quality assurance (IQA) practices. This is measured through a sampling of student work across each module and program. Some EQA's (for example, those representing the ILM), are required to observe the IQA providing feedback to the assessor on his/her marking and to determine what development points are in place to support progression (City & Guilds, 2019). The EQA is also expected to meet with both staff and learners (City & Guilds, 2019). All assessed evidence is measured against its validity, authenticity, currency, sufficiency, and reliability (Gravells, 2016). Indeed, professional bodies invest a considerable amount in the design, checks, and moderation to ensure high levels of reliability and validity. But this investment is available only due to the large number of candidates taking individual courses, thus providing economies of scale (Bloxham, 2009).

The EQA role is largely compliance orientated and ensures that effective quality assurance is in place and that the qualifications being offered meet the awarding organization's assessment practice and procedures (Educating UK, 2017). Essentially, the EQA role is to risk assess the center in terms of its quality standard (City & Guilds, 2019). Martin (2016) argues that the real value of external quality assurance might rest more in the process rather than the outcome. The EQA is geared explicitly toward improving existing practices and to effectively achieve the process that relies on the individual or collective involvement of academic staff at the institutional level.

Quality Assurance in Universities

In UK universities, quality assurance systems have been formalized since the establishment of a single quality assurance agency in 1997. Quality assurance mechanisms provide a measure of student learning in relation to credits and module pathways for degree awards. More than this, they ensure a process for assuring and validating the comparability of degrees across the higher education sector. Indeed, these measures for satisfying public scrutiny and indicators as outcomes are easier to compare than the business of teaching and learning (Jessop, McNab, & Gubby, 2012).

Much of the quality assurance activity in universities takes place in quality support units. Williams (2010) argues that this is because the academic community has never expressed much interest in mechanisms of quality standards. Yet, the quality of provision is most effectively assured by those involved in teaching. Gaunt (1999) purports that external examining is the only quality assurance mechanism that addresses the quality of student output. Most universities now have in place embedded systems for the appointment and induction of external examiners (Universities UK, 2011) yet there is a concern that systems are not always sufficiently transparent (Brooks, 2012).

External examiner requirements are set out in the QAA UK Quality Code which states that the examiner must have had high degree of competence in course design and student assessment. Where possible external examiners should be experienced or supported with a mentor and training (QAA, 2011). In addition, they should be impartial in judgment (indeed, universities are less keen on reciprocal arrangements in their search for external examiners as they are keen to maintain their independence) and have experience in quality assurance and comply with all relevant legislation (Macintosh, 2019). External examiner vacancies are advertised through sector networks and JISCMAIL. Appointments are quite often coordinated centrally through an external examining team or coordinator (Open University, 2017).

Following the review of the external examining process in the UK, there was a desire "to professionalise external examining … so that those conducting the role are skilled and knowledgeable about assessment and the assurance of academic and quality standards" (HEFCE, 2015, pp. 92–93). It was also emphasized that external examiners should engage in activities for the calibration of standards within their subject, discipline or professional community. This requires institutional support for academic staff who are external examiners (Grainger, Adie, & Weir, 2015).

External examiner arrangements for supporting the comparability of standards are increasingly complex arising from modularization and a mass diverse higher education system (Owen, 2010). The UK Quality Code for higher education (QAA 2012) infers a change in the language used to describe the role of the external examiner, from prime guardian of standards to more "critical friend." Indeed, Universities UK (2011) acknowledge that external examiners cannot guarantee comparability of standards and this is reflected in the new Quality Code for UK higher education which states that external examiners can offer an informed view of how standards compare with the same or similar awards at other Higher Education Institutes (HEIs) (in the UK and sometimes overseas) in which they have experience. Yet, this experience is likely to be limited to a small number of comparable organizations as, "external examiners normally hold no more than two external examiner appointments for taught programmes/modules at any point in time" (Chapter B7 External Examining, QAA, 2018, p. 14).

Cheung and Tsui (2010) argue that the external examining system is most effective when built on a collegial rather than an adversarial approach and a crucial part of this is self-evaluation. The process of moderation focuses attention on assessment outcomes to ensure that these are valid, fair, and reliable and that marking is applied consistently (Bloxham, 2009) although Bloxham and Price (2015) argue that the external examining role has shifted from sampling student work to assuring the integrity of the process. Indeed, it is no longer considered appropriate for examiners to change individual student's marks (QAA, 2012).

METHODOLOGY

This research takes a qualitative approach to comparing quality assurance practices across a private education institution specializing in the delivery of business-related courses and a university business school in the UK.

The justification for taking a qualitative approach to designing, collecting, and analyzing data in this research is the need to collect data based on meaning (Bryman & Bell, 2007) rather than collecting standardized data through quantitative approaches (Saunders & Lewis, 2012). A purposive sampling framework was used to ensure that rich data were collected in support of the research objectives (Saunders & Lewis, 2012). Semi-structured interviews were conducted with eleven organizational members from across two organizations including eight academics/tutors, six of whom are also employed as external examiners and/or EQAs.

Using a semi-structured approach to the interviews (Bryman & Bell, 2007) provided a rich source of data (Anderson, 2013) and enabled the researchers to gain deeper insights into the practice of quality assurance rather than the rhetoric understood through policy. It provided the opportunity to "describe the 'gritty' reality of people's lives" (Silverman, 2002, p. 136).

Interview questions were designed to explore the experience of course leaders and managers in engaging with quality assurance processes (Interview Topic Guide presented in Table 1). As some of the respondents also work as external examiners and EQA, it was possible to collect insights into the role and practice of those undertaking these external appointments. This provided further depth to the data collected.

In order to support the data collected through the interview process, a number of documents were considered to support the analysis including institutional policy documents, induction materials, handbooks, module guides, and standard assurance forms. The aim of using documents in this research was to provide an additional dimension to the process of sense making and describing reality (Weick, 2009).

This study interviewed participants from across a university and a private education provider, both offering programs across levels 4–7 (from undergraduate to postgraduate and professional equivalent programs) which allowed an opportunity for comparison (Yin, 2009) (See Table 2 for a summary of the case studies). Case studies provide a useful framework for analyzing a limited number of organizations (Rowley, 2002) and allow the researcher to examine in-depth data relating to several variables (Heale & Twycross, 2017).

Template analysis was used to analyze and make sense of the data (Waring & Wainwright, 2008) allowing a certain degree of fluidity in the establishment of ordered relationships between the themes. This approach is recognized as a relatively new method in data analysis in business research (Waring & Wainwright, 2008). It allows data to be thematically organized using a coding template to summarize themes. The decision to use template analysis as a research method was based on its flexibility as it does not describe, "a single, clearly delineated method; it refers rather to a varied, but related group of techniques for thematically organizing and analyzing contextual data" (King, 2006, p. 268). Although some

Table 1. Interview Topic Guide.

Appointment and induction of External Examiner/External Quality Assurer
Communication with course teams/managers
Consideration of the added value that the External Examiner/External Quality Assurer brings to departments and organizations
Limitations to the process of external review
Recommendation to improve the system of external examining/assurance

Table 2. Case Study Organizations Used in This Research.

Case Study A: Private Education Provider
Based in Central London but with offices in Suffolk and Saudi Arabia and partnership offices in Bulgaria, the private education provider delivers programs that are delivered through part-time study options, offered across weekend, evening, daytime, blended and on-line study options. Qualifications are delivered according to awarding body regulations. The organization is audited by the respective External Quality Assurer as representative for the relevant Awarding Body several times a year. The organization enjoys a top rating for the quality of its provision.
Case Study B: University
The quality assurance and enhancement team in the university are responsible for developing, managing, and supporting policies and procedures for ensuring academic standards and the quality of learning opportunities across the university and its partner institutions. The university expects the external examiner to keep watch over assessment processes and to check that assessments are appropriate.
Course leaders manage their courses and work with external examiners in ensuring standards adhere to relevant national standards (including the Framework for Higher Education Qualifications, subject benchmark statements and professional body standards and expectations).

templates are "too simple to allow any depth of interpretation, or (more often) too complex to be manageable" (King, 2006), this method allows for a period of modification allowing the researcher to impose more structure on the template, thus developing a clear path between theory relevant to this research and data analysis.

DATA PRESENTATION

Case Study A

Appointment of EQAs

EQAs are appointed by the respective awarding body to quality assure the operations of a center to ensure that they meet the standards set out by the awarding body. Awarding bodies rely on their EQAs to ensure that centers can deliver compliant qualifications and deliver quality assessments. Asked about the appointment of their EQAs respondents in Case Study A revealed, "We never know who we are going to get. We just get an email from the awarding body that confirms details" (Interview with Quality Manager).

The CIPD and ILM require their EQAs to attend a one-day induction followed by regular updates and standardization events. EQA's are appointed on an annual renewable contract and are managed by a Senior EQA who samples the quality of their work on an ongoing basis. Performance management systems require the completion of annual continuing professional development and this is monitored by the Senior EQA.

Communication with the EQA

Communication with EQAs tends to be ad-hoc and as required. Centers are contacted when a visit is required and outside of this arrangement the EQA is available to support institutions or to direct questions to the appropriate contact. The main points of contact include:

- To confirm arrangements for visits (both in person and remote)
- To agree the sampling agenda
- Receipt of EQA reports and follow up questions
- In person on day of visit or when remote via telephone.

The center confirmed that, "We tend only to hear from our EQA when he wants to sample student work but we do email him from time to time if we have a query" (Interview with Student Support Manager).

Role of the EQA

The awarding bodies undertake regular checks on centers through their representatives, the EQA. The EQA's role is to ensure that the center staff matrix is up to date and that both delivery and/or assessing staff are approved by the awarding body, that they hold the relevant qualifications and maintain Continuing Professional Development (CPD). The process of review focuses on the monitoring of risk. Generally, the EQA checks the process of learner recruitment, induction, support, and assessment through the assessment strategy, sampling IQA observations and feedback. The EQA checks each center for risk and monitors this through action and/or developmental points. The ratings are based on compliance and responsiveness in relation to center management, recruitment, induction and learning support, assessment and IQA.

The Student Support Manager at the center confirmed that,

> the EQA generally focusses on ensuring staff lists are up to date, that learners are correctly registered, that staff CPD is recorded and that policies and sampling strategies are up to date.

During visits, the EQA also meets with staff and students on-line or via the telephone. The EQA spends time sampling student work, reviewing assessment decisions, and ensuring that IQA feedback to tutors is in place and acted upon.

Value of the EQA Process

The managing director of the center welcomed the feedback received through the EQA process. Indeed, she felt that the EQA visits focus attention on the effectiveness of internal policies and systems and found the feedback from students helpful in enhancing the student experience which "makes good business sense and helps us with repeat business" (Interview with Managing Director). For example, students requested more support with study skills and the center has launched a number of on-line study skills videos accessible to all registered learners. Personal tutorial times have also been incorporated into seminars. The Student Support Manager revealed that, "The EQA has focussed our attention on providing developmental actions to all students no matter the grade awarded" (Interview with Student Support Manager). Feedback from the EQA was also the launching point for the move to electronic submission of assignments. The internal quality assurer at the center suggested that the EQA, "has a good overview as they audit quite a number of centres" (Interview with Internal Quality Assurer) whilst the managing director confirmed that the process, "ensures that we focus on self-evaluation of our internal systems" (Interview with managing Director). Essentially, the process confirms that what the center is doing is effective and this is revealed in recent feedback, "The last review we had said that we maintain high standards of assessment and feedback and there were no concerns raised" (Interview with Managing Director). Indeed, the center holds a top band quality rating and this "gives us confidence that what we are doing is correct" (Interview with Quality Manager).

Limitations of the Role of the EQA

The process of external quality assurance is not without its limitations and these are mostly associated with the limited time the EQA has to review samples of student work and to meet with staff and students and additionally, the time that it takes the center to prepare for a visit. "We have to follow a rigorous process of review and ensure that we have the evidence to fulfil the awarding body requirements at every review" (Interview with Student Support Manager).

The center also revealed that whilst most EQAs are reasonable and fair, there have been situations where actions imposed were deemed to be inconsistent with awarding body requirements. For example, the Quality Manager discussed an example, whereby,

> We had an EQA that recommended that the student declaration sheet be changed so that it removed the reference to the percentage of submission that was expected to be written in the words of the student. We resisted initially as we didn't think this was relevant and at the next visit it was made an action and the centre was downgraded from the Top-quality banding.

The center did not feel confident in raising this issue with the awarding body directly for fear of reprisal.

The Student Support Manager felt that the system was limited as, "The EQA only sees a small sample of student work each time" (Interview with Student Support Manager) and the Quality Manager complained that, "We only see our EQA in person once a year. We do have a remote visit too but there is generally little contact" (Interview with Quality Manager).

Recommendations to Improve the Process of EQA

The center is keen to encourage more EQA involvement and the Student Support Manager advised that the center had asked several EQAs if they would like to observe teaching sessions and attend standardization events and training sessions. This has not yet happened. The center considers that this would provide an opportunity to see policy in action. The Managing Director advised that, "I think this would ensure that action points and recommendations issued by the EQA are supportive and sufficiently tailored to the needs of the business" (Interview with

Managing Director). For example, the center is expanding its delivery options to the Middle East and it is keen to ensure that systems are flexible to meet the needs of a diverse student base. The Quality Manager expressed a need for a more transparent process of appeal with awarding bodies when centers do not agree with EQA feedback. Ultimately, the Managing Director was keen for the efforts of the center to be recognized so that "We are able to use our Top-quality rating to support our marketing. Perhaps the rating scale could become a distinguishing factor for discerning customers" (Interview with Managing Director).

Case Study 2

External Examiner Recruitment

All courses at the university have an external examiner appointed to them in accordance with the university external examiner policy. The process for the appointment of external examiners has recently changed at the institution. Previously, recruitment would take place on an ad-hoc basis, perhaps through networks or recommendation. In 2019, the process was centralized so that a member of the quality team manages the process across the institution.

Participants considered that external examiners should ideally have, "some external examining experience" (Interview with Course Leader A) and "a number of years teaching experience (3–5 years)" (Interview with Course Leader B). All participants expected that an external examiner would have a broad knowledge of the subject so that they are able to cover most of the modules and, "ideally someone that works in a similar institution and who knows the British system of examining" (Interview with Associate Professor A). The Course Leader for professionally accredited programs argued that an external examiner would need, "a masters level qualification as a minimum and professional qualifications as required by awarding bodies" (Interview with Course Leader C).

Communication with External Examiner

The Course Leader manages the course and is the External Examiner's primary contact. Following appointment, all external examiners are invited to the university induction. This provides an introduction to the historical context of the institution, quality assurance processes, and the external examiner contribution expected. The Head of Quality sets out the university's expectations of the external in line with the QAA and Advance HE quality codes. Feedback is sought on assessment processes, the quality of feedback provided, and the quality of teaching and learning. Schedules and dates are communicated at the beginning of the year. Assessment boards require external examiner assurance of the appropriateness of assessment decisions to be able to approve awards. The main points of communication are summarized in Fig. 1.

The Role of the External Examiner

The university expects external examiners to provide an advisory role to ensure that the university is assessing appropriately. The external should assess the

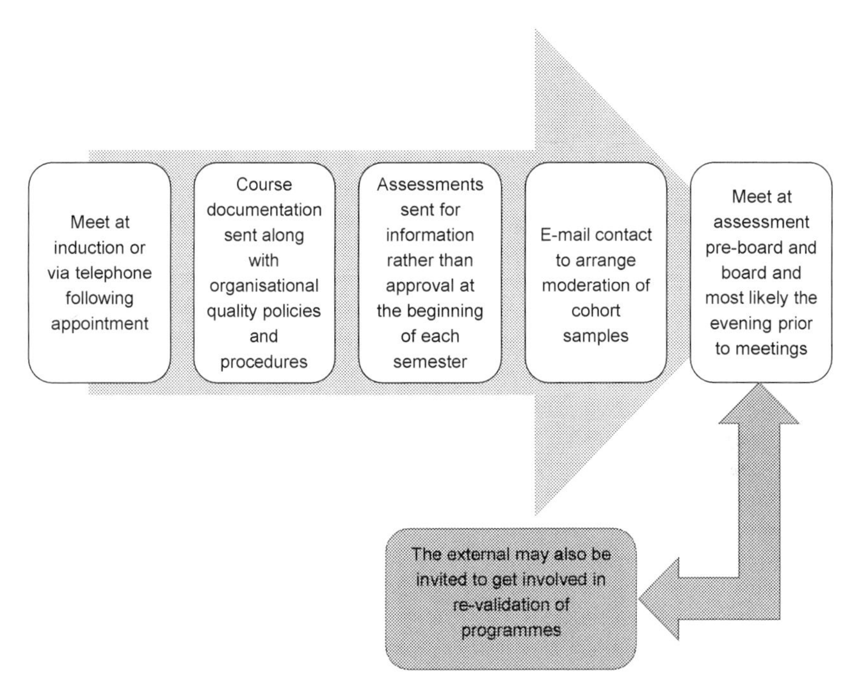

Fig. 1. Communication with the External Examiner.

consistency of marking standards and whether students are being treated consistently. However, the university is equally clear that it does not expect that the external should mark work, change individual grades and act as mediator between first and second marker.

Institutional policy states that externals are encouraged to speak to students as this can be helpful in gaining an understanding of the impact of assessment, teaching and learning, and resources (External Examining Institutional Policy). Yet there is little evidence that this happens in practice.

Course leaders considered that external examiners were most valuable when acting as critical friend, "I like to work with someone who is helpful and friendly but also supports improvements" (Interview with Associate Professor B), perhaps someone who "oversees first and second marking and might also suggest other books and journals to support course delivery" (Interview with Course Leader C). "Providing another set of eyes helps the course team to identify what is going well and what might need to be improved" (Interview with Course Leader D). However, it was also noted that an examiner needs to, "Understand that every institution is different and they need to be easy to get on with" (Interview with Associate Professor A) and "We are certainly not looking for someone that thinks they know better. They should not be given the final word" (Interview with Associate Professor B). However, all agreed that, "The voice of the external is quite powerful and it can be helpful to use this feedback to make changes to courses" (Interview with Course Leader D).

Value of External Examiner Feedback

Respondents were clear that rather than acting as an arbiter of standards, the value of the external examiner had resulted in, "Improving the structure of modules" (Interview with Course Leader D), "Focussed feedback on developmental actions" (Interview with Course Leader C), "Innovative assessment methods" (Interview with Associate Professor B), "Fewer questions asked in exams" (Interview with Course Leader B) and generally, "Improved student feedback" (Interview with Course Leader A).

Managing Differences of Opinion

Respondents acknowledged that significant differences of opinion are rare but where this does happen course leaders are able to reject external examiner feedback if this is not deemed appropriate. Course leaders did not consider that the rejection of feedback would be problematic at either the school or institutional level although this would be discussed with appropriate colleagues. One respondent noted that "On one module the external would not sign unless the grades were changed and the assessment board chair gave in. Everyone was livid" (Interview with Associate Professor B). Another course leader provided an example of an external "Who makes the same recommendation every time and we don't think it is appropriate and this keeps going and it is a waste of time to keep saying the same thing" (Interview with course leader C). Overall feedback indicated that differences of opinion are not problematic.

RESPONDENTS AS EXTERNAL EXAMINERS

Rationale for Becoming an External Examiner

Research participants acknowledged that becoming an external examiner was an expectation in terms of career progression and yet they cited a number of benefits arising from the process which supported their professional development. "I find benchmarking and sharing ideas of particular benefit as it helps in my own course development" (Interview with Course Leader C) and "Actually I genuinely wanted to do it" (Interview with Associate Professor A).

Methods of External Examiner Appointment

External examiners generally became aware of vacancies through both an open system of competition (through JISCMAIL for external examiners) and through direct approaches arising from contacts in their networks.

Key Learning Derived Through External Examiner Experience

Being an external examiner highlighted the fact that the course leader does not know everything and "So it is useful to have an honest discussion" (Interview with Course Leader A). Through the process of review, it is possible to recognize good practice in the home institution in terms of both program management and institutional process. Respondents found the process of external examining reassuring "To find that our internal systems are robust" (Interview Course Leader B). For others the key learning was "What it means to be a critical friend" (Interview with Associate Professor B). Ultimately, respondents highlighted that they, "Never insist on changing anything" (Interview with Associate Professor A) and actually that they need to "Trust the academic team to do their job" (Interview with Associate Professor B).

Communication with Course Teams

Communication with the institution and course teams where the external examiner is appointed tends to be infrequent. Documents are sent for information but the main contact occurs prior to exam boards. Communication tends to be via email with updates regarding regulations and then logistics to support the visit. Respondents noted that communication was largely limited to interactions with the program lead. When asked about meetings with stakeholders other than the program lead, respondents noted that meetings would generally be unplanned and informal as detailed in Table 3.

Limitations to the Effectiveness of the External Examiner Role

External examiners noted that the process is not without limitations, mostly related to time, in terms of dedicated support to the institution and the limitation that this imposes on effective sampling. Respondents also recognized that they were only able to offer an opinion on what they were able to access and review. The advisory nature of the relationship and working in the capacity of a critical friend was found to be both a way of adding value and also a limitation in that feedback to course teams might not be acted upon. Essentially respondents were keen that the process does not become a tick box exercise but rather, a system of producing genuine value for all concerned.

DISCUSSION AND RECOMMENDATIONS

The process of external review provides a degree of external scrutiny to internal assessment systems. Whilst EQAs are appointed as "arbiter of standards" by awarding bodies and external examiners as a "critical friend" in the university context, both hold a powerful voice for supporting change in their respective institutions to varying degrees. The role of the EQA leans toward an audit, as a

Table 3. Which Stakeholders Do You Meet During Visits?

Interviewer: "Do you meet the course team when you visit the university"
Interviewee: "Sometimes, if they are around but I don't schedule meetings with them, so it's a quick hello and a brief chat"
Interviewer: "What about meeting students?"
Interviewee: "I tend to attend board meetings in the summer and the students have left by then"

check of compliance against awarding body requirements whereas the external examiner focus is driven by the extent to which the university is complying with its own practices and this is benchmarked against the externals own experience, therefore in both instances exploring the value in terms of process rather than outcome (Martin, 2016).

The extent to which quality assurance is able to stimulate change and improve teaching and learning is limited only by the imagination of those involved in the process. The main challenge occurs in the way in which systems are employed. EQA's are required to hold specific assessing and quality assurance qualifications (or undertake these on appointment) and they are performance managed by a senior EQA. They are required to attend regular standardization meetings and training. External examiners are generally appointed for their academic experience and qualifications but generally receive little ongoing development specifically related to the role. Recently both new and experienced external examiners have been invited to undertake the professional development course for external examiners delivered through AdvanceHE. Yet, such qualifications were not considered necessary by respondents in Case Study B of this study. Whilst the process of appointment for EQAs is centrally led by the awarding body, there was some variation in the way external examiners were appointed in Case Study B with some evidence of historic personal referral through existing networks. At an institutional level, there appears an appetite for centralizing the coordination of external examiner appointments.

The EQA role generally checks the whole process of the learner journey and organization policy, as well as sampling student work and undertaking interviews with students and staff. The focus is centered on the assessment of risk with a compliance orientation. The EQA checks that assessment practices and procedures are mapped against awarding body requirements (Gravells, 2016). However, the focus of the external examiner appears to concentrate more on building collaborative relationships with course teams and maintaining a watch over assessment processes including initial moderation of assessments, actual assessments, course modification, and assessment issues.

One of the key differences highlighted between the role of the EQA and external examiner is the way in which institutions respond to action points and recommendations. Case Study A considered that they had little redress to challenge an action point issued by the EQA despite the fact that they did not agree with this. Ultimately, as the EQA is the representative of the awarding body he/she is only able to recommend a sanction. All action points must relate to the qualification specification for an action to be capable of enforcement. Yet, respondents in Case Study B did not perceive that it would be problematic to reject external examiner feedback if this could be justified and the correct process followed. This might involve the course team undertaking a mini-audit to address any issued raised. This example highlights the auditor nature of the EQA role and the advisory capacity of the external examiner. Indeed, external examiners emphasized the trust that they had in the academic team to "do their job."

Yet, despite the frustrations felt by Case Study A when issued with action points that they did not agree with and the irritation felt by external examiners in

Case Study B when course teams do not take on board recommendations, there were many examples of where the process has provided added value. Indeed, Case Study A highlighted the benefit of the self-evaluation required in preparation for EQA visits whereby the systems and process review encourage a holistic evaluation of the business. This supports Martin (2016) contention that transformation is achieved through the formal and systematic review of self-assessment procedures rather than the process of audit. Case Study A also cited that achieving the top band quality rating provides recognition of hard work and validates what has been achieved, thus increasing confidence in processes and systems. In Case Study B, respondents revealed that external examiner feedback had been instrumental in supporting course improvement and assessment feedback, in particular focusing course teams on developmental actions to support student progression.

Communication between institutions and their respective EQAs and external examiners appears to be ad-hoc throughout the year with most occurring around the organization of visits. Respondents in Case Study B identify how building a relationship with the external examiner is helpful from inception and this involves arranging to meet the day prior to academic boards where possible. Most discussion is focused on the sampling of student work. During visits, the EQA will meet with both center staff and students. External examiners however do not schedule formal meetings with the course team, albeit they may meet staff informally during the visit. Neither do external examiners meet with students as exam boards are generally scheduled when students have departed for the holidays.

One of the most significant differences between the Case Studies A and B was the extent to which student feedback supports the quality assurance process. Case Study A cites a number of benefits arising specifically from the feedback received from students interviewed as part of the standard review of the learner journey and assessment. The center commented that the feedback provides a valuable addition to internal methods of student evaluation. Yet, respondents in Case Study B did not schedule meetings with students as part of their sampling activity when undertaking their external examining roles and neither was this factored in when externals visited the institution. This is despite institutional policy stating that externals are encouraged to speak to students as this is deemed helpful for gaining an understanding of the impact of assessment, teaching and learning and resources. This is also contrary to the Higher Education Academy guidance on external examining which purports that external examiners carry out their role using a range of measures such as meeting students and staff and reviewing course documentation (Higher Education Academy, 2012). The timing of the exam boards appears to be one of the key reasons why this does not happen although respondents also questioned the value this would bring and the additional time it would take. Notwithstanding the challenges involved in such a review, it appears a missed opportunity to gain valuable feedback on both learner achievement and learner satisfaction (Makhaul, 2019) and particularly as institutional processes have evolved under the OFS to focus further on the experience of the learner in teaching and learning. As external examiner reports are shared with students and student representatives discuss action plans at course committee meetings, there is enormous scope for staff and students to work more closely through the quality assurance process to align teaching and assessment strategy, policies and procedures more effectively.

Notwithstanding the limitations of external scrutiny from both an EQA and external examining perspective including the small sample sizes, limited communication and visits, subjectivity and variability in examining practice (Grainger et al., 2015), the value cited by both case studies appears to offer much more than a check of academic standards and compliance. Indeed, having another set of eyes from which to offer suggestions for course improvements seems a key benefit offered by the quality assurance process.

Although outcomes are often easier to compare than the process of teaching and learning (Jessop et al., 2012), there are a number of examples of process improvements highlighted in this study which enhance the student experience. Of particular note is the addition of an online study skills program and the integration of personal tutorial time in seminars in Case Study A and the implementation of module guides and improved student feedback in Case Study B.

Respondents in this study appeared committed to improving the process of external review through the mechanisms of induction, training, and communication. Case Study A was keen to use their top band quality rating in their marketing as an indicator of their compliance, good practice, and commitment to good practice in teaching, learning, and assessment, and this excellence in quality assurance differentiation might also be considered by the university sector.

REFERENCES

Anderson, V. (2013). *Research methods in human resource management: Investigating a business issue* (3rd ed.). London: CIPD.

Bachan, R. (2015). Grade inflation in UK higher education. *Studies in Higher Education*, *42*(8), 1580–1600.

Bloxham, S. (2009). Marking and moderation in the UK: False assumptions and wasted resources. *Assessment & Evaluation in Higher Education*, *34*(2), 209–220.

Bloxham, S., & Price, M. (2015). External examining: Fit for purpose? *Studies in Higher Education*, 40(2), 195–211.

Brady, N., & Bates, A. (2016). The standards paradox: How quality assurance regimes can subvert teaching and learning in higher education. *The European Educational Research Journal*, *15*(2), 155–174.

Brooks, V. (2012). Marking as judgement. *Research Papers in Education*, *27*(1), 63–80.

Bryman, A., & Bell, E. (2007). *Business research methods*. Oxford: Oxford University Press.

Cheung, P., & Tsui, C. (2010). Quality assurance for all. *Quality in Higher Education*, *16*(2), 169–171.

CIPD. (2019). *CIPD Policy: Language of communication, qualification delivery, assessment and certification*. Version 2.0, June. London: CIPD.

City & Guilds. (2019). *Our quality assurance requirements*. Version 5.4, October. London: City and Guilds.

D'Angelo, A. J. (2017). Leading private higher education providers in Business. *Independent News for International Students. Study International*, 5 October.

Dandridge, N. (2019). The office for students: Reflections on our first year. *Perspectives: Policy and Practice in Higher Education*, *23*(4), 158–161.

Educating UK. (2017). *The Function of EQA (External Quality Assurance)*. Retrieved from http://www.educatinguk.com/the-function-of-eqa-external-quality-assurance/. Accessed on January 5, 2020.

Federation of Awarding Bodies. (2019). Policy Hub. Retrieved from https://awarding.org.uk/. Accessed on January 4, 2020.

Filippakou, O., & Tapper, T. (2008). Quality assurance and quality enhancement in higher education: Contested Territories? *Higher Education Quarterly*, *62*(1–2), 84–100.

Gaunt, D. (1999). The practitioner as external examiner. *Quality in Higher Education*, *5*(1), 81–90.

Grainger, P., Adie, L., & Weir, K. (2015). Quality assurance of assessment and moderation discourses involving sessional staff. *Assessment & Evaluation in Higher Education*, *41*(4), 548–559.

Gravells, A. (2016). *Principles and practices of quality assurance: A guide for internal and external quality assurers in the FE and Skills Sector*. London: Sage.

Heale, R., & Twycross, A. (2017). What is a case study? *Evidenced Based Nursing,* [e-journal] 21(1). http://dx.doi.org/10.1136/eb-2017-102845.

Higher Education Academy. (2012). *A handbook for external examining*. York: The Higher Education Academy.

Higher Education Funding Council for England (HEFCE). (2015). A review of external examining arrangements across the UK. Report to the UK higher education funding bodies by the Higher Education Academy. Retrieved from https://awarding.org.uk/about-awarding-bodies-uk/. Accessed on February 5, 2020.

Hughes, T., Porter, A., Jones, F., & Sheen, J. (2013). Privately funded providers of higher education in the UK. *BIS Research paper No 11*. Department of Business Innovation and Skills.

Hunt, S., & Boliver, V. (2019). Private providers of higher education in the UK: Mapping the terrain. *Centre for Global Higher Education*. Working Paper No. 47. London: Centre for Global Higher Education.

Institute of Leadership and Management (ILM). (2018, April). *ILM customer handbook (for ILM centres and providers): Policies and Guidance (v4)*. Burntwood, UK.

Jessop, T., McNab, N., & Gubby, L. (2012). Mind the gap: An analysis of how quality assurance processes influence programme assessment patterns. *Active Learning in Higher Education*, *13*(2), 143–154.

King, N. (2006). Using templates. InC. Cassell & G. Symon (Eds.), *Essential guide to qualitative methods in organisational research* (pp. 256–270). London: Sage.

Macintosh, R. (2019). Careers Intelligence: How to become an external examiner. *Times Higher Education*, 25 July. Retrieved from https://www.timeshighereducation.com/news/careers-intelligence-how-be-external-examiner. Accessed on January 6, 2020.

Makhaul, S. (2019). Higher education accreditation, quality assurance and their impact to teaching and learning enhancement. *Journal of Economic and Administrative Sciences*, *35*(4), 235–250.

Martin, M. (2016). External quality assurance in higher education: How can it address corruption and other malpractices? *Quality in Education*, *22*(1), 49–63.

Middlehurst, R., & Fielden, J. (2011). *Private providers in UK Higher Education: Some policy options*. Oxford: Higher Education Policy Institute.

Open University. (2017). Guide for external examiners of open university validated awards. Retrieved from http://www.open.ac.uk/cicp/main/sites/www.open.ac.uk.cicp.main/files/files/ecms/web-content/032-ai-external-examiners-guide.pdf. Accessed on January 9, 2020.

Owen, R. (2010). Review of external examining arrangements in the UK. *The Law Teacher*, *44*(3), 404–406.

QAA. (2012). *UK Quality Code for Higher Education*. Gloucester: QAA.

QAA. (2018). *UK quality code for higher education: Part B assuring and enhancing academic quality – Chapter B7 External Examining* (p. 14). Gloucester: QAA.

Ramsden, P. (2003). *Learning to teach in higher education*. London: Routledge.

Rowley, J. (2002). Using case studies in research. *Management Research News*, *25*(1), 16–27.

Saunders, M. N. K., & Lewis, P. (2012). *Doing research in business & management: An essential guide to planning your project*. Harlow: Pearson.

Shury, J., Adams, L., Barnes, M., Huntley Hewitt, J., & Oozeerally, T. (2016). *Understanding the market of alternative higher education providers and their students in 2014*. London: BIS. Retrieved from https://www.gov.uk/government/publications/alternative-providers-of-highereducation-the-market-and-students-in-2014. Accessed on January 3, 2020.

Silverman, D. (2002). *Interpreting qualitative data: Methods for analysing talk, text and interaction* (2nd ed.). London: Sage.

Stensaker, B., Langfeldt, L., Hervey, L., Huisman, J., & Westerheijden, D. (2011). An in-depth study on the impact of external quality assurance. *Assessment & Evaluation in Higher Education*, *36*(4), 465–478.

Universities UK. (2011). Patterns and trends in UK higher education – 2003 to 2011 reports. Retrieved from https://www.universitiesuk.ac.uk/facts-and-stats/data-and-analysis/Pages/patterns-and-trends-uk-higher-education-2011.aspx. Accessed January 9, 2020.

Waring, T., & Wainwright, D. (2008). Issues and challengers in the use of template analysis: Two comparative case studies from the field. *The Electronic Journal of Business Methods*, *6*, 85–94.

Weick, K. E. (2009). *Making sense of the organization: The impermanent organization* (Vol. 2). Chichester: Wiley.

Williams, P. (2010). Quality assurance: Is the jury still out? *The Law Teacher*, *44*(1), 4–16.

Wolff, R. A. (2009). *Future directions for US higher education accreditations*. Higher Education in Asia/Pacific. New York, NY: Palgrave Macmillan.

Xu, L. & Zhu, Y. (2019). Does the higher education expansion in the UK reduce the returns to education? A comparison of returning-from-work versus fresh out-of-school graduates. *Economic Modelling*, *79*, 276–285.

Yin, R. K. (2009). *Case study research: Design and methods* (4th ed.). London: Sage Publications.

CHAPTER 10

BUILDING WITHOUT A FOUNDATION: EFFORTS IN HIGHER EDUCATION TO MEET EXTERNAL EXAMINERS REQUIREMENTS IN THE ABSENCE OF STATEWIDE DATA

Megan Schramm-Possinger, Lisa E. Johnson and Beth G. Costner

ABSTRACT

The United States (US) has accreditation agencies that assess higher education in a manner analogous to external examiners in the United Kingdom. An example accreditor, the Council for the Accreditation of Educator Preparation, requires university-level Educator Preparation Program providers (EPPs) to evaluate the degree to which (a) their graduates feel prepared to assume their professional roles as a result of their EPP training and (b) their impacts on PK-12 students' learning. These are meaningful forms of programmatic assessment, however, governmental agencies in the United States do not uniformly collect these data. This has required many EPP providers to do so, with unintended negative consequences. The authors use this context as a case study to examine what must be done when reporting guidelines do not align with the data available. Although a single example, readers are asked to consider

The Role of External Examining in Higher Education: Challenges and Best Practices
Innovations in Higher Education Teaching and Learning, Volume 38, 159–172

ISSN: 2055-3641/doi:10.1108/S2055-364120210000038010

analogous situations within their own contexts. Presented in this chapter is the accreditation landscape, a description of the challenges listed above, common solutions, and recommendations for greater coordination among stakeholders in order to expand the systematic conferral of data in safe, ethical, and meaningful ways.

Keywords: Accreditation; compliance; continuous improvement; data collection; data quality; external examiners; PK-12 teacher impact data; programmatic assessment; state departments of education; teacher education

The British tradition of having external examiners assess the quality of post-baccalaureate programs is analogous to the roles assumed by assessors from accreditation bodies in the United States. The US's accreditation process has long been fraught with a tension between evaluating programs as a compliance exercise, versus evaluating programs to inform continuous improvement. Although it can be prudent to examine levels of competency in disciplines such as nursing (ensuring graduates of these programs "do no harm"), many have criticized accreditors for requiring post-secondary institutions to indicate they have met certain criteria in the absence of having engaged in substantive, meaningful assessment.

In response, the Council for the Accreditation of Educator Preparation (CAEP) now requires the Educator Preparation Program providers (EPPs) that they accredit to ascertain and present richer data on the placement and success of their graduates. Specifically, the expectations of CAEP Standard 4 (one of 5 Standards for this accreditation body) for the initial preparation of teachers requires EPP providers to showcase a variety of post-graduate outcome information as indicators of how well they have prepared pre-service teachers to assume professional roles (CAEP, 2020). Post-graduation data requirements include demonstrating the degree to which completers' skills are associated with positive impacts on their PK-12 learners' academic growth.

CAEP's current mandates are evidence of external examination moving in a positive direction given the long-standing desire for accreditors to require post-secondary institutions to collect data that could inform their *continuous improvement*. At the same time, the paradigm shift that occurs with the creation of the current standards presents logistical challenges. Specifically, it is difficult for colleges and universities to track their alumni (Lambert & Miller, 2014). Tracking alumni has traditionally been overseen by state departments of education (DOEs), whose licensure requirements, ostensibly, enable them to locate students who have passed their examinations and graduated from EPP providers. However, the degree to which state DOE's track and share data on job placement and the performance of EPPs completers varies greatly throughout the United States. Additionally, the conferral of examination and performance measures has become more complicated as concerns for data privacy and data misuse increase. Variability in state tracking and fears of improper data use has resulted in disjuncture between mandates for EPP providers to engage in data-driven programmatic improvement and access to required data. Consequently, the evolution of assessment into a meaningful external examination now sits unevenly with EPP providers who have neither the infrastructure nor the consistent state-driven support to gather the data needed to enact this process (Peck et al., 2009). Regardless of the local expectations under which one may be working, this disconnect must be examined and considered as an area of change and growth.

To circumvent these obstacles, many EPP providers have ascertained the required information described above (through a variety of procedures that will be described in this chapter) at great cost, both in time and money to themselves and to their school district partners. This comes at a time when EPP providers' student enrollments are trending downward and budgetary constraints and competition from alternative providers increase. To further complicate matters, when faculty were asked, "To what extent do you agree that the benefits of national accreditation for faculty outweighed the costs?" half either disagreed or strongly disagreed (Hail et al., 2019, p. 22). Admittedly, one could argue that the "glass is not half empty, rather it is half full" since half of the faculty agreed that the costs of accreditation were worth the benefits derived. Still, it is important to note that one out of two faculty members did not feel the process was "worth it." These beliefs may be associated with faculty members' corresponding actions that include the degree to which they are willing to creatively and tenaciously ascertain needed information from completers through novel, sometimes time-consuming means. Acknowledging these considerations in the context of (often complex) highly diverse relationships between state organizations and higher education institutions (Peck et al., 2009), this chapter explores the challenges of meeting external accreditation (or external examiners) requirements in the absence of statewide data systems.

ACCREDITATION IN HIGHER EDUCATION

It is important to consider these variables in the broader "universe" of higher education accreditation (HEA) in the United States. Specifically, HEA is executed by a variety of regional agencies (RA), national faith-related agencies, program-specific agencies, and national career-related agencies (SACSCOC, 2018). In general, the goal of all these agencies is to ensure that institutions of higher education are maintaining a common level of quality per agency standards. Those that lose their regional accreditation or are placed on a probationary status of some kind can face penalties ranging from the loss of federal financial aid to a tarnished reputation. Although this chapter is focused on accreditation-based considerations pertaining to EPPs, institutions are managing various, agency-based processes, and these responsibilities are relevant to the overall quality assurance landscape in the United States and internationally.

General Differences Among Accreditors – The US Landscape

Degree-granting institutions within specific geographic regions are held to the same accountability standards by their regional accreditor, of which there are eight in the United States. These standards are applied to the institutions' main campus, satellite campuses, and distance learning programs. All regional accreditors are reviewed every five years by the National Advisory Committee on Institutional Quality and Integrity (NACIQI), which is an entity within the United States Department of Education (USDE). Specifically, RA must maintain approval from NACIQI because of the RA's power to control access to federal financial aid. Meaning that if institutions lose their regional accreditation, they will also lose access to federal financial aid. Loss of federal financial aid is likely to result in the closure of an institution. Thus, there are an array of accreditors to which many institutions find themselves aligned (from programs to institution) and each has a unique set of expectations and requirements. This complex web of agencies suggests that various types of data will be (and are) needed to meet the panoply of accreditation standards.

A CASE STUDY IN TEACHER EDUCATION ACCREDITATION

Limitations

Beginning in the 1980s, states assumed a more central role to ensure that colleges and universities assessed student learning outcomes and institutional effectiveness. By the early 1990s, however, all *regional* accreditors adopted the requirements formerly under state purview. States were then confronted with budgetary cuts, including those for funding institutions of higher education. Perhaps due to shrinking budgets, many states promoted performance-based funding programs, so that finite dollars could be allocated to institutions that demonstrated specific gains related to key indicators (Jones & Paulson, 2001). Consequently, institutions shifted their focus on assessment according to state requirements – other than those pertaining to meeting performance-based funding metrics – to accreditation agency requirements (Ewell, 2007). Despite this shift, some program-specific and regional accreditation requirements were gradually integrated into state regulations/laws, resulting in the continued need for state-specific compliance data.

Embedded within the accreditation landscape is a tension between conducting assessments to inform the process of continuous improvement versus conducting assessments to demonstrate performance compared to one or more benchmark(s). Most institutions find they must do both. The former is focused on analyzing the results of several mixed measures to identify strengths and weaknesses related to locally defined program and student learning outcomes. The latter is focused on determining whether a standard was met as an indicator of compliance. Although not always true, most states oversee whether higher education institutions have met or exceeded certain thresholds of quality according to quantitative metrics. Thus, the emphasis, for most state agencies, is on posting outcome measures that are compliance-based in nature. This struggle between compliance and improvement are not unique to the case study in this chapter.

Users of compliance-based data face constraints regarding the kinds of conclusions they can draw from them (such as the types of programmatic improvements that may be associated with enhanced student learning outcomes). Yet, in many respects, it is pragmatic for states to enforce, and in some instances, reward, schools/institutions that meet or exceed compliance-based outcomes. For example, if a college or university's 6-year graduation rate hovers at 25% over the course of 5 consecutive years, then it makes sense to not only inform the public of that outcome, but to hold the institution accountable for its lackluster performance. To support the use of relevant information such as this, a subset of states such as Tennessee have established robust assessment systems that track the degree to which its statewide institutions have met a set of well-defined objectives (e.g., graduate students from underrepresented populations).

Furthermore, as indicated previously, institutions can become eligible for outcomes-based funding incentives relative to performance (Jones, 2016). This can be a positive catalyst for refining and continuing to cultivate a culture of continuous improvement. For example, the University of North Florida aligned its mission, vision, goals, and targeted interventions in accord with statewide performance measures, which has been associated with positive student success outcomes (e.g., relatively high earnings among its graduates) (University of North Florida, 2020).

Several unintended consequences can result from performance-based funding such as increasing graduation rates by lowering criteria for degree completion. Other consequences include significant cuts to financing institutions of higher education in states like Louisiana. For example, Shihadeh and Reed (2019) reported that if Louisiana State University did not increase its overall retention by three percentage points, per the LA GRAD Act, it could have lost a total of $54 million (from losses in tuition-based revenue coupled with fiscal sanctions imposed by the legislature). These considerations are not the focus of this chapter but are important to acknowledge. Additionally, in states that require EPP providers to maintain their accreditation from organizations such as the CAEP, yet have neither the necessary structures nor the apparent willingness to share data with institutions of higher education, the consequences may be even more detrimental.

PK-12 Districts – A Common Struggle

Higher Education is not alone in this struggle. Most school systems are required to use and report PK-12 student impact measures. These outcomes are often calculated by states with some deemed unreliable, inapplicable to specific groups of students (such as those with disabilities), and largely irrelevant in explaining test score gaps that are ostensibly associated with teacher quality (von Hippel & Bellows, 2018). For example, due to a variety of reasons that go beyond the scope of this chapter, scores from Value Added Measures (VAM) are imprecise – as are all test scores (to some degree)– and are often unreliable. More specifically, given the amount of error in these scores due to a myriad of factors between students, within schools, within districts, and calculation factors (such as the size of the group or the number of years of test data used to compute the value), every VAM measure has a point value (or actual value) within a confidence interval. The confidence interval indicates the range of scores within which the true score exists.

Individual VAM scores by teacher; however, are often close to the predicted score. The reason why this is consequential is best illustrated by using an example: In the state of Florida, if a teacher's students' predicted growth score equals his/her students' actual scores/performance, then the teacher's VAM score will equal zero. If a teacher's students' actual growth scores are *lower* than the values the VAM algorithm predicted, then the teacher's VAM score will be below zero (or a negative number); similarly, if a teacher's students' actual growth scores are higher than the values the VAM algorithm predicted, then the teacher's VAM score will be above zero (or a positive number). Despite the statistical complexity of calculating VAM scores, their interpretation seems quite simple. However, it is not uncommon for a teacher in the State of Florida to have a VAM score of –0.3, with a confidence interval of ±1.5. This means that the teacher's *actual score* could be anywhere from +1.2 to −1.8. Thus, it is as likely for the teacher to have "earned" a VAM score of zero (per his/her students' performance on standardized testing) as it was for him/her to receive a positive or negative VAM score. This presents challenges regarding how to accurately conclude a teachers' impact on student growth.

Additionally, if a teacher scored markedly above or below zero (despite the wide confidence interval), the score was likely to be above or below the predicted value. This information still has minimal value in pinpointing what factors influenced the students' performance. As is the case with various state score reporting that exists today, measures and scores offer little to inform changes to programming that could increase PK-12 learners' growth.

For these reasons, publishing certain types of state data, such as teacher's VAM scores, could unintentionally mislead stakeholders. This is because when members of the public are presented with numbers or tables that indicate one person, school, or state is "doing better" or is more effective than another, then that becomes a core determinant of that person or institution's value. For example, the Long Beach Unified School System in California regularly presents color-coded growth scores for mathematics and English (EdSource, 2019), thus implying strengths and weaknesses among schools. There are numerous reasons, most of which are outside of a teacher's control, that can account for variance in students' growth scores. Not one of these is described in the context of these colored indicators. Considering that such practices are common in the PK-12 environment, there are reasons for states and EPP providers to be cautious regarding what data are collected, how these data are shared, and how these data could be misused/misinterpreted.

Of central concern to the points explicated in this chapter is that compliance-based state reporting is often of limited utility to stakeholders, accreditors, and advocates of results-based assessment in higher education (Flores, 2018). Another representation of this relates to measures that do more to indicate whether practitioners have demonstrated the minimal level of proficiency required to perform their roles. For example, many states report licensure test pass rates or the percentage of test takers who scored at or above a "cut score" on a licensure exam for disciplines such as teaching. Although considerations of minimal levels of acceptable performance may provide some indication of pre-service teachers' preparation and readiness to perform their roles, this is primarily a practice designed to ensure that completers of higher education programs "do no harm." It does not reveal candidates' strengths and weaknesses in relation to constructs assessed by the exam, nor how this variance is associated with test takers' race, ethnicity, socio-economic background, or gender. This is evidenced by the fact that students whose scores on licensure tests are much higher than the cut score (or value indicating whether students passed or failed) are not predicted to have far more expertise in the areas assessed by the exam. Thus, pass rate data tell users very little, if anything, regarding how to engage in programmatic improvement and only indicate whether the test takers' level of knowledge is below the value required to satisfactorily perform his/her roles.

Considering the issues explicated above, it is reasonable to assume that relationships among state agencies, PK-12 districts, and EPP providers are somewhat tense and replete with unresolved matters pertaining to data sharing (Data Quality Campaign, 2015). Thus, state standards for the accreditation of institutions, their commitments to continuous improvement, and the relative availability of meaningful data to inform these processes and procedures are certainly both an accreditation *and* a political issue. Again, all stakeholders in examination process have a responsibility to consider what is used, the merits of data, and the goals for data use. Whether involved with CAEP examination, state compliance, or national systems of accountability, the struggle between what data are used and available must always be placed within the context of what the data can and cannot indicate in relationship to individual and program efficacy.

CURRENT LANDSCAPE FOR EDUCATOR PREPARATION PROGRAMS (EPPS)

Accordingly, most states' limited provision of useable data is all the more problematic given current accreditation standards, which, as noted previously, require institutions of higher education to (a) prove the degree to which their students demonstrate a spectrum of competencies and (b) construct data-driven plans for continuous improvement. For example, close to 1,000 EPP providers throughout the United States are seeking national accreditation from CAEP. One of the standards defined by CAEP – Standard 4 – requires EPP providers to demonstrate, using multiple measures, that completers of initial teacher certification programs positively impact PK-12 students. EPPs are also required to assess the degree to which the employers of their recent completers are satisfied with the completers' job performance/impact on student learning as well as the degree to which completers' themselves feel equipped to assume their professional roles as a result of their pre-service teacher training.

CAEP's focus on using data to inform continuous programmatic improvement is one that is increasingly evident among accreditation bodies (Head & Johnson, 2011). After all, candidate impact, employer satisfaction, and completer perceptions seem like reasonable points of examination for programs preparing teachers. Yet, the mechanisms to track candidates and ascertain the level of data specificity needed to make judgments on their performance and associated improvements to EPPs greatly hinder this process for many institutions (regardless of their size). For example, university–school partnerships can be leveraged to collect data at a cost to both the institution and district. Still, low numbers of early career teachers in a single district and/or differences in the types of evidence collected across districts yield data of limited reliability and utility for impacting change in preparation – the goal of CAEP standards (Peck et al., 2014). The authors acknowledge that some of these limitations are indeed specific to the United States where there are no national systems for tracking graduates and locally defined assessment expectations. Yet, this disconnect is only an example that can be used to consider individual inconsistency that are seen across the program evaluation landscape in the United States as well as internationally.

As noted, EPPs are mandated to uphold the standards/regulations/laws in the state(s) in which they are located and that may include being CAEP accredited (Hail, et al., 2019). For CAEP Standard 4, the processes by which EPP providers must ascertain in-service teacher and alumni data vary by state. For example, some states provide EPPs with one or more of the following: PK-12 learning data; employer survey data; completer employment rates and retention in the field over time; and/or completer survey data. Others provide data that have been stripped of identifiers to the point that the EPP cannot link the results to a specific program (also a requirement of CAEP Standard 4). Yet, others provide no data to the EPP even after having already collected such information from districts. Whether the state in which an EPP is located does or does not provide some, or any, of this information, CAEP will not alter its requirements.

Many EPP providers are requesting assistance to ascertain this information from administrators and staff in PK-12 school districts. However, district partners often struggle to find available PK-12 student data, particularly if they are not provided with a list of completers that includes identifiers used within the human resources software specific to the district. This process is even more taxing for districts in regions served by multiple institutions of higher education or small rural districts that have limited resources for such data mining. Interestingly, the authors of this piece were struck by the confusion of many school leaders in response to having been asked for data (from EPP) that they had already provided to the state through teacher effectiveness databases. Thus, despite their concerted efforts to provide the EPP with data in a timely manner, they voiced frustration regarding having to provide data to the state that it would not then (securely and legally) disseminate to the EPP.

Nonetheless, it is clear that a state's systematic provision of data is fraught with complications and reasonable considerations. Further resistance to collecting data, identifying data by institution, and sharing data is not the sole state department concern. Many EPPs are reluctant to encourage state data sharing due to the possibility of data presented outside the EPP in a manner that "grades" programs without context, as has been the case for many in PK-12 education. Within this political and practical issue, there are also concerns about the meaning of student performance data collected by the state. As previously illustrated, PK-12 student impact measures are unreliable, inapplicable to specific groups of students, and often irrelevant in explaining variance in student growth (von Hippel & Bellows, 2018). Complicating the situation further are examples of states that tie higher education funding to accreditation expectations. States such as Tennessee, whose state-level reporting is elaborate, allocate portion of higher educational performance-based funding according to whether academic programs are accredited. Emergent from these variables are extant questions for thoughtful discussion and review.

CURRENT QUESTIONS FOR CONSIDERATION

How do EPP providers within institutions of higher education, who have few extra resources, fiscal or otherwise, meet evolving accreditation requirements, as states endeavor to devise future plans to confer needed data? One approach has been to conduct elaborate case studies of recent completers. In the absence of other options, this is a wise strategy, yet it requires considerable resources and will only provide findings for a relatively small sample size. Some institutions are attempting to mitigate investments of resources by using proprietary tools – such as video recordings – that can be used to assess their impact on student learning. Although cost to EPP providers (both personnel and fiscal) and PK-12 districts is an important factor, arguably more important are considerations of the possible impacts the information gleaned can have. Low sample sizes and questions surrounding the conclusions that can be made put into question whether such practices are related to continuous improvement or compliance.

How can the federal government and accrediting bodies advocate for support or consider differences in state reporting services? What resources are needed to support, fiscal and otherwise, data sharing that is responsible to all involved? Enacting such systems would require political support for a paradigm shift moving from presenting data on percentages of students, faculty, or others who met or exceeded a threshold to providing qualitatively different, more meaningful information. Additional research and commitment would be necessary to use measures that provide PK-12 partners, EPP providers, and state agencies with data that considers context in the evaluation of students, teachers, and programs. Agreements must exist on the use of such systems and associated data to ensure that the affordances and limitations of what this information can provide is explicit. Stakeholders have recommended that the federal government create a student-level data system to include information required of all regional accreditors in the United States. Suggestions such as this raise the question of which agencies – state, federal, or both – could, or should, play the more central role in the provision of data for institutions of higher education and how this would be orchestrated. Such a system could then have an impact on the time currently spent generating reports for other regulatory state and federal bodies. Again, the cultivation of such federal systems requires deliberations that are extremely political in nature. Could repackaging similar data for reports with different definitions be redirected into more robust use of meaningful data for continuous improvement?

How can one consider these questions in other contexts? Regardless of one's role in accreditation or external examination, cooperation between agencies and stakeholders is essential to the meaningful use of data for program improvement and not solely compliance. Further users of data must consider the context of the data while balancing the ethical use of the data. International scholars and agencies have a responsibility to engage in scholarship that allows for a balanced looked at reporting of data so that where appropriate the focus can be either compliance or program improvement. Finally, the consideration of data for program improvement should be the responsibility of local, state, and national stakeholders. This, in turn, requires the consideration of systems that support such examination.

RECOMMENDATIONS

The question of whether reports providing users with pertinent, actionable data versus a list of scores for the purpose of "accountability-based compliance" has fostered fruitful research regarding how to generate documents, such as PK-12 testing outcomes, of consequence to stakeholders including parents, teachers, and students. Zenisky and Hambleton (2012) suggest that score reports indicating test takers performance on exams include dissemination in a timely manner; careful crafting for intended audiences; assessment for usability; presentation in multiple formats (graphic, tabular, etc.); interactivity; clear and accessible language for non-technical users; and, supplemental technical manual(s). Although PK-12 standardized test score reports differ from other outcomes-based state-level data, conceptually, the idea is the same: provide stakeholders with data that is not just indicative of having met a standard or cut score and instead provide them with usable information of practical utility. Jones and Paulson (2001) advance the argument while focusing on a cultivation of state-level data infrastructures. In the context of doing so, they report the salience of presenting higher education measures of students' "academic achievement, attainment level of workplace skills, state employment by occupation, and, acquisition of key competencies (at the transition point from lower to upper division, and again at graduation)" (Jones & Paulson, 2001, p. 16). The authors of this chapter assert that the recommendations outlined above could serve as useful guidelines to state agencies who wish to advance data democratization for assessment, accountability, and accreditation.

Due to the demands of accreditation expectations, EPP providers must find solutions to meet immediate, high-stakes requirements for data and information. Collaborating with local districts for case studies is likely the most accessible option to explore in states without robust data systems. Such collaborations can provide opportunities to provide data for compliance with accreditation standards while also providing insight for program improvement and piloting of data processes that may eventually be housed at the state level. These processes are time-consuming and the amount of data are limited, but case studies do serve as a reasonable first step.

Meeting immediate needs is important, but it is vital that institutions, state DOEs, and professional organizations begin to examine long-term solutions that can better impact program improvement and compliance. The authors provide three areas to consider as systems and processes are examined. These are collaboration, data quality and ethics, and advocacy.

Collaboration

All involved in the creation of a state system for data and information sharing must be willing to collaborate, and at times compromise, to establish systems that meet the needs of all entities while being manageable at the state level. One possible area of collaboration could be to have a satisfaction survey for completers and employers that is collected statewide and disaggregated by institution and program. Such an undertaking is no small task, but would allow for the conferral of comparative metrics that can be used to assess the degree to which accreditation standards have been met (e.g., institution average/standard deviations to state averages/standard deviations). Furthermore, the statewide data collection process could expand opportunities to explore data beyond the traditional geographic regions associated with existing EPP providers/PK-12 partnerships.

Employers could also receive a standardized set of questions enabling them to evaluate all new teachers hired. Such a system may limit the ability of institutions to ask questions regarding the quality of unique programmatic offerings or services although would save significant time and manpower. It should be noted that the existence of comparison data could make some EPP providers feel vulnerable or at risk of incurring adverse consequences.

Other areas for collaboration could include sharing teacher performance measures and student learning outcomes, many of which are already collected by several states. Although considerations of data security and personal information are not always straightforward, working together to develop reasonable standards of use and privacy measures can facilitate the provision of more robust information to programs. This will require EPP providers, state DOEs, PK-12 teachers and school districts to collaborate and formulate the structure of such a system to ensure it is safe, secure, and efficient.

Data Quality and Ethics

As stated above, data ethics and proper data governance are unequivocally critical in the context of devising methods for the timely, secure dissemination of information needed by EPP providers to meet accreditation requirements. Three key sources of legal and procedural information can be utilized to inform this process. First, state representatives, EPP providers, and accreditors are mandated to disseminate data in accordance with the Family Educational Rights and Privacy Act (FERPA). FERPA is a federal law that protects the confidentiality of students' educational records (USDE, 2018). Second, stakeholders must adhere to FERPA guidelines as well as procedures defining proper data governance according to the considerations enumerated by the USDE's Privacy Technical Assistance Center (2015). Third, data users, whether they be statisticians or accreditation experts, must follow all guidelines for the ethical dissemination and use of statistical data that are enumerated in the American Statistical Association's (ASA's) Ethical Guidelines for Statistical Practice (Committee on Professional Ethics, American Statistical Association, 2018). Integrity, confidentiality, transparency, objectivity, data quality, and a myriad of other considerations such as maintaining the privacy and security of data systems are prerequisites to the establishment of consistent state information dissemination for the purposes of accountability and accreditation.

Despite the clarity of these guidelines, issues of proper data utilization remain. For example, the ASA indicated that, "VAM scores or rankings can change substantially when a different model or test is used" (ASA, 2014; Amrein-Beardsley, 2014). However, in 2015, VAM scores in Florida were calculated according to two different standardized tests: the first being the Comprehensive Test, in 2014, and the second being the Florida Standards Assessments, in 2015. Thus, the recommendation to calculate VAM scores according to student performance on the same test over time was not heeded, possibly resulting in misleading conclusions. Although only one example is provided, the reality of data collection and dissemination within the guidelines from groups such as the ASA is an ongoing consideration.

Additionally, some states endeavor to provide consumers with comparative information of teacher preparation programs, and some of this data are quite helpful (e.g., whether the program is nationally accredited and the school's cost of tuition). Other forms of information such as "Licensing Exams Pass Rate," as noted above, have little or no utility, particularly when reported pass rates are all the same (at 100%) considering all students have to pass the exam in order to be licensed (Teacher Certification Degrees, 2020).

Of tremendous benefit to EPP providers would be the dissemination and collection of completer survey data regarding the degree to which they feel prepared to assume their professional roles. There again exist considerations pertaining to data quality; specifically, how many questions will the state pose, what is the relevancy of the questions, and what is the overall psychometric quality of the instrument? If a small set of queries are posed, and there is no variance in completer responses, then the utility of those scores will be commensurate to the utility of posting Praxis pass rates of 100% – limited at best.

Along the same lines, presenting information such as the average evaluation score for a statewide teacher evaluation system and an average evaluation score for the graduates of an EPP provider, per the same statewide evaluation system, is a step in the right direction. However, the only way to actually compare whether the EPP provider's average scores are meaningfully different from the statewide average is to include the standard deviation for both samples (which would enable EPP providers to calculate effect sizes or determine the magnitude of difference between the two scores). Continual information sharing and expeditious work moving forward must be supported and shaped by EPP providers, statewide experts, and CAEP so that the true purpose of evaluating EPP provider's quality through the accreditation process can be achieved.

Advocacy

In tandem with state and EPP provider efforts to collaborate to create systems of data sharing, legislative and professional bodies must increase the efforts to provide necessary resources, guidance, and influence to encourage and shape systems yet to be created. With the authority to require data, such as that seen in CAEP Standard 4, comes the responsibility to ensure that access to meaningful data is equitable for all. Although suggestions such as the use of partnerships and case studies can be seen as a solution to fill a gap in availability of data, case studies are not a long-term solution. As previously discussed, low participation rates, limited comparison points, and significant cost to EPP providers and PK-12 districts characterize such processes. Therefore, professional groups must help EPP providers lobby for increasingly systematic mechanisms for sharing data. Professional groups can not only leverage their voices and expertise to encourage participation in collaborative efforts to build and sustain such data systems. They can also be a conduit through which more standardized definitions of common measures are created while supporting a collective understanding of data integrity and security considerations. Through encouraging and conducting research on such systems, identifying best practices, and working with all stakeholders, professional groups have the opportunity to guide collaborative efforts while serving as external arbitrators. Finally, the authors suggest that many professional groups have the platform from which to explore and develop example measures that better address the concerns and expectations outlined here as well as included in many calls around the ethical and meaningful use of data.

CONCLUSION

Although it may seem too late and too daunting to begin the process of building the collaborative systems needed, teacher education can still serve as a case study in collaboration and efficiency. However, the work must begin now, with a true commitment to change and solution development. There are examples from which much can be learned. From 2015 to 2018, the Alabama State Department of Education created employer as well as first-year completer surveys, disseminated them, and sent the results to respondents' EPP providers. There must be a clear commitment to and support for a renewed process for seeking a resolution to this data-related issue. Professional organizations, state departments, EPP providers, and PK-12 districts can and should come together to consider the next steps in making real change in the landscape of data for program improvement, students' development, and compliance.

REFERENCES

American Statistical Association (ASA). (2014). *ASA statement on using value-added models for educational assessment.* Retrieved from https://www.amstat.org/asa/files/pdfs/POL-ASAVAM-Statement.pdf

Amrein-Beardsley, A. (2014, April 13). *American Statistical Association (ASA) position statement on VAMs.* A Vamboozled Blog Post. Retrieved from http://vamboozled.com/american-statistical-association-asa-position-statement-on-vams/

Committee on Professional Ethics, American Statistical Association. (2018). *Ethical Guidelines for Statistical Practice.* Retrieved from https://www.amstat.org/ASA/Your-Career/Ethical-Guidelines-for-Statistical-Practice.aspx

Council for the Accreditation of Educator Preparation (CAEP). (2020). *The CAEP Standards*. Retrieved from http://www.caepnet.org/standards/introduction

Data Quality Campaign. (2015). Student data privacy legislation: What happened in 2015, and what is next? Retrieved from http://dataqualitycampaign.org/wp-content/uploads/2016/03/Student-Data-Privacy-Legislation-2015.pdf

EdSource. (2019). How California measures academic success is changing at some of the state's largest districts. Retrieved from https://edsource.org/2019/how-california-measures-academic-success-is-changing-at-some-of-the-states-largest-districts/620361

Ewell, P. (2007). The 'Quality Game': External review and institutional reaction over three decades in the United States. In D. F. Westerheijden, B. Stensaker, & M. J. Rosa (Eds.), *Quality assurance in higher education. Higher education dynamics* (Vol. 20). Dordrecht: Springer. https://doi.org/10.1007/978-1-4020-6012-0_5

Flores, A. (2018, April 25). How college accreditors miss the mark on student outcomes. Center for American Progress Blog. Retrieved from https://www.americanprogress.org/issues/education-postsecondary/reports/2018/04/25/449937/college-accreditors-miss-mark-student-outcomes/

Hail, C., Hurst, B., Chang, C., & Cooper, W. (2019). Accreditation in education: One institution's examination of faculty perceptions. *Critical Questions in Education*, *10*(1), 17–28.

Head, R. B., & Johnson, M. S. (2011). Accreditation and its influence on institutional effectiveness. *New Directions for Community Colleges*, *153*, 37–52.

Jones, D. P. (2016). *Outcome-based funding: Taking stock*. A white paper for Complete College America through the National Center for Higher Education Management Systems. Retrieved from https://nchems.org/wp-content/uploads/2018/01/OBFTakingStock111516.pdf

Jones, D., & Paulson, K. (2001). *Some next steps for states: A follow-up to Measuring Up 2000*. San Jose, CA: National Center for Public Policy and Higher Education. Retrieved from http://www.highereducation.org/reports/next_steps/jones.shtml

Lambert, A. D. & Miller, A. L. (2014). Lower response rates on alumni surveys might not mean lower response representativeness. *Educational Research Quarterly*, *37*(3), 40–53.

Peck, C., Gallucci, C., Sloan, T., & Lippincott, A. (2009). Organizational learning and program renewal in teacher education: A socio-cultural theory of learning, innovation and change. *Educational Research Review*, *4*, 16–25.

Peck, C. A., Singer-Gabella, M., Sloan, T., & Lin, S. (2014). Driving blind: Why we need standardized performance assessment in teacher education. *Journal of Curriculum and Instruction*, *8*(1), 8–30.

Privacy Technical Assistance Center. (2015, June). *Data Governance Checklist*. Retrieved from https://studentprivacy.ed.gov/sites/default/files/resource_document/file/Data%20Governance%20Checklist_0.pdf (Original work published in December 2011).

SACSCOC. (2018). Handbook for Institutions Seeking Reaffirmation. Originally published in 2011. Retrieved from https://sacscoc.org/app/uploads/2019/08/Handbook-for-Institutions-seeking-reaffirmation.pdf

Shihadeh, E., & Reed, A. (2019, October 28). Comparing two methods for predicting student retention: Implications for best practices. Consortium for Student Retention Data Exchange (CSRDE), Conference Paper, New Orleans.

Teacher Certification Degrees. (2020). Best teaching schools and degrees in Louisiana. Retrieved from https://www.teachercertificationdegrees.com/schools/louisiana/

United States Department of Education (USDE). (2018). *Family Educational Rights and Privacy Act (FERPA)*. Retrieved from https://www2.ed.gov/policy/gen/guid/fpco/ferpa/index.html

University of North Florida. (2020). *Strategic Plan*. Retrieved from https://www.unf.edu/uploaded-Files/president/president/UNF%20Strategic%20Plan%20to%20BOG.pdf

von Hippel, P. T., & Bellows, L. (2018). Rating teacher-preparation programs: Can value-added make useful distinctions? *EducationNext*, *18*(3), 1–9. Retrieved from https://www.educationnext.org/rating-teacher-preperation-programs-value-added-make-useful-distinctions/

Zenisky, A., & Hambleton, R. (2012). Developing test score reports that work: The process and best practices for effective communication. *Educational Measurement*, *31*(2), 21–26.

ABOUT THE AUTHORS

Patrick Blessinger, EdD, is an Adjunct Associate Professor of education at St John's University, a math and science teacher with the New York State Education Department, and the Chief Research Scientist of the International Higher Education Teaching and Learning Association (in consultative status with the United Nations). He is the editor and author of many books and articles, and he is an educational policy analyst and contributing writer with *UNESCO's Inclusive Policy Lab*, *University World News*, *The Hechinger Report*, *The Guardian*, and *Higher Education Tomorrow*, among others. He teaches courses in education, leadership, and research methods and he serves on doctoral dissertation committees. He founded and leads a global network of educators focused on teaching and learning and he is an expert in inclusion, equity, leadership, policy, democracy, human rights, and sustainable development. He provides professional development workshops to teachers and professors and regularly gives presentations and keynote addresses at academic conferences around the world. He has received several educational awards, including: Fulbright Senior Scholar to Denmark (Department of State, USA), Governor's Teaching Fellow (Institute of Higher Education, University of Georgia, USA), and Certified Educator (National Geographic Society, USA).

Mikhaila Burgess is an Associate Professor and member of the Academic Administration team at Noroff School of Technology and Digital Media, Norway. They have a PhD from Cardiff University (UK) in Computer Science, focused on data and information quality. Prior to joining Noroff, they were a Senior Lecturer in the Information Security Research Group at the University of South Wales (UK). An experienced external examiner, at Noroff Mikhaila is responsible for external examiners and annual assessment boards for Noroff University College. Mikhaila is also a Fellow of the Higher Education Academy and a professional member of BCS, the Chartered Institute for IT.

Sarah Cooper is a Senior Lecturer at York St John University, and specializes in magazine journalism. She has worked as a journalist in the UK, Australia, the UAE, and Hungary, and has freelanced as a sub-editor for the *Sunday Times*. She is working on her PhD exploring haptics and its impact on reading journalistic content. As part of this research, she has worked with former colleagues, now publishers of the magazine *Delayed Gratification*, to examine how different paper stock affects the reading experience, with a review to proposing more robust business models for journalism. She has held three external-examining roles, at Solent University, UAL, and UCR Rotherham. At Solent University, she is the external examiner on the BA(Hons) Fashion Media course; at UAL, she was the external examiner on the MA Arts and Lifestyle Journalism degree, and at UCR Rotherham, she was the external examiner of the BA(Hons) Media and Moving

Image course (accredited by the University of Hull). She is a Senior Fellow of the HEA and has been nominated as Best Lecturer (2019), was shortlisted as Best Course Team (2014), and won Motivator of the Year (2015) as part of the York St John University "Golden Robes" awards.

Beth G. Costner is an Associate Dean and Professor in the Richard W. Riley College of Education at Winthrop University in Rock Hill, SC. Having coordinated assessment and accreditation efforts in a College of Education and a College of Arts & Sciences, she has interacted with a number of different expectations and processes for program and university examination. In addition to college level leadership, she has a background in mathematics education, helped established the department assessment system as chair, and has served as are viewer in that for that discipline for many years. Her scholarship has primarily focused on the preparation of K-8 teachers in mathematics and local, state, and national grants that support the development of STEM teachers.

Barbara Cozza, PhD, is the Department Chair and a Professor of Education in the Department of Administrative and Instructional Leadership Program within the School of Education at St John's University in New York, NY, USA.

Juliet Hinrichsen has extensive experience of educational development and learning design, gained in several UK universities. Her research has focused on the development of end-user methodologies and tools for pedagogical development. In her former role as Head of Academic Professional Development at Sheffield Hallam University, she led on professional development, covering internal and external teaching awards, professional recognition and cross-institutional CPD provision. She is a Fellow of the Staff and Educational Developer's Association (SEDA) and a Principal Fellow of the Higher Education Academy (HEA).

Lisa E. Johnson is an Associate Dean and Professor in the Richard W. Riley College of Education at Winthrop University in Rock Hill, SC. As the director of a ten-district school university partnership network, she facilitates teacher development through collaboration and shared professional learning. She leads the Department of Education Core, which serves all initial preparation programs by providing foundational experiences focused on diverse and inclusive practice. Her research includes investigation of school university partnership impact, teaching as a moral endeavor, and teacher dispositions. Additionally, she is the co-author, recipient, and principal investigator of multiple million-dollar grants that serve to strengthen teacher impact by providing students with equitable access to a high-quality education.

Helen Kay is a Senior Lecturer in Academic Development and Inclusivity at Sheffield Hallam University. She is an experienced educational developer with extensive knowledge of curriculum development, course/program leadership and institutional research. Her practice is research informed and underpinned by a wealth of experience in evaluating the implementation of academic practices. She is a Senior Fellow of the Higher Education Academy (HEA).

Fareeda Khodabocus is currently Director Quality Assurance at the University of Mauritius. Prior to which she was the Head of Department at the Faculty of Engineering (2005–2010) and has more than 25 years of experience in Teaching and Research in the field of Quality Assurance at Faculty level. Her current mandate is to Lead Quality Assurance and Good Practice, contribute to the formulation of the Quality Assurance and Enhancement Policies, their implementation and monitoring across the University.

Henri Li Kam Wah is currently an Associate Professor of Chemistry at the University of Mauritius, the first established university of the country. He joined the University of Mauritius in 1988. From 2002 to 2006, he was the Director of Quality Assurance before assuming the post of Dean of the Faculty of Science from 2006 to 2009. His areas of research and interest include coordination, environmental chemistry, forensic chemistry, quality assurance in higher education, and audit in tertiary institutions. He acted as a member of audit or scrutiny panel for several tertiary institutions in Mauritius.

Kay Maddox-Daines, PhD, is a Leadership and Management Consultant, External Assessor for the Institute of Leadership and Management, External Examiner for Leeds Beckett University, a Career Development Institute UK Registered Career Coach, and a qualified Executive Coach. She manages and delivers executive education at the University of Suffolk and oversees academic development for a number of private sector education institutions. She is a Fellow of the Higher Education Academy, a Fellow of the Staff and Educational Development Association, and a Chartered Member of the Chartered Institute of Personnel and Development. https://www.kaymaddoxdaines.co.uk

Victoria L. O'Donnell is the Dean of Research and Academic Development with Laureate Online Education. She is also an Expert Assessor for the UK Quality Assurance Agency, and Principal Fellow of the Higher Education Academy. She holds a PhD in Psychology from the University of Stirling, UK. She has had a long career in UK public higher education and in the private, commercial HE sector, with particular experience of alternative provision, contemporary pedagogies, digital education and online learning. With an academic background in psychology, she has published widely on the psychological aspects of learning and teaching, transition to higher education, the experiences of non-traditional students in HE, inclusion in higher education and HE organizational change.

Sara Pearman has an MA in Cultural Policy and Management, with Distinction and an undergraduate degree in Media Production. She is also a Fellow of the Higher Education Academy. As a qualified teacher, she is passionate about the importance of creative curriculum. She has focused her research on funding in the creative sector and the creative economy. Her background has mainly focused on moving image and radio. She is currently a Curriculum Team Leader at a college in South Yorkshire, she is responsible for the Media, Photography and Graphics department, from levels one to six. She has 18 years of experience working within the Further

Education (FE) sector and 9 of those years has encompassed responsibility for Higher Education (HE) in the FE sector. She is well versed in the complexities of managing, designing, and delivering HE in the FE environment. She has held various posts externally verifying for FE provision. She has worked for both Pearson and UAL. She has visited numerous colleges verifying standards of FE provision. She has seen first-hand, the positive impact of creativity and how it has transformed the lives of young people, this has driven her attempts to keep creativity firmly on the curriculum. She has also been involved in writing course content for Pearson at HE level and has written a degree, validated by the University of Hull.

Helen Phillips is a Senior Lecturer within the School of Computer Science and Informatics, and the Assessment and Feedback Lead for the College of Physical Sciences and Engineering at Cardiff University. She has a M. Phil from Cardiff University, in Computing Mathematics "Prime Numbers and Elliptic Curves" and a PGCE, Secondary School Mathematics from the Open University. An experienced external examiner, she is currently the primary external examiner for all computing bachelor programs at Noroff University College. She has been actively involved in the design and re-development of undergraduate and postgraduate degrees whilst at Cardiff. She is also a Fellow of the Higher Education Academy and a professional member of BCS, the Chartered Institute for IT.

Amudha Poobalan is a Medical Doctor trained in Public Health, with 20 years of experience as an educator and researcher. She is a Senior Lecturer in Public Health at the University of Aberdeen in the UK. She graduated from Christian Medical College, Vellore in India and worked as a Leprosy clinician before becoming an academic. She is a Senior Fellow of the Advance HE (formerly Higher Education Academy), leads the Masters in Public Health (MPH) and teaches on several undergraduate and postgraduate programs. She supervises national and international masters and doctoral students, acts as external examiner for MPH and doctoral degrees and conducts CPD workshops for academics and health care professionals on cutting edge research methods. Her pedagogical interests are improving student experience through socio-cultural coaching and effective teaching of research methods. Her public health research focusses on modification of lifestyle behaviors for prevention of non-communicable diseases during "TRANSITIONS." With expertise in mixed method study design, qualitative research, and systematic reviewing, she has established international teaching and research collaborations with India, Singapore, Australia, Nigeria, Kenya, Bangladesh, and Nepal. She is an Adjunct Faculty Member of the School of Public Health at Manipal Academy of Higher Education (MAHE, India).

Megan Schramm-Possinger is an Assistant Professor in the Richard W. Riley College of Education and a Senior Research Associate, both at Winthrop University. Her work as a methodologist is focused on examining the cultivation of teacher expertise, assessment of educational preparation providers completers' impacts on their K-12 learners, as well as the efficacy of pedagogical practices and experiences used to advance undergraduates' skill sets and corresponding preprofessional development. She also conducts research on the associations between the beliefs, behaviors, and cognitions of undergraduates and their academic work ethic; and, is examining the considerations for use of relatively new predictive modeling analytics.

Enakshi Sengupta, PhD, serves as an Associate Director of HETL and is responsible for the advancement of HETL in Asia, Middle East, and Africa. The associate director works closely with the executive director to fulfill the mission of HETL. She is also the Director of the Center for Advanced Research in Education (CARE), Associate Series Editor of the book series, Innovations in Higher Education Teaching and Learning, Emerald Group Publishing. She is the Managing Editor of the *Journal of Applied Research in Higher Education*, Emerald Publishing, and serves as the Vice Chair of the Editorial Advisory Board of the Innovations in Higher Education Teaching and Learning book series, Emerald Publishing. She is a Senior Manager of the Research, Methodology, and Statistics in the Social Sciences forums on LinkedIn and Facebook and responsible for managing all aspects of those forums. She is a PhD holder from the University of Nottingham in research in higher education, prior to which she completed her MBA with merit from the University of Nottingham and Master's degree in English Literature from the Calcutta University, India. She has previously held leadership positions in higher education institutions.

Padam Simkhada is a Professor of Global Health and Associate Dean International in the School of Human and Health Sciences at Huddersfield University, UK. He is interested in different aspects of international health particularly in public health problems in developing countries. His current research interests are in the areas of health systems, reproductive and sexual health including HIV/AIDS and migration. He has published a wide range of peer reviewed journal articles and book chapters related to his research field. He has published over 170 research articles in international peer-reviewed journals. He has received many prestigious awards of his field such as Global Health Award 2013. He is currently serving as an External Examination for two British universities. He has completed MSc in Public Health and Health Promotion from Brunel University and PhD from Southampton University, UK. Before he moved to Huddersfield University, he was a Professor of International Health at Liverpool John Moores University (2015–2019), a Senior Lecturer at Sheffield University (2010–2014), and a Lecturer at the University of Aberdeen (2002–2010). Previously, he worked for Save the Children (UK) and Ministry of Health in Nepal. He is also a Visiting Professor in Nepal, India, and UK universities.

Andrew Ssemwanga is the Founder and Executive Director for Family Enterprise Support Initiative (FESI) that undertakes research, capacity development, and advocacy for family enterprises. He previously served as the Vice Chancellor and Acting Vice Chancellor for St Lawrence University and Cavendish University Uganda, respectively. He is trainer, consultant, and researcher in various aspects of Higher Education, such as Business Ethics, Academic External Examining,

Teaching and Learning Strategies for Sustainable Development, Assessment, Institutional Evaluation, etc. He is also an expert in Corporate Governance; Finance, Insurance and Accounting. He previously served as an international expert for the Association of African Universities (AAU) on an Institutional Evaluation Programme in one of the universities in Nigeria. For another assignment, he produced a Code of Business Ethics as a Policy Tool for Building Linkages between African Higher Institutions and External Stakeholders in the Productive Sector. He holds membership in several professional bodies, such as Chartered Institute of the Education Assessors; Centre for International Governance Innovation; Africa Governance Institute; Oceania Comparative and International Education Society; British Institute in East Africa; Institute of Financial Accountants; Institute of Public Accountants; Institute of Financial Consultants and others. His academic background is in Corporate Governance, Finance and Accounting.

Edwin van Teijlingen is a Sociologist. His degrees were awarded by the University of Aberdeen: MA (Hon); MEd and PhD. He is a Professor of Reproductive Health Research at Bournemouth University. He has an interest in health promotion/ education and health services research. He has published more than 300 papers. He has an interest in socio-cultural aspects of health and health care. He is a Member of the UK Research and Innovation International Development Peer Review College (2020-23). He has edited 10 books, including *Psychology & Sociology Applied to Medicine* (2019), a widely used textbook for medical students. He has published on academic writing and had presented sessions on publishing academic papers at various universities in Europe and South Asia. He has experience of external examining on undergraduate and postgraduate courses at various UK universities, including Aberdeen, Dundee, Edinburgh, Glasgow, Leicester, Newcastle, and Sheffield. He has examined over 40 PhDs in 7seven different countries, including Belgium, Finland, Nepal, Australia, the UK, and Ireland. He is currently a Visiting Professor at the University of Nottingham (UK), two colleges affiliated with different universities (Tribhuvan University and Pokhara University) in Nepal and at Mahatma Gandhi University, in the State of Kerala, India.

Dionisia Tzavara, PhD, is the Director of Online Studies of the University of Liverpool Online DBA and EdD programmes offered in partnership with Laureate Online Education. She has a long career in Higher Education in Greece and the UK, in academic and managerial roles, and a long career in online education. She is an active researcher with a broad research portfolio, and she has taught multiple undergraduate and postgraduate courses in Economics, Business & Management. She holds a BSc in Mathematics from the University of Crete in Greece, and an MSc in Economics and a PhD from the Dept of Economics of the University of Surrey in the UK. She has completed two post-doctoral fellowships, funded by the ESCR and the Jean Monnett fellowship program.

Deepanjana Varshney is a Full Professor and has around 18 years of academic experience in India and overseas universities apart from four years of corporate experience. She had conducted training and development programs and involved in talent acquisition activities. She has been extensively involved in research publications focusing on dysfunctional employee behavior, gender issues, employee migration, and employee attitudinal dimensions. In the field of higher education and learning, her areas of research encompass student perception and attitudes, curriculum design and development, learning methods and different university systems. Her research has consistently been published in Scopus-indexed journals with publishers like Brill, Emerald, and Wiley.

NAME INDEX

SUBJECT INDEX